CONTENTS

Foreword

Karl Lutze is not my father. But he is my father's age — and *of* his age. I mean that each is as old as the other, and that they are both of the same generation.

Early on, Karl's person was shaped by the same traditions, culture, faith, and church that shaped my young parents. Karl grew up in Wisconsin, my mother in St. Louis, my father in Kentucky, Illinois, and Michigan. No matter the wide geographies: it was the same world that welcomed them all three, taught them to see and to speak, then sent them forth to *be* the world — sight, insight, and languages — that since has shaped this writer, too. Me. Walt Wangerin, Jr.

It is from generation to generation that we are what we are. The elders bequeath to their juniors more than memories or money or treasures in countable measures: more powerfully, they bequeath a sense of self. They bequeath unto us — if we can find it and accept it — our identity.

In times past — I mean, while I was still young — there existed manifest paths for this passage of identity. Whole communities still lived in a visible continuity; children walked in the footsteps of their parents and their grandparents: to the same churches, the same schools, same county fairs and funeral homes and softball diamonds.

Karl Lutze and I, in fact, attended the same six-year boarding school which prepared (in those days) boys for the Lutheran ministry: Concordia Junior College in Milwaukee. So had my grandfather attended there, Walter Wangerin, the first of three Walters and one generation older than Karl's. There at Concordia, in moments both common and incandescent, children were etched in the images of their parents. Identity was both declared and delivered.

7

For example….

On the first day of class — in Karl's day as in mine — a teacher would gaze with searching scrutiny upon the fourteen-year-old freshman who had just timorously answered, "Here."

The teacher had just called a name. "Karl Lutze?" And "Walter Wangerin?"

The student said, "Here" among the L's in the midst of the classroom, said "Here" back by the double-u's and then — if he did not know the drill — grew increasingly uncomfortable while the teacher paused to probe him with an unwinking eye.

Karl Lutze: small and pale, skinny as a hoe-handle, confident enough to look back, probing the teacher's face with an equal and twinkling intensity. Walter Wangerin, likewise small, but so treacherously shy that he could not hold the gaze, fearing rather that some secret sin was about to be announced….

Instead the teacher would repeat the last name, "Lutze, Lutze, hmmmm," and then ask, "Are you the son of *so and so Lutze,* or of *such and such Lutze?*" Each possible parent the teacher would identify according to church profession: *"the son of so and so Lutze,* pastor in Detroit? *Of Charles Lutze,* school principal in Sheboygan?

And little Karl would smile, swinging his bony legs beneath his desk: Yes that one. The principal-Lutze-one, yes! That's his dad!

And the teacher would nod: Yes, of course. As he knew the father, so he knew the son here in the classroom before him.

And the small Karl, and small Wally one generation later: we sighed profoundly at this brief exchange, for now we too were known. Far from home — abroad as it were, and strangers in this place — we had been granted a traveling identity. It came forth from the persons of our parents. Acknowledged by the larger community, it gave us a present personhood here as well. It gave us both legitimacy now and a pathway to our future selves.

By such manifest paths as this did we receive our shape and at the same time come to realize the shape that was our *selves.*

But those schools are passing away. And the common pathways by which the legacy of identity once descended from one generation to the next: these too have largely passed away.

It is as true of our society as of our Lutheran traditions that the old intimacy is dissolving, children moving to places where their parents' names (or even their parents' ways of life) are unknown; cities destroying the old places in favor of new places without memories or meanings; churches abandoned, churches rebuilt, churches changing their primary focuses.

And what do my children know of the horrid and heroic fights for civil rights? It is their heritage. In them they may discover not only their history, but also their *selves*, for identities were forged in those fights.

Ah, but Karl Lutze knows those fights. He, my senior, participated.

And Karl remembers in details both tender and whet-sharpened what sorts of ministries shaped all of us in the past. He participated. He remembers the grand acts of our parents and our parents' parents; the subtle traits they shared; remembers even the "lesser" among them, struggling single parents, people in poverty, those who would go unheralded except for Karl's memory and his affections and his sweet capacity to tell a story. But they *should* be remembered, the poor and the burdened and the mute and the inglorious: for they are parents for us all, from whom come our identities, in whom we discover our own selves.

———

In other words, in this book Karl Lutze accomplishes for us something of central importance to the continuity of our communities. He tells the stories of the generations just before ours. For he participated. He tells in small the true stories of the past of us all.

It is from generation to generation that we are what we are. Karl — by his personal experience and its narrative here — connects

9

the generations. His book makes a pathway, therefore, for the passage of identity, the transmission of shape and behavior and goodness and substance from our grandparents to their grandchildren.

As society more and more neglects the connections, we may be grateful to those who live their lives twice: once in its own time, and once by stories in *our* times and for our sakes.

Karl, thank you!

Walt Wangerin, Jr.
September 1, 2001

Prologue

It has been helpful for me to raise the question, "What's going on here?" — that is, beyond what I see of what lies before me.

So, when I see an infant cradled in the arms of its loving mother, I get to see more than a nursing scene.

My probing brings me to realize that this little one had been for months snuggled safely enclosed within the walls of the mother's womb, which afforded warmth and protection. Enough now; further confinement would be disastrously fatal.

So the little one emerges through the door of the womb to embark on its journey of life. I *know* that. What I begin to *see* before me is the mother, with her arms, her warm bosom, and the downy blankets, surrounding the helpless one with a soft wall to shield her treasure from cold — or anything that might threaten its well-being.

And there'll be more to wall this child in, and into childhood and beyond, providing shelter from ice and sleet, and germs and viruses, and countless other menacing realities that well might jeopardize development or growth — or even threaten life itself.

And caring parents teach the child to erect its own walls against all dangers.

And as in a womb, the walls intended to protect, can — and often surely do — confine and ultimately quite diminish life. Walls can become deadening — even deadly.

I'm grateful for the many walls provided me through the years — the diphtheria shots, the guards around my crib, the good nutrition, the safe home, the good counsel, the small town setting — the list could be far longer.

But I am grateful too for doorways in my life, doors that opened to me unexpected experiences, increased understanding, new visions.

Surely, situations, places, and events have often, in their own way, provided me with such doors. But, even more, people I have encountered along my way have presented me with vitally important doors — in conversations I had with them, things they did, their very uniqueness as persons.

There's been an amazing parade of such people passing through my life. It is about some of these that I write here. The stories I tell hardly serve as adequate biographies of any of the people I have included. Much less is this my autobiography.

In vignettes I have hoped to communicate how these people have enriched my life and have endeared themselves to me. Some are famous, some hardly known. In every instance, I suppose, not one of them realized how profoundly they affected my life and, of course, my ministry.

The ones I've chosen to recall here are only a small number of the people who have marched in this *Procession Through My Life*. They are some of the many who have graced my life. Others have been so lavish in their care for me I cannot fully comprehend their contribution to my life and I'm not yet prepared to tell their stories as they should be told. As days are added to my years, I have little doubt that more such personal benefactors will come to mind and I will want to share their stories too.

And there are surely some around me still who enhance and enrich my life, about whom I am not ready to write, because I am still luxuriating in their friendship and solicitous concern for me. And some day they may be the substance of another book.

The song goes, "I love a parade!" — and few can match the one I've been enjoying.

Part One: *The Wisconsin Years*

```
┌─────────────────────────────────┐
│                                 │
│            My Dad               │
│              I.                 │
│        Before My Arrival        │
│                                 │
└─────────────────────────────────┘
```

---

children at our door open new doors for us

"Dad" wasn't just another word for "male parent." "Dad" was Mister Charles F. Lutze, *my* Dad — well, of course, my sisters' Dad too, but nobody else's Dad. And years before I was born he was that special person all along — Dad.

It's not as if he became Dad when I was born. Long before I came along, he was there. Dad was there.

It was about 1910 when he was graduated from what was known back then as Oshkosh Normal, the young teacher became the principal of a little two-room country school not far from Howards Grove, Wisconsin, where he also taught eighty children, grades five to eight.

Eighty! Imagine eighty boys and girls crowded into one room! After two hours, can you picture all that pent up vitality exploding and spilling out into the schoolyard in wild recess? After playing with them, he can't have found it easy to corral them inside once more to resume an orderly setting for shaping and challenging those young lives. He loved it all — the job and the children too.

And although some of those farm boys towered above their five foot, four inch teacher, he apparently was much respected and loved by both students and parents. In later years, my sisters and I would repeatedly beg him to tell about those experiences and we'd have ever so many questions to prompt his telling and retelling us those stories. And he'd happily oblige.

Oh, and he should be remembered for his traveling in those days on a little black bicycle on dirt — and sometimes gravel — roads. Not only to and from his rooming house but the ten miles or more back for weekends at home when weather permitted. And he carried with him his own tire repair kit — replete with patches and glue for those skinny vulnerable tires — and an air pump.

Oh, and it should be remembered that the farm family with whom he stayed were gracious folk. Mrs. Emma Westermeyer cooked his meals and laundered his clothes. And, infinitely more important, she introduced Dad to her younger sister Alma, who lived with her parents some half dozen miles away. So the bicycle got even further use.

After a five year courtship, Dad had skimped and saved, purchased a lot at the site of the Lutze homestead, had his Uncle Carl,

the carpenter, build him a lovely and expansive two story house, and finally took Alma to be his bride.

None of their offspring ever achieved his capacity for planning and organization. Admiration, completely. Emulation, hardly! This was Dad — competent, thorough, industrious, thrifty, logical, creative — all those wonderful attributes and more assembled in this energetic, diminutive frame — who, however, would surely never be regarded a man of small stature.

In addition to the aforementioned ingredients of exceptional personhood, I'd do well to toss in an additional pair, acknowledging two that were his in significantly large portions: confidence and a penchant for adventure.

With a broad grin that stretched straight across his face from left ear lobe to right ear lobe, he would recount the story of his entering the automotive scene. By this time he was already married and had become Principal of Washington Elementary School in Sheboygan, a position he held till his retirement.

Very few others in the area had purchased one of these horseless carriages. No dealerships seemed to have been established as yet. However, advertisements appeared in magazines. So Dad clipped out the printed ad, and together with his check, folded them neatly into the note he had written, licked and affixed the required two cent stamp on the envelope, and mailed in his order.

Weeks later he received a call from the local freight agent: his new car had arrived and he could pick it up. He took his younger brother, Ernst, with him and they walked to the station together. The railway employees helped them roll the vehicle from the flat car. The two brothers climbed inside the brand new Flanders automobile and proceeded to leaf through the "Directions for Operating" booklet.

They read the instructions to each other aloud and carefully started the engine. With a release of the hand brake and a somewhat noisy engaging of the gears, they lunged forward into what must have been a slightly terrifying maiden voyage. I can see them now, Dad mounted high, his knuckles white in his death grip on the steering wheel, and Uncle Ernie holding on to his flat-topped straw hat with one hand. Shouting above the engine's roar, he would read from the booklet the instructions appropriate to the moment. They probably zigged and zagged their way down the unpaved streets, appearing to be nonchalant about their dramatic entrance into the Twentieth Century, past gawking pedestrians and panicking horses, till they finally arrived, safe and surely shaken — and likely altogether triumphant — back at 801 South Fifteenth Street.

The car rested there for a few days until the instruction book's warnings were fully comprehended and, apparently, Dad's driving proficiency improved dramatically.

That was the kind of experience that contributed to the shaping of the Dad who became my very own on June 24, 1920. He never acknowledged this, but Aunt Marie, his older sister, recounted the story so often that I almost feel I witnessed it. "He was standing there at the side of the house that morning when they called out, 'Dr. Elvers says it's a boy!' He just stood there and beamed," she would tell me. There had been four children earlier. Little Thusnelda had died of a serious illness at only two weeks. And then came Gertrude Henrietta, Cordelia Elizabeth, and Hildegarde Lenore. None of these had been family names. They were all adopted from English and German literary sources. Dad treasured books and reading.

Dad loved those little girls and was altogether pleased with the joy they brought to the household. He did not speak of hopes that this last child be a son. He was deliberately poised to be grateful for any child God would give. He was modest about fathering, but, obviously and ostensibly, a humbly grateful Dad.

```
+--------------------------------+
|                                |
|            My Dad              |
|              II.               |
|         Years of Growing       |
|                                |
+--------------------------------+
```

surprise on the other side of a door

One of my earliest memories of Dad finds me following him through deep, drifted snow in a path that the dairy delivery wagon had carved in its early rounds. Those buckled galoshes so warm and so heavy on my feet, my own brown woolen cap pulled down over my ears, and a scarf wound around my face so that my eyes could barely see over the top where he was leading. We were on our four-block trek to church, of course. And, of course, we wouldn't miss church.

Very little of our nights at home seems to have been memorable. There'd be gathering around the piano to sing while Dickie — that's Cordelia — played, and sometimes Gert would take out her flute. We had no phonograph and I must have been a fifth grader before we were given a radio by Uncle George and Aunt Ida. Its power source was an automobile battery that upon regular intervals required nourishment from a squirt of distilled water. And nobody had given a serious thought about television back then.

I remember my sisters with homework and their own creative play and their ukuleles, and early bedtime. But not without prayers and hymns that accompanied the tucking in. And, if we were still awake, we could hear downstairs the gentle bonging of the hours on the clock and the glass doors of the bookcase gently opened and closed, and Dad's voice reading to Mom the evening devotional and Scriptures.

One night in particular I remember. One of Pastor Krause's sermons had especially impressed me. I decided to heed his urging to read and study the Scriptures. I was stretched out on the floor near where Dad was sitting with a book of his own, my head propped on elbows as I paged through some verses in Genesis which I'd started perusing somewhat randomly. I would stop each time I'd encounter an unfamiliar word and Dad would help me out. However, when I arrived at some passages that dealt with adult infidelities and I asked for explanations, his mood suddenly changed and he told me I shouldn't be reading such things. I immediately invoked Pastor Krause's words to counter his comments. Unwilling to gainsay our pastor he quickly regained his composure and tried to assure me that the New Testament would prove more rewarding and easier to understand — or something like that.

I suppose a part of growing up is learning where the sensitive spots lie in certain adults' lives and ways. So without knowing exactly why — or which, I did learn there are some subjects to broach somewhat gingerly.

Dad had through the years cultivated the countenance of — maybe the best way to describe it — a competent administrator. Eloise Lindow, my high-school-age sometimes tennis partner once said to me, "You know, your Dad never smiles."

Oh, she was wrong, I insisted. He loved to chuckle at funny happenings and could even guffaw at a good joke. Truth was, Eloise *had not* ever seen him smile. And I began to realize that. Cordial, friendly, not severe, but his face usually communicated seriousness. His offers of friendship too were serious — neither casual nor superficial.

I recall — in the days long before United Way or other community social agencies — on one occasion Dad answered a knocking at the kitchen door. Ever at his side, I was there to behold the spectacle of a pitiful looking man. I'd judge him to have been in his forties. He mumbled his words as he begged for some food. Unshaven, hair tousled under his small dirty cap, eyes bloodshot, his face colorless. The ragged coat too long, his baggy trousers torn, his shoes were coming apart. He was obviously very weak.

Dad at once stepped back into the kitchen and pulled out a chair to the little porch and asked the man to sit down. As his trousers crept up his legs, we could see blood on his shins and ankles. Dad called to my mother asking her to bring a bowl with warm water, boric acid, and a cloth. Dad sank to his knees and slowly and carefully removed the man's shoddy shoes and his filthy socks. Then he gently — almost reverently — washed his feet and put some sort of ointment on his sores. He left the man's feet to rest on a towel Mom had brought. He stepped inside, whispered some words to Mom, and came out again with a small pan of water and some soap with which the man might wash his hands. Then he handed the man a towel and mother appeared at the door once more with a bowl of soup, a sandwich, and a cup of coffee. The eating went slowly. The man savored each bite, each swallow, each moment.

21

I cannot remember that through all this the man had said a word. In a solemn sort of silence we waited and afforded him quiet company as he ate. When he had finished, with a long gratified sweep he wiped his sleeve across his satisfied face. Dad took his place again at the traveler's feet, bound them in clean white gauze, and with a cautious tenderness pulled a fresh pair of his own socks over those bruised toes and heels. The man winced a bit, and he almost smiled. Dad carefully fitted those feet into the old, tired shoes. Mother handed him the sandwich she had wrapped for him and he rose to resume his journey. There were no words of gratitude that could express his obvious feeling. Mom and Dad both wished him well — no sermon. And he walked down New Jersey Avenue to the belt line where such homeless travelers would often find their travel accommodations in an empty boxcar.

Dad disappeared into the center of the house without a word. Mom gathered me to her lap. I looked up and her eyes were wet.

I had never seen Dad cry. Without having ever been told, I simply knew men do not cry.

Grandma Lutze died when I was seventeen. I traveled by interurban from Milwaukee, where I was in prep school, and arrived just as the undertaker and his assistant were carrying Grandma into her house. She had lived next door to us. Her sons and two daughters were there. The house was filled with people and muffled whisperings. Different ones around the room made their comments — as if someone had written their scripts. They were saying things that seemed to be expected to be said. "She looks like she's sleeping. She looks so natural."

Someone hung a floral spray near the front door intended to announce to passersby that Grandma had died, and, by the way, they were of course invited to come in "to view and pay respects."

More quickly than I might have imagined possible, everyone of the family had dispersed — to the barber, to the hairdressers, to the stores to buy clothing suitable for mourning — wherever. And quite suddenly I was left alone — with instructions to welcome anyone who might see the flowers and drop in. This was my assignment — till the family would return.

Well, they didn't return and they didn't return and I thought they'd never return. And no one else dropped in. I was alone with a dead person. I'd never been alone in a room with a dead person before. I reasoned — after all I was seventeen: "This is my Grandma. She loved me and I loved her. And she's dead." So I walked close to the casket.

I had never touched a casket before. I touched it. But not the silky stuff around the sides. I looked at her closely. Of course it was Grandma. But she really didn't look like Grandma. And I didn't think she looked like she was sleeping either. She looked dead. And the room smelled stuffy. And the blanket of roses spread on the casket exuded a thick and heavy fragrance, sweeter than roses should.

As I stood there wishing someone else would be there too — or that I had been a thousand miles away, all kinds of weird stories about people in caskets waking up and not being really dead came to mind. I looked closely at Grandma's hands and watched her fingers. They didn't move. And there wasn't the slightest indication that she was breathing. And maybe if I touched her hand — just for a moment. But what if it would be really cold?

Never did touch her. And I wasn't very proud of that at all.

She was a dear lady, a small gentle and strong woman. And truly a matriarch. Bright, she would read English novels, as many as my father would bring home to her from the library. And she crocheted. And she was a lively conversationalist, but preferred to speak her native German. We grandchildren could understand her; but, as I recall, we'd talk to her in English, and for the most part she'd respond in German.

Her three sons knew better than to fail checking in with her at least once a week for conversation — often long conversation, while their wives might have preferred more time with them. Their attentiveness was not mere filial duty. They genuinely loved this mother of theirs.

My cousins and I were chosen to be pallbearers. That was a first for me. The funeral was of course conducted in German — a short service first at the house, to be followed by a second at the church when the loved one was brought for a final worship hour. It was in the setting of the home that I experienced what I'd never at all anticipated.

Except for the casket and the flowers — by now there were many more wreaths and sprays and vases and baskets — chairs and tables had been removed from the room to make space for the people who had come.

Grandma's two daughters and her three sons were standing in a row only a few steps away. Of course I expected Aunt Marie and Aunt Fi (that's from Sophia, which was also Grandma's middle name) to be touching a handkerchief to their cheeks.

In churchly voice, Pastor Krause was reading some of her favorite passages and hymn stanzas, when suddenly Uncle August, the youngest brother, reached for his handkerchief and was reduced to tears. "Oh no!" I thought. "He's crying!"

Then I glanced at Uncle Ernie. His hand dove to his pocket to retrieve a handkerchief as he burst into tears. This was a bit more than I was prepared for. And then it was Dad who was no longer in control. My own Dad was burying his face in his handkerchief to stem the flood of tears. What had happened! The whole family is falling apart!

It was almost like a revelation and I realized, "They loved their mother and it's okay to cry."

And I took out the handkerchief I had been clutching in my pocket and put it to my face too.

———————

It was probably our last Christmas the whole family observed together in our Sheboygan home. My siblings and I were well into our working careers. It was magnificent, as all our Christmases always had been.

Caroling around the piano followed the church service. The beguiling aroma of Mom's Spanish Dish filled the house (flying in the face of German cuisine tradition). We were all there, family and as many other relatives as we could round up, settled in our seats. The little Santa and his sled and six brown reindeer in red ribboned harness took over the center of the table. The ordinarily open door to the living room was closed.

As the meal ended and conversation would center at the east end of the table, Dad would quietly disappear. We all knew he was gone, but no one would mention it. Some five minutes later when the doorbell rang we knew the magic moment had arrived, and bursting open the door to the living room we could see, in the front room, the beautiful tree, bright with its blazing candles.

There was again, as always, an abundance of gifts. I don't remember what anyone in particular got that Christmas, except Dad. As usual, he received a supply of White Owl or LaPalina Cigars and a huge tin of Velvet Tobacco, which he would manage to use sparingly to last him till July tenth, when his larder would again be replenished on the occasion of his birthday.

It was approaching midnight. Most of the relatives had left. It was then that my sister, Dickie, the poet laureate of the family, brought her Christmas gift to the family. It was a poem she had been busily writing for days, a longer poem, recounting different events in the passing of our years as a family.

Aside from its elegance, her choice of content, her deep insights, the piece probed so many hours of our life together and wrung from them their richest and sweetest juices. We all marveled at her recall and could not help being moved by her eloquent rememberings.

And when it was over Dad quickly left the room, handkerchief in hand.

I imagine that early on — long before Grandma's funeral — I knew the tenderheartedness of Dad — and that he simply didn't know how to cry in front of others.

That's probably why I never asked him about tiny Thusnelda.

Up and down the blocks from our house, wherever there were boys — the Sonnenbergs, the Schnells, the Damrows, the Eisemanns, the Lindows, the Ziereths, and the Peasleys to the west;

the Falks, the Meiferts to the north; the Haacks, the Ferschlands, the Messners, the Prislands, the Mohrs, the Bartzes, and the Brauns to the south — none of the fellows there had dads who played catch with them. At least I never saw them tossing a ball back and forth.

But *my Dad* was the best Dad in the whole world. When the weather was accommodating, at quarter till noon I'd rush home from Sheridan School (the schoolyard was just 100 feet away in the same block). I'd be waiting at the curb with my bulky catcher's mitt, a baseball, and a fielder's glove which I'd hand to Dad as soon as he'd climb from the car. He'd drive home the two miles from Washington School to have his noon meal with us. Before he could even go inside to greet Mom, I'd have him pitching to me. He'd stand on the sidewalk at our front steps and I'd be up against grandma Lutze's house next door. Because there were no windows on her north wall, the building served as an effective backstop to catch an occasional errant pitch Dad threw or a fast one that slipped through my mitt, each of these miscues accompanied by an embarrassingly loud bang against the wall. Since we'd try to squeeze in as many throws as possible in the fifteen or so minutes before Mom would call us to the table, a lot of talking didn't get done during those very intense sessions but a lot of bonding did.

I was very proud of Dad. I was proud to be seen with him.

Although he was principal of Washington School, he did not choose to seek a waiver from the rule of children attending their respective neighborhood schools. He would brook no slightest suggestion that he might ever show favoritism in his role as principal. That possibility was surely avoided by enrolling us in nearby Sheridan School.

Aside from not wanting to be away from my many neighborhood friends at Sheridan, I would have loved going to Washington, to "Dad's school." It was the newest, most attractive of all of the city's elementary schools. He was its first principal. Washington also had a gym, while Sheridan's building was a bit old, with creaky, well-worn wooden steps, noisy doors, and windows that rattled when the winds blew hard. The school's recreational activities were limited to the out-of-doors.

Occasionally, if some task called Dad to return to his office on a Saturday afternoon, he would respond favorably to our begging to go along. The school was a full two miles from our home and we had little occasion otherwise to be familiar with the neighborhood. I remember his pointing out to us little white frame buildings. Interspersed between small groceries and shops and modest houses, they were quite unlike any structures elsewhere in the city.

Dad explained that these were the places where Jews worshipped. We knew of course that many of the children who attended Washington School were Jews. Dad would tell how rabbis would often drop in at his office to explain some of the customs and especially the festivals their people would observe. Dad always spoke appreciatively of their visits and his deep respect for these leaders was obvious. He also explained to us the importance of not imposing our Christmas customs on others, and he told of his attempts to provide opportunities for others to exercise their religious liturgies and customs.

And these rabbis, gray, bushy-bearded, and garbed in black, seemed to appreciate Dad and the welcome he accorded them. We knew that because each spring he would bring home for our happy consumption a box of matzo — unleavened bread — which his friends had brought by for him.

Most Jews in Sheboygan lived on the North Side. Probably all of them were first or second generation immigrants and for the most part had not achieved significant social or economic recognition. Some of the older men would pass through our streets somewhat regularly on their horse drawn wagons, shouting "Rags! Papers!"

People who had been saving cloth and paper items would take their bundles to curbside, where the bearded gentleman would lift them to his large dialed scale. Then, digging into his purse, he would produce the payment for the exchange and continue his slow journey.

In many ways, Sheboyganites were generally regarded as good, neighborly, morally responsible folk. Yet in the matter of human relations with their neighbors who were Jews, they were found wanting. Negative stereotypes persisted. People still passed on to their children the false myths and legends. The unkind names found a comfortable niche in community vocabulary.

I remember coming home for lunch one noon and announcing that a new student had enrolled at Sheridan. "His name is Abie Raffelson. The teacher calls him Harold, but everyone calls him 'Abie'!"

Dad's eyebrows arched far up into his forehead — as it did whenever I crossed a slight bit over his line of expectation in something I'd say or do. That surprised me now because I didn't think anything I'd said merited this kind of response.

Then Dad said, simply, "When you get back this afternoon, ask him whether he would prefer your calling him Harold or Abie."

I did.

That evening after school, Harold invited me to walk home with him and I met his mom and dad. He told them I was his new friend who didn't call him Abie.

The Raffelsons operated a small neighborhood grocery and Harold was their only child. Somewhat haltingly they studied me, then they smiled. And they nodded "yes" when Harold asked whether he might step out of the apartment with me into the store. He headed straight for the candy counter and I was close behind. He drew back the sliding glass door, reached in and emptied out a fist full of candies into my open hands. And any stereotype of Jewish selfishness that might previously have seeped into my head was forever erased.

And the bonds of friendship did not consist solely of confectionery involvement. The harmony finally found its expression in a musical duet. Our debut and only performance occurred in 1930 as we played to my sister's piano accompaniment over Sheboygan's radio station WHBL, "The Chant of the Jungle."

That little ballad isn't remembered today. Neither is the Raffelson/Lutze Harmonica Team who became as little renowned as their song!

During the Lenten season, our church offered worship services in the German language out of respect for some of the older members of the parish — all of whom, I suppose, could understand English very well. There may have been some who thought German would be the language of heaven, because each time God was quoted in their German Scriptures he was speaking in German. More likely for most, however, there were sentimental notes and nostalgic chords struck for them when they would sing again the hymns they had learned and sung in earlier years.

Dad would sometimes take me with him to such services. He'd open his miniature hymnal with its tiny words in German print. I recall one evening when the hymn to be sung was one he remembered from his early days as pupil at the parochial school. All teaching of religion (and probably a few other subjects as well) had been done in German. He handed me the hymnal then and sang the entire hymn (often such hymns had ten or more stanzas) from memory.

He was devout — a studious Bible scholar, familiar with theological writings. I sensed a pride in my sister Dickie, who, together with some of her close friends, was enrolled in his Bible classes for high schoolers at Immanuel Church.

Each Sunday noon during our biggest dinner of the week, around the table we would discuss the service we had attended. Well, not each Sunday.

It seemed that every September, Lutheran pastors greeted the arrival of a new school term as an occasion to extol the virtues of the parochial school. So did our pastor. Inevitably, by implication or in unabashed and undisguised forthrightness, such sermons would draw unfavorable comparisons with the education offered in public schools.

My sisters and I would bristle with resentment. We all were enrolled in public schools and our Dad was a public school principal. We could hardly wait till we could air our feelings at that Sunday's meal. Without wishing to disparage Immanuel's school and always speaking with great respect for its staff, Dad would simply explain that he wanted the education best for us. He felt sure that the public system offered what would be the best.

So, though we really wanted to discuss the sermon, Dad would have none of it, reflecting his own high regard for Pastor Krause. And he would remind us of Dr. Martin Luther's explanation of the Ten Commandments, assigning to the Christian the responsibility to " ... defend [our neighbor], speak well of him, and put the best construction on everything [the neighbor says or does]." And, with that, the matter was closed.

Dad's high regard for the "holy ministry and those who serve in it" was unshakable and unswerving.

```
My Dad
III
Days of Separation
```

the hesitancy imposed by unfamiliar doors

While Dad never ever even so much as suggested I consider the role of pastor as a possibility in my future, the thought had surely occurred to me. One of my Dad's very favorite cousins, Uncle Hans Kleinhans was a pastor, and each of his three sons followed him into the church's ministry. I had a deep respect and admiration for all of them. And there were a half dozen other fellows from our congregation off at school preparing for the ministry — as was my cousin John Lutze. Pastor Krause obviously had been an active recruiter for church related ministries, so it was not surprising he should ask me. But I *was* surprised.

Don't misunderstand. I loved church. I loved my Lord. The thought of serving God as a minister was exhilarating and prompted all kinds of scenarios in my thirteen-year-old head, as I envisioned myself as a clergyman. It would mean I'd already that fall be away from home, enrolled at Concordia College in Milwaukee (it really was only a four year high school academy with two years of junior college courses tacked on — but going "off to *college*" was a pretty heady idea).

Dad made no comment, either encouraging me or dissuading me. I began begging him for permission to apply and he'd dismiss my adolescent nagging with neither acquiescence nor rejection. I knew if he once were to say "No," it would be his final word on the matter. On the other hand, I knew that unless he would say "Yes," I should not count on his favorable verdict.

Finally, well into the June that preceded the opening of the term, he gave his approval.

I began to realize what a serious, solemn choice I had made, and that it was indeed my choice and not my parents'. The commitment was mine and, as much as the more frivolous factors had been part of my desire to enroll, I was stepping into something awesome, something holy.

And I'd be leaving behind Fritz and all the rest of the neighborhood — Fritz and Art and Bob and Marvin, Jim and Grace and Eloise too. And mainly from now on, I'd have classes with only boys, all male instructors.

The opening-of-school banquet for freshmen was a sort of formal goodbye to our parents who were attending the event with us.

In his address Dr. Barth, Concordia's president, told us that people often asked whether his students ever got homesick. His reply: "Our students are young men who never get homesick — but sometimes when they think of home they get a funny feeling in their stomachs." And then he said that if we were at all human, we'd all get that funny feeling once in a while — and if we didn't, he was sure there was something wrong with us.

Well, I got that funny feeling once in a while.

We would make our way to the chapel each weekday for short worship services. We had devotions in our rooms. Each night as I crawled into bed I would say my prayers.

And I had classes in religion too.

There was something about this life away from home that I'd not anticipated. Five hours of Latin every week, and the same for English and German, plus the other subjects of math and history and science. Six years — and after the first two years they'd add four years of Greek. And to keep our minds off things like girls and such, we had an extracurricular schedule of singing, athletics, and other little interest groups dangled before us.

Compulsory three hour study periods each weekday were marked by visits by different faculty members who'd walk through our dormitories each evening — and some mornings, ostensibly to encourage us in our studies, but realistically to be sure no one had sneaked off or gone to bed, or might be brewing up some sort of exciting mischief. Such attentive surveillance, paired with evening curfew (9:30 for fourteen and fifteen year olds and 10:30 for students in the four higher frames), the life style oscillated somewhere between a monastery and a reform school experience.

However, with some 350 plus resourceful, bright, and venturesome youth assembled in such a situation, there were, of course, plenty of distractions to keep the experience from being a bore. And at times it was hard to remember we were on a career track towards becoming ministers.

33

Mercifully, there were summer vacations, occasional weekends at home, and the Thanksgiving, Christmas, and Easter recesses. These gave us connection again with a different world. And how good it was to be back home in my own room, in my own bed. And to sit up late at night and talk at the kitchen table with my Mom and Dad and gain refreshened perspectives.

I had been a fairly sharp eighth grader before I'd left for Concordia. Once enrolled, my grades slipped a bit. They were okay, but they weren't what they might have been, or should have been — or what my parents had hoped they'd be. There were times during my Milwaukee days that I thought seriously about wanting to quit it all. I knew though that Dad would have said, "You know, I never said you should go off to school. I never said you should be a minister. This was your choice." I knew he would say that, and I knew he'd be right saying it. It was then too that I realized I didn't dare turn back from what I knew to be the course I should follow.

I think there were times he had more commitment to my becoming a pastor than I did. And I'm not proud of that either. But I am grateful for the role he filled.

Neither Mom nor Dad ever scolded me or even chided me about my grades. Time and again, their low-key way of standing with me, supportively and quietly, their weekly letters to me, and the care-packages they sent helped me survive that strange adolescent period of my life. Now, as I reflect, I find myself — despite the good times experienced during my Milwaukee days and some wonderful friendships cultivated there — deeply resentful of those six years. I regard them a serious disruption which stole from me precious time to be with two wonderful, wise, loving, and caring parents.

In the days while I was still at home, Sheboygan saw little of African American people. Nor, despite its name, did Sheboygan have American Indian residents, nor Hispanics. People who lived there were almost all ethnically derived from northern European countries. And, as for us younger ones, we gave recognition to just two categories, Catholic and Lutheran (and in a general way we included all the rest of the Protestants in the latter category).

Oh, we learned the hearth-side singables of Stephen Foster and a few more from the *Golden Book of Songs* and the *Twice 55 Favorites*. We even learned them in school — songs whose lyrics introduced to us such terms as "darkies," "colored," and even "pickaninnies," which were explained to our little innocent ears as titles of endearment that referred to "dark-complexioned people of the South."

When a Pullman porter would step down from his train to help passengers off at Sheboygan and take on new ones, it would be one of those rare occasions when we'd see an African American in our city. And then, of course, there was circus time when the Ringling Brothers or Wallace Shows came to town.

Their entourage would always include a significant number of black workers to unload wagons in preparation for the evening's opening. We would watch in awe as in perfect rhythm as many as six workers would bring down their sledges in quick successive blows to drive enormous stakes deep into the ground in order to secure the massive tents they'd raise.

Other than that, our opportunities to learn about African Americans, their history, and their "place" in America were severely limited. And the adults in our community were equally ignorant.

Uncle August was somewhat an authority on the subject. Because he had married Aunt Lugie, Texan by birth, he'd visited in the South a few times. When he spoke about southern culture we listened. I recall him speaking in clearly authoritative tone, "You never use the term 'nigger' if there are Negroes nearby because they don't like that and can get very angry."

My six years in Milwaukee afforded me little more opportunity to be a learner in the matter of racial concerns. Milwaukee was a big city, maybe not as large as Chicago, but certainly a lot bigger than Sheboygan. It had its own high numbers of Lutherans and Roman Catholics, but a few black refugees from the segregated South had found their way there too. But they were not a significant number. In all my days there I would see few more than the occasional queue of school children lined up for morning mass outside St. Benedict the Moor Church, to the east, on State Street. However, when I would be visiting Frank Sage's Barbershop on 27th Street, I got to observe the man who was hired to shine shoes and to sweep away the clippings that fell from the five chairs the busy barbers kept serving. His skin was very dark. With a large smile he would welcome me — and anyone else who entered. His hopes, obviously, focused on the customers asking him to shine their shoes. On my small allowance, that was at best on his part dreaming "the most impossible dream."

There were mirrors on both of the long walls of the shop. I don't recall the barbers looking at those mirrors much — the scene remained fairly constant — all the barbers with their tiny shears, snipping away. And not many customers looked up. The sight of being captive under the barber's sheet was probably not inspiring.

I kept looking because I was engrossed by the appearance of this lone white-coated gentleman who went about his work so diligently. I realized that not many really used his shoe polish services and, although no one was abusive or rude to him, he was clearly there at a different — and lower — level. Between sweepings, he would retire to a little corner nook assigned to him, furnished sparsely with a short stool, a hook for his coat, a little set of shelves for his brushes and shoe polish paste, and a bin for a mop, bucket, broom, and dust cloths.

Ever so often he would emerge from his corner, armed with the tools of his trade, to engage in short sorties between the chairs, scooping up the newest little piles of unwanted clippings that had floated to the floor. I never had been much for sitting still while someone would be snipping away at the back of my neck. So I'd often become intrigued by this custodian's activities.

On one such occasion I was studying his actions rather closely. Looking in the mirrors, I followed his moving about. Suddenly, after a quick furtive scanning of the room to be sure no one watched, he turned quickly to the barbers' shelf behind the chairs. He grasped a bottle, removed its lid and downed a large, swift swallow. With an assumed nonchalance, he quickly and quietly set the bottle down and returned to his corner. Obviously no one else had seen him.

When my chair was turned about I realized the bottle contained an after-shave lotion, and because of its alcohol content, the man had a rather strangely perfumed product to quench his craving.

My initial response was sheer surprise. There was an element of humor here. Neither barbers nor customers would ever have asked this man to join them at a tavern across the street for a short, refreshing beer. They simply wouldn't want to be seen with him as their drinking companion. Yet here he was, having one "on the house" in their very company.

I couldn't even bring myself to a smile, however. What I had seen here I would never forget. I felt chilled, realizing that this man had this job to come to, day after day after day. I couldn't imagine the home he'd left in the morning and would return to again each night. Was there a family to feed? Would anyone ask — even dare to ask: "Well, how was work today?" What were his hopes for the future, or was this daily routine in store for him for the rest of his life? And I wondered how long before this horrible selection in drinking would eat away at his health.

Things didn't cost much in those days. We could — and did, when the meals at school were less than appealing — run down to Torres Café, where we could buy a small bowl of wonderful spicy — and greasy — chili for five cents. But we really didn't have the money to do that very often.

I could supplement my modest allowance (five dollars a month that came from home) by signing on occasionally with the college kitchen crew at fifteen cents an hour. This also entitled us on Saturday nights to have a piece of our baker's wonderful coffeecake he'd prepared for the students' Sunday breakfast.

Saturday night would also be the time we usually would see a black police car parked near the kitchen door. On one particular night the officers dropped in, as was their custom, to enjoy a free cup of coffee and some bakery. Somehow, the administration probably felt comfort in this tacitly negotiated alliance that would provide special protection in exchange for some munchings.

The uniforms, the billy clubs, the handcuffs dangling from their belts, and their holstered guns lent them a special kind of awesome presence. So when they would speak, their words were always immersed in authority.

They began telling about what they anticipated as they were setting out to patrol Milwaukee's Saturday night. They indicated that they would of course be cruising through "the colored neighborhood." The younger of the two told how much he hated that because of all the fights they'd probably encounter. His senior partner responded by informing him — and all of us who were there listening — that "you have to know those people. Take Joe Louis the boxer. He keeps winning because they keep hitting him in the head and he doesn't feel it. You see, niggers have hard heads. They're different that way — real thick skulls. If you hit them on the head with a night stick it'll split right in two." Then, stretching out his hand and pointing to its center, he added, "You have to hit 'em on the side of their head as hard as you can, and they'll just buckle under. It's not easy, but it's how you show you're the boss."

At fourteen years old, I didn't know anything significant about anatomy. His comments about the thickness of skulls caused me to wonder why, if that were true, I'd never heard of it before. But after all, police were experienced and informed. Beyond having doubts about authenticity of his comments, I recall feeling almost sickened by what he had said. I was disappointed and confused at the thought that any kind of racial confrontation would warrant such a response by the police.

After I had returned to my room, still troubled by the dining hall episode and all the officer had said, I recalled an event of my early childhood. I must have been five or six at the time.

———————

It was summer vacation time and one of those very warm, almost steamy Sheboygan nights. We didn't have electric fans at our house, but our windows were wide open as we waited — and hoped — for a late evening Lake Michigan breeze to rescue us from the sweltering heat.

Uncle August and Aunt Lugie had dropped by for a visit, when suddenly an almost blinding flash of lightning, followed immediately by a crashing explosion of thunder, shook the house and left us in sudden, total darkness. Torrents of rain slammed down on the pavement outside and rain began blowing through the screened windows. As more brilliant shafts of lightning streaked from the sky, I could see why it was called lightning. At each flash, the outside was lightened to a brightness that made everything as visible as midday sunlight. The storm had snuffed out the streetlights, making the night darker than usual. Yet it was phenomenally clear outside. At each flash — always accompanied by a deafening crash, we could see everything. We had already rushed to the windows to close them against the rain. Mom and Dad had meanwhile scurried about and found candles which brought some light to the inner rooms.

We huddled together at the bed room window to watch the dazzling, awesome display. Suddenly Aunt Lugie exclaimed, "There's a man out there, standing under the tree — and he's colored!"

No less excited, Dad added, "He shouldn't be standing out there — close to a tree like that is the worst place he could be."

Mom grasped his arm and whispered, "Charlie, you've got to go out there and bring him inside right now!"

Dad must have realized that above the roar of the rain his call to the man would never be heard, so, snatching his cravenette and throwing it over his shoulders, umbrella in hand, he went out into the storm to bring the stranger to cover.

Aunt Lugie became anxious and raised the caution, "But he's colored and you don't know how dangerous this might be!" Uncle August tried to calm her and, taking her by the arm, brought her to the "safety" of our upstairs for what would be a rather lengthy time.

Mother and I met the two men at the kitchen door. The rescued one appeared both frightened and relieved. And physically and emotionally fatigued. And grateful.

In candlelight and with soft voice he told his story. He was one of the kitchen crew for the circus that had come into town. An oversight by the chef found them to be without sugar for breakfast, so our guest had been dispatched to find a store and purchase at least a small amount to tide them over till a larger supply could be found the next morning. In his roving all over the city the poor man learned what every resident in Sheboygan already knew, that no grocery stores were open after six o'clock. When the clouds unloaded this deluge, he had run as fast as possible to find his way back to the circus. Finally he had to stop to catch his breath. With no other shelter in sight he chose to stop under the Lutzes' broad-leafed chestnut tree until the rains might relent. And, obviously, they hadn't.

A small pool of water had begun to form under the man. Mother had already begun warming the oven and she invited him to take off his shoes and drape his socks and denim jacket before the open oven to dry. Dad took the shoes to the sink, poured water from them, and placed them on the oven shelf.

As our visitor stood warming himself he became more comfortable with us and gladly answered the many questions we had about circus happenings. Sipping his hot cup of coffee, he regaled us with tale after tale of this intriguing kind of life. It was a wonderful visit. He was such a warmly human and kindly person. To paraphrase the famous song, "We could have talked all night...."

Eventually the storm subsided. Moments later the power was restored and the lights in the house went on again.

His socks were dry, and he commented how comfortably warm the shoes had become. Over and over again he thanked us for the hospitality as he prepared to leave.

It was Mom then who asked, "But what will you people do for breakfast when you have no sugar?"

Because in our pantry we had two deep bins — one filled with flour, the other with sugar, she offered to sell him some if he wished. He was overwhelmed. Dad found a large bag and measured out fifteen pounds of sugar for the man to carry back to the circus. The chef had supplied him with cash to buy whatever amount he could find so he offered to pay a generous amount for it. My parents would not hear of it and insisted he pay no more than our grocer had charged us. He laid the exact number of coins on the table, thanked us again, and went out into the night that had been pleasantly cooled by the rain.

We never did ask his name, nor he ours.

We remembered him and his visit and we often talked of the experience.

And now I remembered him again. And tonight's experience with the policemen left me chilled.

```
My Dad
IV.
The Later Years
```

a door of privacy

Among the virtues regarded particularly high in our family life was modesty. In my earliest years I was already sure that my Dad was one of history's greatest, finest men. He certainly had to be the best school principal in Sheboygan. He even admitted that he had played helmetless quarterback on an intramural football team during his college days. And he was smart. I was sure he had read every one of the many shelves of books in his library cabinet. We could ask him questions about flowers or famous figures of history or sports or political figures or carpentry or birds or farming or about distant countries and he would always have answers for us. He'd surprise us with recitations of poems appropriate to our conversation when we'd be at table.

My sisters and I were so very proud of him. I remember once asking him, when I was still very small, why I had never seen his name or a picture of him in the *Sheboygan Press*. He replied, quoting an adage I heard him repeat from time to time through the years (I don't know that I had ever heard the words from anyone else's lips before — nor have I since). However, they were important for him to invoke when he felt it fitting:

"Fools' names and faces
Are always found in public places."

He clarified his pronouncement, adding that he did not mean to imply that all people whose names or pictures appeared in the *Sheboygan Press* were fools. He was simply trying to say he wished for neither himself nor our family to be regarded as "fools" in some exposure in the local press.

Of course, it was impossible for him to conceal his pride in his family. He would certainly hope that others thought well of us. If we should be thus regarded, however, it would have to derive from others observing our lives rather than our telling people of our performance or our own listing whatever virtues we might have.

Years later, upon receiving a copy of the first book I authored, he wrote back almost immediately, thanking me for sending it and telling me he had already read it.

He heard me preach several times through the years and though we might have conversation about the content of any homily or address, he would quite deliberately side-step any assessing or critiquing of the presentation.

I knew, of course, he approved of what I did, yet I yearned for his commendation. But I should have known better — and really did. I'd come not to expect it.

I was about four years into my Oklahoma ministry when Mom and Dad came to spend a few days with us. I was not yet thirty and still enjoyed participating in athletics, so I'd been enrolled in a summer adult softball program. I asked Dad if he'd like to come along to watch.

I wanted so much to play well because my Dad was watching. I actually played one of my best games ever. I had a hit each of my four times at bat — a single, a double, a triple, and a home run. I made five good fielding plays. Near the end of the game the batter swatted a sharp grounder through the pitcher's mound. I raced toward the ball from my second base position and managed to knock it down, but not in time to throw the batter out at first base. The next man up hit a line drive directly at me. I caught it and tagged the runner who had been on first base. We had snuffed out the rally and won the game with an unassisted double play.

As Dad and I drove off toward home, I asked him whether he liked the game. He cleared his throat, harrumphed slightly, and noted that I missed getting the batter thrown out on the grounder behind second base. And I grinned broadly to myself.

This stubborn resistance to anything even suggesting pridefulness was of course a part of adapting to his German Lutheran culture. But already, while still a toddler, I learned that though Dad respected that culture, he was not its captive.

For years a long-set pattern of seating had been established in Lutheran churches, and in our Sheboygan church as well — providing for women to be seated in the section to the right of the center aisle (with the children of course). Men would sit on the left side. Who knows where the custom started? Most likely — since men made all the decisions anyway — the voters viewed the altar as the place where God was gathering all His people, the worthy ones on His right side and the less worthy on His left. This, of course, would be to the right of the aisle, where the women would then be expected to sit.

Early on, Dad would lead us along the wall on the *left* side of the church and would stop at the fifth row to let us all slide by him into the pew he selected. Uncle August and Aunt Lugie, followed by my cousins, selected their *left side* pew as well. Apparently other women of the parish who observed this aberrant move badgered their own husbands to accord them that kind of respect. And so, save for the instances of a few chauvinistic die-hards, in an unbelievably short time, gender segregation disappeared in our church. Dad and his younger brother, the unobtrusive mavericks!

Retirement years did not come easy to Dad. He was in fine physical condition. He was mentally sharp. Suddenly — as if before the final act in the drama could be completed, he became sixty-five years old, and the curtain closed abruptly on his career.

I was miles away when it happened. His letters spoke briefly about the formalities of closure. But there were the clippings from the press and the printed programs that Mom sent along that told the story of his splendid record as teacher and administrator, with tributes from colleagues, community leaders, and former students. Flowers, cards, letters, and other celebrative expressions attested to the love and regard he had won through the years.

However, his letters to us hinted at his frustrations of being put to the side when there was still so much he could offer.

Months went slowly by. One morning, however, his day was significantly brightened by a call from the pastor of a neighboring parish. The new school term was about to get underway and Bethlehem Lutheran School had just lost its eighth grade teacher. Would Dad be able to fill the position? Of course he would, and he did.

The tone of his subsequent letters breathed his gratification. He had been remembered, recognized, wanted. He had been chosen.

The euphoria did not last. The workload was heavy, working under a different system called for significant adjustment and adapting. Equipment and materials were not of the quality he'd been used to. But he liked his colleagues and admired their dedication and appreciated the way they welcomed his counsel and drew on his years of experience. He felt good about the appreciative parents. And he loved the excitement of the classroom and the rewards of growth in his pupils.

The position did not last. After all, it had originally been agreed. The arrangement was only to be temporary.

At this same time, however, Mom's health began to fail — a fractured hip, severe arthritis, the dimming of her vision all beckoned to his best instincts of kindly care. All of us in the family were so very delighted and grateful to see him pitch in as he took on roles of kitchen help, housekeeper, and genuine colleague to Mom.

This was the same Dad who, in the early days of their marriage, had cautioned Mom (as she told us later), "the children are growing now and becoming more perceptive, so we'll no longer have display of affection in their presence."

At eighty-nine Dad's own health diminished. His doctors scheduled him for surgery.

On the night before he was hospitalized, Mom told us, she had been sleeping in her special adjustable bed and was wakened as if a butterfly was touching down on her forehead. She was about to brush it away, when she realized it was Dad leaning over her pillow, caressing her forehead with repeated kisses. She finally gave him leave, reminding him, "You must get some sleep now, Charley; you have a big day tomorrow."

Once he was settled in — in his hospital bed, my sisters tried to put him in touch with my Mother. His hearing had faded and he was unable to distinguish the words Mom spoke to him on the telephone. In frustration and tears he handed the phone back to my sister. Sadly, that never-quite-completed tryst proved to be their final goodbye.

There are times I spot a strangely marked bird, or some wild flower I've never seen before, and my impulse is to call Dad to ask him to identify my find for me. And there are times I'd like to report to him on how things are going and how my perspectives are honed. I would so value the chance for conversation.

I have missed him.

My Mom

though confined to indoors
one can find new doors to open

January, 1945. It was one of the last days of Christmas recess. We were at home sipping cocoa together at the small kitchen table. I was to be graduated from the seminary only a few days later. On February fourth I would be ordained. She told me how deeply she regretted that she'd not be able to go to Oklahoma to attend the ordination ceremonies.

The conversation drifted. We got to talking about my arrival back in 1920.

She tried to describe the birth pains. They must have been unusually severe. Birthing was nothing new to her — she had had four daughters. This time, however, the pangs were intolerable and she cried out, asking her Lord to allow her to die. The dear friend and family physician, Dr. Elvers, in the midst of his working furiously, reprimanded her. Aloud, she burst out, "All right then, Lord, let it be twins!" (I've always felt God answered her prayer by giving her only one of me — obviously enough to handle.)

"However," she confided, "quietly in my heart I was praying the prayer of Hannah who had had no sons, and who bargained with God, 'If you give me a son, I will give him back to you for your service.' So I have always wanted you to be a minister and now my prayer is answered."

I was astonished. "Mother! You *never* told me you wanted me to become a minister. You never suggested that for my future, never even mentioned it! In fact, when I was finishing eighth grade, I was begging you and Dad to let me go to Concordia so I could become a pastor. The months passed, and you gave me no encouragement at all! It wasn't until only a few weeks were left before the fall term that you and he finally relented and agreed to let me enroll."

She smiled.

I don't remember Mother attending any Sunday Bible hour. Perhaps none was offered. I remember all the rest of us — five in a row — going off to Sunday school each Lord's Day — Dad to teach a class of high schoolers. Then we'd all regroup with Mom to worship together at the Lutze pew. About five rows back on the left.

50

Once I was at school in far away Milwaukee (sixty miles down the road), more letters came from Dad's typewriter than from Mom's pen. But she communicated well.

We had two choices for getting clothes laundered — the college laundry (for a fee of course) or sending it home. Most students saw the decided advantage in the second option. I did too.

The system put to use inexpensive, suitcase-sized corrugated boxes, fitted into a canvas covering, fastened with heavy knit straps. To make mailing convenient, the canvas casing provided a plastic or celluloid pocket to hold a reversible card bearing the student's address on one side and home address on the rear. What we would send home was always a crumpled mess (for about 22 cents, as I remember); but, oh, what a beautiful thing to behold when returned. Fresh, sweet smelling shirts and socks and such and, most important, cookies, or cake, or fruit were the really important items. And for me, Mom more often than not would include a dozen of her culinary specialty — Danish rolls with pineapple filling, liberally iced. No need for her to write — she communicated her love for me quite adequately — and gratifyingly.

When she did set her hand to letter writing, her news was more often than not domestic — names of relatives who'd dropped by, reports on my sisters who were off to college by this time, inventory on her flower garden, and a few motherly hints on hygiene, dress, and the use of clean handkerchiefs.

One of her letters I especially remember. By this time I was already a pastor.

I had been serving the little parish in Muskogee, Oklahoma's black community for barely a year when, to my surprise, I received word from St. Paul Lutheran Congregation, Chatfield, Minnesota, inviting me to become its pastor. In a letter to my parents I shared the news. By return mail Mother wrote to tell me how pleased she was. She acknowledged that I indeed had been working hard in what certainly was a difficult setting, but she was overjoyed at the prospect of our leaving Oklahoma to be "closer to the family" back in Wisconsin.

A few days later I wrote home, announcing my decision to stay on in Muskogee. She wrote no letter of response to mine. Her

51

silence left little doubt in my mind that my declining the call to Minnesota must surely have disappointed her.

In the summer that followed, Mom and Dad drove down to Oklahoma to visit us and got to see where we were serving. The nave, which accommodated about sixty worshippers, was in the front of the large old house that also served as both church and parsonage. A small corner of carpeting that covered the chancel floor had torn loose and Mom was sitting alone with me as I tacked it into place. When I stood up she placed her hand on my forearm and said, "I'm so happy you are here and I am so glad I could meet these people. I know that many churches would not welcome them. I am so happy to see how you and Esther love them — and how much they love you!"

Then with moist eyes she apologized, "I've been so ashamed that I wrote what I did when I told you I was hoping you would leave Oklahoma and move closer to us. You did right to stay. You belong here and you are serving our Lord well here. I'm very proud of you."

I don't know of any affirmation I've ever received through the years that has meant more to me.

I can't possibly draw a list of the good people who have been supportive to me in my ministry, but I count my mother as my most enthusiastic fan. I recall visiting with her at home in her parlor in days shortly before she lost her sight (I almost said "vision," but she never lost that!). I noticed on the table at her side the book I'd written, *To Mend the Broken*. It was already out of print by then. Her copy lay there, open. She explained that reading had become a chore and she did little of it any more. "So," she confided, "instead of reading from my daily devotional booklet, I read a page in your book each day."

Mother didn't become totally blind till she was well into her eighties. In 1977, when at last her days were ended, she had garnered enough physical impairments that may well have warranted declaring her small, embattled body a medical disaster area. As I remember, the list included a fractured hip and deteriorating cartilage that ruled out surgical correction, arterial sclerosis, rheumatoid arthritis, pulmonary emphysema, and residual glaucoma.

Once Dad died, and her well being had further diminished, we found for her the kind of care she needed in a nursing home. Confined to bed and wheelchair, now completely blind, she began the final chapter of her life in a room that she came to know only from our descriptions and by the sounds and smells around her. Whenever we visited her we would sit close to reach and gently stroke her stiff but remarkably soft hands.

On one of my visits I found her weeping. I asked her "Where does it hurt, Mom?" She quickly told me that the tears were prompted not by any physical pain, but by the death of her roommate that morning. And she added, "And she was so young!"

"How old?" I asked.

"Only 86." You see, Mother was 94.

During her eight years in that room six roommates had died. These were women she had never seen. Yet she was with them each day from dawn to sunset, and slept only five feet away from them at night. She knew their voices — and she got to know them well as they would talk about their earlier years, their families, their disappointments, their pains, their happier times, their grandchildren.

If a contest were offered, inviting participants to submit an additional four or five to the original list of our Lord's Beatitudes, youth would surely post as a winner: "Blessed is the parent who refuses to be preachy." Mother was not preachy. She was teachy.

With endless patience and soft persistence, even in (*especially* in!) her later years, she would brush to the side questions we'd ask about her situation or well being. She would manage to steer our conversations that pressed me to reflect on and assess my role as parent, husband, and pastor. All this she would do without prescribing what kind of a father, husband, or pastor I ought to be.

She had cultivated the art of unruffledness, and was eager that we learn from her to take the crises of life in stride and to stand ready to move in with "plan b" when "plan a" would fail. On one occasion a visitor to our home, eager to be helpful, was on tiptoe to replace a dessert dish on a high shelf. Mother and I both watched with apprehension, as it surely seemed a mite beyond her reach. We saw it slip from the young woman's hand. Even before the glass struck the floor my mother calmly said, "That's all right." Our guest, already in tears, stooped to pick up the thousand splinters of shattered glass. And Mom gently explained, "We have more glasses and we can always get another. Now come, let me help you."

In an instance of far greater consequence, Mother exhibited the same sort of disciplined serenity. Dad had come home from a meeting with the principals of all the other city schools. Mother was in the kitchen behind her ironing board. He was clearly troubled. She stopped ironing to give her complete attention to his report. The moment was so intense that neither of them bothered to shoo their little nine year old off to play. I didn't understand it all, but I was able to grasp the main message.

Apparently the dramatic dimensions of the Depression had left city funds woefully short for meeting the costs of administering and maintaining the city schools. It seemed that the only recourse for the school board was to shut down Horace Mann, the smallest of Sheboygan's elementary schools. This move would save a considerable amount in salaries of the dismissed faculty and staff. In resourcefulness and unselfish loyalty and in care for their colleagues, the principals had now in this meeting unanimously agreed to ask the school board to curtail their own salaries so that there would be sufficient funds with which to keep Horace Mann's staff on the job.

Mother had only words of appreciation and commendation for the decision. I remember her saying, "How could those people ever make it otherwise? What else would they be able to do?" If I remember correctly, their voluntary salary reduction amounted to fifty per cent. Both Mom and Dad sat right down together then at the kitchen table to determine at what points they might best attend to and manage the impending austerities. And I remember being very, very proud of them.

Years later, on a visit to her nursing home, I walked into Mom's room as she was listening to her radio — a program out of South Dakota called *Lutheran Vespers*. Normally when I'd arrive and her radio was playing, she would shut it off at once. Not this time. Not in the middle of a church service. The customary greetings would have to wait. Without speaking a word, she was still teaching me something about priorities.

Once the broadcast was ended she turned off the radio. She proceeded to tell what she had found helpful and useful in her long life of having heard probably six thousand or more sermons through the years. Of course she also told me what she had found boring — and at times, to her annoyance, utterly useless. And I listened to her teaching and learned.

She also taught me something that could prove especially valuable should I myself some day be in a place where I would be receiving institutionally prepared meals. This learning experience occurred on a Sunday evening. A worker in dining services informed Mother that the evening meal would consist of a wiener (along with sundry other side items). When asked what beverage she preferred, Mom ordered, "Coffee without cream"

When the woman had left us, I expressed my surprise, "Mother! I didn't know you drink coffee anymore — and when you used to, you never drank it black!"

Mom explained that on Sunday nights wieners were a regular fare, and by the time they were delivered they were invariably cold. She would dip her wiener into the hot coffee and warm it up a bit before indulging. "It really works nicely, " she noted.

When our children were very young, almost every summer we would drive from Oklahoma to Wisconsin "to see the folks." The 1952 trip carries the most vivid memories for me. It was July, and because of small lumps on her throat, Esther had agreed to undergo an examination while in Sheboygan. Dr. McRoberts urged immediate surgery.

The operation lasted far longer than anticipated. I was feeling a new anxiety. While I was waiting, hoping to make the time pass more quickly, I drove around the city with our three boys. Quite suddenly and shockingly I was overwhelmed at the realization of my own inadequacy and unreadiness to fill the role of single parent. I found myself almost smothering them in my attempt to be a good father. I stopped to get them popcorn, soda, ice cream. They, of course, reveled in my extravagant affection. But they also sensed the seriousness of what was going on in the hospital — and in my head.

It was then that little four year old redheaded Steve brought me up short with his Sunday School theological observation: "Dad, it would be okay if the doctor's knife would slip and Mom would die, because God would take her to heaven!" Out there in the parking lot, all four of us huddled together in the front seat and prayed.

When Dr. McRoberts emerged, he asked me to sit down while he explained why the operation procedures had lasted so long. This former Mayo Clinic surgeon explained how in all of his eight years of doing thyroidectomies, he had never encountered a cancer that had called for such drastic and complete invasion. The surgery had proved so difficult that it would be hazardous for her not to stay on in Sheboygan several weeks in his care.

This we'd hardly expected. Even before we had left for Wisconsin on this trip I had already agreed to accept the pastorate of the newly begun Prince of Peace Church in Tulsa. Immediately upon our return in two weeks we were to vacate our home in Muskogee and move into our new house in Tulsa.

My Mom was in her seventieth year when all this happened. Without hesitation she urged me to return to Oklahoma and attend to all the responsibilities of packing and relocating back there. I was "not to worry!" She would take on the role of Florence Nightingale with Esther and Mother Superior for the three boys, all under six, for fully three weeks.

Years later, long after Esther's complete recovery, and after a fourth son had been added to the family roster, Esther would try to put into words the deep gratitude all of us — but especially she — felt for the generous, attentive care Mom had shown us during that rigorous ordeal. And Mother would tell her time and again, "This is the way it is in the Christian family — we all take our turns loving and the times come when we need loving and someone else is there who cares."

And she was right, of course. During her long years of almost total dependency, my "in-between-sister" and I (we both lived a good distance away from Sheboygan) would come to visit her as often as possible. However, my oldest and youngest sisters, Gertrude and Hildegarde, who lived nearby proved the constant ones. Day after day, they would take turns to be at mother's side at lunchtime and supper. They would be there to describe for Mom what was going on in her room as well as the world outside and what items were on the tray of food before her. They would identify each forkful and spoonful of food they would bring to her lips. They would comfort and cheer her when her spirits were low. In her perpetual darkness they would prompt her to recall, in all their full color, people and events of her past to help her relive happy moments of her earlier years. And at day's end they would sing with her the prayers her own mother had sung at crib side, prayers she herself had prayed with us at bedtime, and which we've taught our children too.

For the loving care these sisters have brought to her that I could never bring, I shall always be grateful. They learned much and they learned well from our Mother how to be dispensers of grace.

My Friend Fritz

the best doors make possible traffic in both directions

The Ferschlands lived in the little brown brick house, owned by Ben Haack, father of Reuben, who ultimately married my sister Gertrude. The Ferschlands lived directly across from Fritz Mohr (my favorite childhood friend) and kitty-corner from Bartz's grocery.

For the benefit of serious students of geography, the Haacks lived directly to the north of the Ferschlands in the big-porched white two-story house, across the street from where the Zieraths lived. He was a doctor. Silver-haired Mrs. Zierath reminded me of Eleanor Roosevelt, stately, dignified, and much better looking than the first lady. Their son Frederick was the very kind of young man who would go to West Point. And he did. Three daughters, Gretchen, Marian, and Charlotte, were of about the same ages as my sisters.

Twelve feet north of the Haacks' house lay the cindered alley that cut through the block, right across the Sheridan School playground, emptying into Fourteenth Street across from Mr. Baehler's barber shop where Dad and I used to get our haircuts at fifty cents each. His wall was covered with shelves containing the personal mugs of different customers who would come in for their shaves, each requiring personalized, customized service. Dad shaved himself at home.

There were other barber shops around. One, two blocks away next to Marholz's butcher shop, and another, next to Eisenmann's saloon and bowling alley across from Schreier's brewery, which was kitty-corner from our house. Nickels were sparse, and when one would come our way, we'd go to the saloon for an ice cream cone, where the bar tender would invariably ask, "Which flavor do you want, plain, white, or vanilla?" We probably went to Mr. Baehler for tonsorial attention because of Lutheran connections. His daughter Elizabeth, a classmate of one of my sisters, was, as I recall, a member of my father's Bible Class at Immanuel Church.

Next to Baehler's was Schmidts' grocery. The Lutzes didn't buy groceries there because Schmidts didn't get their insurance from the Lutze Insurance Agency which my Grandfather had developed and was now operated by Dad's youngest brother, Uncle August. But we did buy our Thompson's Chocolate Covered Malted Milk Balls and Mr. Goodbars at Schmidts' when we'd have scraped together the necessary five pennies for that kind of transaction. We liked the two Schmidt kids. George and Junior were both younger, but athletic enough to get in on the softball game we'd regularly have across their street at Sheridan playground. I don't remember them well, but I do recall the time they were wearing roller skates in the back of the grocery delivery truck. Their granddad was driving and collided with another vehicle and there was broken glass all over the place and the boys got banged around and cut up rather badly. All of us kids in the neighborhood learned that you should never be in the back of the truck with their grandfather driving, especially if you're wearing roller skates.

Back to the Ferschlands. Harold Ferschland was in first grade with Fritz and me. I don't remember him throwing footballs around with us or playing catch. I don't remember much about Harold at all because, early on, they moved away. But I do remember his mother who, when I first met her, wore a fresh white patch/bandage across her left eye. She'd been frying bacon, and some grease had leaped up from the pan and struck her eye. And I remember promising myself that if ever in my lifetime I would fry bacon, I would keep my eyes closed. And to this day on those infrequent occasions when it's my turn to do the bacon, I still squint.

I recall being at their house one day when Mr. Ferschland dropped in for a cup of coffee. The streetcar tracks ran west from Eighth Street, down across the Pennsylvania Avenue bridge, and after steep climbs and right angle turns, passing Sheridan School, finally rounded the corner on to South Fifteenth Street. And that of course is the corner where we lived. One block to the south is where the Ferschlands lived.

Mr. Ferschland was the conductor on this little trolley and, when he chose to do so, he would simply leave what passengers there were on board, in their seats out there in the middle of the street, while he would dash inside to sojourn with his wife. Considering the "fast" pace which marked life in Sheboygan at that time, no one particularly minded or appeared to be disturbed about the unscheduled stopover. When he had completed his rest stop, he would climb into the car again and resume his seat at the controls, register two or three noisy clangs and be on his way again, guiding his little orange machine down the tracks. Sometimes we'd run alongside

61

of the streetcar to the end of the line, about a half-mile farther. We'd watch Mr. Ferschland dismount and walk around to the rear of the coach to pull down the trolley pole from the power line above. Then he'd go to the opposite end, unhook the other trolley pole and, mid loud flashing sparks flying in every direction, he'd fit the small wheel at the end of the rod against the power line. The motor would start its pulsating hum, the interior lights would go on once more and he'd climb aboard again. Then, noisily pulling the backs to each of the seats so they'd face the opposite direction, he was prepared for the return trip to the downtown car barn, wheels ascreeching and bell aclanging.

There were of course other youngsters that moved in and out of my life. None of these, however, grew into the deep friendship I had with Fritz Mohr. We had not known each other before the day we both showed up at Sheridan School in front of Ms. Gertrude Hinske. Then and after proper medical certification we were declared fit to emerge from our quarantined status and be reinstated as totally acceptable kindergartners.

In the previous weeks both the Mohr and the Lutze houses had been marked by the city health department with huge red signs posted near the front doors, declaring us unclean and warning people to avoid these premises, lest they too become victims of scarlet fever. I am not sure what happened at the Mohr household during those days. However, my two uninfected sisters and Dad moved next door to spend the time of quarantine with Grandma and with Dad's unmarried sister, Aunt Marie.

It was a bitter winter, but our house was warm because each morning and evening Dad would slip into our basement through the outside trap door in the rear and would attend to furnace requirements to keep the home fires glowing.

Our house had a long porch on its south side and my sisters and other relatives would come to the window each day for mini-reunions. That year we missed out on many of the traditional Christmas happenings, but a highlight for me was showing, through a porch window, my new wind-up train circling its little oval track, and how my partner sister would help me fill its cars with pine needles for its short runs.

Fritz and I hit it off immediately in our new uncontaminated status. Details of collaborative activities are a bit blurred, but deportment cards my mother should have thrown away reveal symptoms of *my* being a slow learner. One entry announces my having learned to skip with one foot, and a subsequent missive reports my having forgotten how to skip. Still another informs my parents of difficulty I was encountering in learning to tie my shoes.

Fritz would never have had such entries on *his* cards. He was very athletic — could turn somersaults perfectly, while I would fall over sideways in my attempts. He could do hand springs. I would really try, but I'd sort of crumble before getting even half way up. Fritz was also very good on the merry-go-round. I would be holding on for dear life in sheer terror when the big kids got on and would send the contraption on dizzying speeds.

His dad had bought him membership in the *Turn Verein*. I'd sometimes go along and with awe and envy I'd watch him and these other very athletic youngsters go through their gymnastic routines. I couldn't even touch my toes (except when I'd bend my knees just a little). Fritz never made me feel inferior to him in any way. We were really friends. And while he pursued his gymnastic training, my natural preference for the fine arts found me — though I was only in fourth grade — awarded the position of president and drum major of the Sheridan School Harmonica Band. However, these activities did not define for either of us our future careers.

But, oh, we played. And played. And played. Hardly a day would pass when we weren't together. And when such times did occur — because of family priorities or because we were with other neighborhood kids — it was a sort of mini-reunion when we'd be together again.

We wouldn't call each other up; we'd never knock at the door; we'd never ring the doorbell. We'd simply stand outside and at the top of my voice outside his door I'd yell (always in two syllables): "Fri-yitz! Fri-yitz!" or he'd shout from the bottom of our porch steps: "Kah-rull! Kah-rull!"

Afternoons and evenings and Saturdays we'd be playing. If we weren't over at Sheridan School in some pickup softball game, he'd come over with his glove. I had a catcher's mitt. The positions were natural. Fritz was a fine pitcher — I never did learn how to throw a curve.

I did pretty well at catch. Dad would often — every day the weather was right — throw a baseball with me when he'd come home for lunch (Dad could throw a curve!). When Fritz and I would be out throwing together, however, it was no longer Fritz and Karl playing catch. He was Jerome Dean and I was Chicago Cubs backstop Hartnett. I'd commend him, "Nice pitch, Dizzy!" and he'd respond, "Good catch there, Gabby!"

And Sundays? The Mohrs were Evangelicals. The subject was painful and not much discussed. It seems that they had indeed been Lutherans too. Fritz's grandfather had not been deemed "active-in-good-standing" or whatever, and so at his death the Lutherans denied the family a church burial for their father.

I never learned much about the Evangelical Church. My father confided that they were very close to the Lutherans. That signaled to me that Fritz and his family were okay. Which I knew anyway. Fritz and I, each in our own church, were confirmed as we were finishing eighth grade. I was not allowed long trousers until confirmation. Fritz wore long trousers already in seventh grade. I began to see some difference between my church and his.

Another thing I remember about St. John Evangelical Church was that a woodpecker had some sort of a grudge or dislike for St. John's metal steeple. This bird would perch on it and beat it relentlessly with his beak, making a horrible racket and becoming a serious nuisance not only for the neighborhood, but especially for people seeking the quiet dignity that a church ought to offer its worshippers. The *Sheboygan Press* carried a front-page article about the matter, showing a magnified photo of the bird perched in its percussion position. On the same page was a picture of a marksman posing with his weapon of choice fully equipped with telescopic lens. He had been dispatched by the local police to eliminate this threat to community serenity and he did indeed fulfill his deadly mission. Sheboygan's Lutheran churches really offered nothing of dramatic significance that could match this Evangelical Church event.

Another thing — I knew that Fritz could go to the movies on Sundays but I was not allowed such Sabbath compromise. Later — I must have been sixteen or so — my father, who'd probably by this time seen some epic film which had particularly impressed him, relented and, urging good judgment on our part, reluctantly agreed to our occasional Sunday trip to the movie.

I don't recall that this no-movies-on-Sundays practice represented an official Lutheran stance. However, Lutheran sermons certainly took note of the latent evil in the entire cinematic enterprise.

In many locales across the country so-called "blue laws" governed the activities of the citizenry to ensure a minimizing of opportunities for ungodly activities on Sundays. In many communities this meant that even baseball was prohibited. And, in some communities where there were no such laws, preachers nonetheless would deliver tirades of admonishment for those who indulged.

Sharp in their marketing skills, the management of the Sheboygan Chairmakers, our local baseball team, every year would mail each of the city's clergy a free season pass to the team's reserved sections. The games were always played on Sunday afternoons and there was usually a full complement of ministers on hand to cheer the home team on to victory.

So much for the ministers. For kids the cost was a dime. And dimes were hard to come by. But when there'd be a home game, Fritz would come by and invite me to walk out to the ballpark. It was a mile and a half walk but we'd always stop on the way at his Aunt Amanda's. Her cookies alone made the trip worthwhile. But I'd always feel so uncomfortable when we'd get there. Fritz's dad — who also happened to be Sheboygan's city clerk — would be in the front office of the little ballpark selling tickets. He, of course, knew we were there and for the most part appeared to ignore us. And then occasionally he would say something like, "What are you kids doing around here?" or "Why don'tcha kids go home!"

I'd always want to leave, but Fritz, who knew his dad well would say, "Nah — just stay around." And I'd be so uncomfortable.

And eventually, just before game time — after we'd been standing around for an hour or more — Mr. Mohr would finally relent and motion us to come over where he was and he'd let us go into the grandstand — free! And we'd scream our heads off.

These were the days before mercury arc lights. Sheboygan's city fathers, employing appropriate municipal thrift, had arranged for the streetlights to be parceled out, one to an intersection. Huge maple trees, evenly distributed at fifteen-foot intervals, shaded the sidewalk between the Mohrs and the Lutzes. This became a very dark distance for us to travel at nighttime. In our earlier days when we'd be with each other at the Mohrs' house, Fritz would walk half way home with me rather than send me on the 350-foot journey in the dark alone. That would bring us to the alley at mid-block. Then I would walk with him half the distance to his corner. Then he'd walk with me half the distance to the alley. And ultimately we'd both run quick as lightning for our respective home bases.

As absurd as this may seem, a sobering encounter we had experienced together warranted such a mutual security pact and ritual.

One night Fritz and I were returning from a rendezvous at Flader's Drug Store, where we had just indulged in our not-too-frequent-because-we-couldn't-afford-it-more-often purchase of double dip strawberry cones. We had barely arrived at the huge tree that spread over the Mohrs' house when from behind the stocky trunked tree stepped Mr. Steffen and his son. They were carrying between them a long, dark brown wicker basket. Mr. Steffen owned the funeral parlor and furniture store across the street, right next to Bartz' Grocery.

They were almost as surprised to see us as we them. They said nary a word — which made it all, even more, a spooky moment. We quickly figured out that it must be the elderly Mr. Leikup they were carrying. Well, we watched it all with wild and whispered curiosity and stood stunned for a moment. Desperately needing to regroup, we dashed into the Mohrs' enclosed front porch where we could sort things out in low-voiced excitement.

66

The Leikups were nice people who had no children — at least none our age. They'd lived next door to the Mohrs for years and Mr. Leikup had been very ill. The Steffens did have a funeral coach, but they apparently felt that since it was night they could just cross the street and carry this neighbor without attracting a whole lot of unnecessary neighborhood attention.

Once we'd caught our breath and our heartbeats slowed, we eventually arrived at a kind of tacit agreement. We did not want to have this close a brush with death ever again — at least on our street — and especially without each other's company.

As we grew older, years of separation were inevitable. We would correspond less than semi-occasionally.

When I'd be home from school for a weekend or any recess, I'd hardly be in the house when I'd call Fritz to see if we could get together. And if he didn't have time, he'd make time. And we'd walk. And talk and walk and talk. Late into the nights we'd bring each other up to date on what we'd been doing and what we'd been thinking.

When I came home from my first year at the Seminary I was asked to conduct a service for a vacationing pastor. Fritz Mohr came with me to a small, rural white-frame Lutheran church on the highway in Town Wilson, a few miles south of Sheboygan. Fritz was my friend sitting out there in the little congregation. He heard my first sermon. And he approved! It was a great ride back home.

The years have passed. He's Lutheran now too — not because of that sermon, I'm sure. Though he lives only seventy miles away, we seldom see each other, but we still stay in touch. And I remember our visits and conversations when we forged together so many of the ideals that have shaped our lives. He will always be one of my very best friends.

I
Never Learned
His Name

---

some who open doors are hard to forget

At last! At long last! My prep school days were over. I was on my way to the seminary. I was finally going to become a pastor.

For graduation Dad had given me a handsome gold Hamilton watch. I would pull back my sweater cuff again and again — not to find out the time, but to admire this new possession with my name engraved on its back.

Mother had given me a beautiful black leather bag. I'd never ever seen one quite so elegant — or large. I had packed it full of almost everything I owned: suits, jackets, extra shoes, blankets, books. I had had to hold my knee against it to force it closed. It bulged a bit, but the strong straps held it together valiantly.

I was proud of that suitcase, but to lift it was no small matter and I trudged along with it, barely able to keep it more than an inch above the pavement. These were the days when traveling cases didn't come equipped with wheels. When I finally got beyond the gate and onto the passenger ramp at Union Station in Chicago for the last leg of my trip, I hoisted my burden to the platform and mounted the steps to the coach. Nick May, another Wisconsinite, who was to be my seminary roommate, was wrestling with luggage of his own. When he had attended to his own, he gave me a hand in lifting my impossibly heavy piece to the rack above. We were among the first passengers aboard, so we took seats nearest the exit, not wanting to tote our belongings a single step farther than we had to. We were slightly fatigued by the ordeal and welcomed the chance to sit down.

This was 1940, when only business people and the more prosperous utilized the airlines. Trains were reasonably efficient and a less expensive way of getting around the country.

More and more travelers boarded the train and began to fill all the seats in the car. It became crowded, and some men had to stand in the aisles. The train was almost ready to depart when two women came through the door. We regarded them elderly (of course we were only twenty, so that term applied to most anyone who was older!) — and they were *ladies* — and therefore we rose to give them our seats. We remained standing — and did so for some seven slow hours into St. Louis. We commented that this was almost like going to St. Louis by foot.

There's not a great deal of scenery to enjoy from a standing position in the aisle. And the poles planted next to the tracks along the way came by a bit too quickly to count — if we had even wanted to. The hours dragged by.

Finally, we began crossing the long bridge across the Mississippi, people were gathering their packages and such in anticipation of our arrival. And I began to worry. It was obvious that we were to be the first ones to disembark. How was I ever going to be able to work myself into a place in the already crowded aisle so I'd be in a position to retrieve my suitcase from the rack above — and to do it without it falling down on some passenger's head and breaking someone's neck?

Well, the porter suddenly appeared, coming through the door in the front of the car, announcing in a deep, resonant voice which the Metropolitan Opera Chorus would have coveted, "We're arriving in St. Louis."

People squeezed together in the aisles to make way for him. He was large — really large — probably could have played right guard for the Green Bay Packers, had the rules allowed non-whites on their rosters in those days.

He wore a soft smile and when he came to where I stood he looked at my big black leather bag, and then at me. "Is that yours?" Nodding, I answered, "Yes."

Then this towering giant of a man reached his long, strong arm up, grasped the handle, and in a single motion — almost effortlessly — brought down the bag and told me he would have it waiting for me outside on the platform when I'd leave the train.

I was completely surprised and blurted out, "Thank you, thank you! That was really white of you!"

I said that. I really said that!

I couldn't believe I had said it. And, oh, I wish I hadn't said it. I was so ashamed. I wanted to crawl under the nearest seat.

He looked at me only briefly. And I could not look at him at all.

Here I had used a phrase that I'd been hearing for years — never in my home — but it was a common part of my peers' vocabulary back at prep school. And none of us had ever given the phrase a second thought or even reflected for a moment that these words really implied that if some act was particularly commendable it would of course be performed by a white person, rather than by a person of color. What arrogance! And it had become so much a part of me that I could say the words without any discomfort at all. Until now.

And now, as I'd be stepping down from the coach, this man who had been so helpful and to whom I had been so thoughtlessly rude would be standing there. How would I be able to face him?

Indeed he was standing there, keeping guard over all the bags he had removed and had lined up for our convenience.

He pointed to my large black bag. I walked over to it. I could not find a word to say, but my face must have displayed my anguish, because as I looked up at him to say my thank you, without speaking a word to me, his face showed me nothing but kindness and forgiveness, bespeaking a sort of silent benediction, *looking upon me with favor*, as if to say, *"Peace!"*

I was thrilled when I finally arrived at the seminary campus. The moon was reflecting off the high pitched slate roofs. I was overwhelmed with awe and reverence. I was stepping into something new and holy. Ministry. Bringing God's love to people. And I felt so small.

My big suitcase and I.

I had finished two years of college. The teen-age years of having all my personal radar antennae reaching out and picking up anything and everything had certainly brought a lot of data into my head to assess and organize.

For a long, long time the topic of race had been one of great concern to me. And though, admittedly, my exposure to the issue had been embarrassingly minimal, I had felt that I had a fair grasp on the matter. I had a bitter feeling towards this country's tolerating of slavery. Stories about "lynching of Negroes" were abhorrent to me. I was deeply troubled when I learned about the caste system and the pariahs of India. I resented hearing reports that told how Jim Crow laws were still being observed in the South. I resented use of the term "nigger" and other uncomplimentary names. I spoke out against derogatory and degrading humor at the expense of people of color.

Now I had been confronted with the reality that I actually had been engulfed in a white culture that assigned lower status to non-whites. So deeply was it a part of me that I couldn't even recognize how immersed I was in such prejudice!

My encounter with this stranger on the train — the entire episode — my spontaneous words, my embarrassment and shame, and that man's gentle forgiving countenance — stayed on my mind all that night and for days and nights that followed.

I finally realized that when my sisters — or any of my cousins, for that matter — had left home after high school, whether for college or the military, or for a post in the workplace — none in the family would be surprised if that young person might some day return to us, married. We might even have conceded — though probably with reluctance — that the person might return, married to someone who was not Lutheran. I realized, however, that no one would have expected such a marriage to have involved a non-white spouse.

In my mind I pushed the matter a bit farther. Suppose one of our relatives — say Uncle George and Aunt Ida who loved children, but had none of their own — suppose they would decide to adopt a child into their home. We'd probably all be happy that they would be bringing such a little one into their lives — into our larger family.

However, it most likely would not have occurred to any of us — nor to the adopting parents either — that the child they would adopt might be a child of a race other than white. Could I infer from this that I — and my family as well — believed — or at least had taken for granted — that people of a race other than white simply weren't good enough to belong to our family? What subtle racism! What unthinkable arrogance!

And now, young embryonic Christian pastor, how do you square all this with the desire you have expressed to be a faithful servant of a God who is parent and Savior of all the children of God?

That large, strong porter had already become my first instructor of my seminary years.

Part Two: *The Baltimore Year*

```
The Chaplain
I.
His New Intern
```

the welcome mats at some doors never wear thin

In my mind I try to reconstruct the scene of a long ago meeting that would pretty well determine the seminary education required to equip young people to be pastors. There would probably have been six — no, more likely twelve, an important Biblical number — sober faced men. *All* men. Most of them bearded. Some with shiny baldheads surrounded by halos of brown fur. Seasoned clergymen themselves, some of them serious and proven scholars, all dedicated and determined to give their very best wisdom to this effort to make sure that congregations seeking a pastor from the graduates of their program would be competent, dedicated, and ready.

Can you see them? Each brings his own idea of what the ideal young minister should look like, and what input would be needed to achieve that kind of a product. There would be the classicist, who insists that students be able to handle the Scriptures in their original languages. The historian would indicate those facets of his discipline that would be essential for understanding where the church had been through the years and what its future might be. The champion of doctrinal studies would not compromise his position that the statements of faith developed through the years be given prominent place in the curriculum. And surely development of each candidate's spiritual life and personal devotional practices would deserve prime attention.

There would be a dozen or more other passionate appeals to include other areas of concern — maybe even a few voices were raised about grooming, conduct of home life, control of temper, physical exercise, and how to get along with clergy of other denominations.

Possibly, as the hour grows late, the confusion mounts. Committee members manifest irritability. Fatigue is setting in so the chair assumes control and wisely observes, "Brethren, if all that you propose is to be included we'll have to provide more years of study before these young men will be adequately prepared. At length then, upon their graduation, they will in fact not only be mature, they may well be senile!"

That moment it would have been appropriate for an angel to appear among them to suggest, "Reverend and venerable sirs, might you limit the prescribed courses as best you can, yet insert a year of internship for the young men? Might not such arrangement provide a first hand learning experience at the side of a wise and seasoned pastor and thus better equip them for a useful ministry?" The motion probably was accepted and, very likely, the weary committee adjourned with a profound sense of accomplishment.

And so it came to pass in those days of completing my seminary experience that my classmates and I were to separate from one another, to receive, in a year of internship, the education we still lacked. This was to be the year that all the gaps in our preparation would be exposed and filled in by our participating in the "real ministry out there." We would return one year later having experienced everything needed to make us productive and happy ministers.

My classmates had a thousand stories to share when we came together again. Not a few told how their pastor/mentors pushed off on them chores that they themselves disliked doing. Some had been asked to fill a vacancy in the parish's day school as teacher. Some reported that they had learned to do little more than to operate a duplicating machine and to print, slip-sheet, and fold weekly bulletins to be distributed in Sunday worship services. Most were assigned to corral a youth group and to teach Sunday School. Few of them got to preach even as many as eight times.

When I had been given my internship assignment, it read simply: "to assist the Reverend Leslie F. Weber, Chaplain for Lutheran City Missions of Baltimore, an institutional ministry." I, of course, readily conceded that I was not yet ready for pastoral ministry. But I felt good about this assignment, excited. I was ready for Baltimore.

It would be a long train ride, so I arranged for a stopover with a seminary graduate who had lived across the hall and was now a pastor in the black community of Pittsburgh. He was ready for my coming, and had old clothes waiting for me. I was barely in his house when he was showing me how to use a huge, unwieldy floor sander that kept running away from me. He was redoing the entire floor of his little congregation's worship center. I'd not done this sort of thing before, and it was a hard job. But it was fun working

79

with Roland Gerhold, because he was so excited about his ministry and his enthusiasm was contagious. He saw all the hard work in terms of the people he was serving. I got to meet a few — and wonderful people they were. My pulse was still running fast as I left the next day. So this was ministry! I was ready for Baltimore.

I was not ready for Baltimore.

For each of my first five days in Baltimore, the thermometer topped the 100 mark. On three of those days the heat exceeded 105 degrees. Baltimore itself was not ready for that.

Pastor Weber met my train and took me at once to Mrs. Elgin who was to be my landlady. She was sitting at her second floor bay window, in her regal chair, keeping watch over everyone who chanced to near Augusta Avenue, reminding me more of a hall monitor back in my Sheridan School days than a guardian angel.

Although I was the only one who roomed at her house, she communicated with little messages that remained tacked to the walls in strategic places, reminding me to turn off lights, keep radio low, remove ring from tub after bathing, and similar bits of counsel. The room was incredibly small with space enough only to accommodate a chest of drawers and a twin bed which I had to hurdle in order to get to the window. Yet, fortunately, the rental cost was unbelievably low, because my monthly paycheck was parsimoniously small.

The room — sans fan — was stiflingly hot. I'd barely unpacked my belongings and transferred them to the chest of drawers, when my host reappeared and rescued me from there into the basement of his house up the street. There he had set up a sort of workplace/office that offered a semblance of coolness.

I was to find out later that Leslie F. Weber invariably signed his letters "cordially." This for him was not simply a variant of "yours truly" or "sincerely." He had signed his name that way in his first letter to me when I was still at the Seminary. What I discovered early on, was that Leslie F. Weber really was a very cordial man, a man with a heart, a large heart. To his very core he was a genuinely caring person. A real pastor. I wouldn't doubt but that his middle initial stood for "Freehearted."

His welcome to me was a hearty one. He had done everything possible to make my arrival comfortable. His care for me was obviously genuine. He wanted to know everything about me — my likes and dislikes, my interests and my personal history. He wanted to know all about my family. He made it clear, too, that he was regarding me as a co-worker and not as mere errand boy. All through our conversation he would excitedly interject references to his ministry and he would manifest his excitement about the prospects of our working together.

Already on our trip from the train station, the chaplain had begun to describe the scope of the ministry. He was serving two mental hospitals, an orthopedic hospital for children, a large municipal general hospital, a state prison, two institutions for the mentally ill, and four hospitals for tubercular patients, all within 75 miles of Baltimore.

With such an ambitious agenda, Pastor Weber had to squeeze as much work into every day as possible. So even my first day with him was not to slip by without attending to a few tasks. He explained that a good bit of the ministry involved preparing and distributing literature for those we'd be visiting. Purchase of such materials would prove prohibitive for the limited budget we were given. He said we'd be doing much of that work ourselves on our duplicating equipment. Without wishing to waste any precious time, he immediately unveiled this stone-age machine and proceeded to teach me how to operate the bulky tool.

He patiently brushed the thick ink on the cloth pad that covered the drum. He called it a diaper because it would need changing ever so often. Then he securely attached the edge of the stencil he'd prepared earlier, painstakingly stretching the thin waxed sheet of printed material across the pad, careful to avoid tearing or wrinkling. Fastening that end of the stencil to the drum, he loaded the feeder tray with paper. With a hint of triumph in his voice, "And now all we have to do is take the crank by the handle and give it one turn counter-clockwise" — which he proceeded to do — "and out comes the printed page!" he exulted.

He then invited me to give it a whirl. I protested, pleading that nothing in my past personal performance suggested any potential for majoring in mechanical engineering. I was reluctant to try. He insisted. Mounting up all the confidence and courage I could muster, I stepped forward, gripped the handle firmly and gave the crank a firm steady turn — clockwise.

"Oh, no!" he gasped. Then achieving a remarkably speedy recovery from shock and summoning all the patience and serenity he could, he assured me I had not broken the machine and that the obvious mess I had made was really a small matter after all. Then he took to the task of showing me how to clean up after such an "accident." What a euphemism!

Blushing with shame, eager to make amends, yet knowing full well my capacity to botch things up even more, I stood back, awkwardly watching. A million thoughts were going through my mind: "Accident?" — stupid *bonehead*! What had my mother told me about how important first impressions are? This man has to be thinking, 'What has the Seminary bestowed on me here?' "

He dismantled everything. He removed the rubber rollers and wiped the greasy ink from each one and carefully replaced them. Then with delicate touch he wiped ink from the soiled stencil. Finally he wiped his own hands clean and tossed the towel in a large waste basket, already almost filled with crumbled paper towels smeared black with the thick stubborn ink.

With saintly patience, he once more went through the procedure, step by step, so that this time I might get it right. And in my innermost mind I was in terror saying to myself, "And what if I might not!"

Then, in tones best intended to generate confidence and equanimity, he said to me, "Now, try it again — and, remember, counter-clockwise."

Edgy? Hesitant? Rattled? Scared? Embarrassed? Wishing I might be a million miles away — *any*where else? Bad dream and wishing I would wake up?

All of the above.

Resolutely and determined, I stepped to the machine. Once more he said, "Counter-clockwise." Handle in hand, with a deep breath I turned the crank — clockwise.

The pastor sighed a long sigh and after a silence that seemed endless, but really was only about five seconds, he said — almost cheerfully, "I'll bet Wanda has supper ready for us. Let's climb the stairs and we'll come down later to do our cleanup."

In their book, "Teaching as a Subversive Activity," Postman and Weingartner bemoan as useless the division of education into two parts, teaching and learning. They point to the lament raised so often by teachers who claim "we taught the students that but they didn't learn it." Leslie Weber surely had taught me — I simply hadn't learned. But *he* had. He never let me near that machine again for the entire period of my internship.

The supper was waiting for us. Two sweet little daughters, Grace and Barbara, shy and beautiful, and the woman who was to become one of my best friends ever, Wanda Weber, were there waiting for us. It was to be the first of countless delicious meals I'd be having with the Webers who warmly embraced me as a member of the family.

The Chaplain was eager to tell me about our work and the meal was hardly underway when he started in. When he and I picked up towels to help Wanda with the dishes, he was still well into describing more about the ministry. And when the dishes were all back on the shelves and the silverware back in their drawer, we sat down and long after the children were bedded down and prayed to sleep, Leslie had still more to tell me. And the more he spoke, the more excited I became about getting to work.

People in institutions, he had learned, invariably miss going to church. His view of chaplaincy ministry was broader than stopping at a bedside, speaking a word of comfort and prayer, and then moving on to the next patient. Wherever it was possible he would have the beds or the wheel chairs moved into a circle in a ward or in a dining hall and he would conduct a mini-church service there. For one of the hospitals he had arranged for construction of a portable altar. It was very carefully built, and equipped with wheels for easy guiding from one worship site to another. A built-in cabinet, below, in back, held a set of hymnals, an altar crucifix, and a pair of candlesticks.

He asked whether I liked to preach. I conceded that I'd only done so a few times and I found it a gratifying experience. "Well, you'll do a lot of it while you are here," he promised.

He acknowledged that Baltimore's torrid summer was near unbearable. We would delay making trips to the hospital till the heat wave would break. He invited me to join his family for a bit of respite with friends on the Eastern Shore of Maryland.

The cottage was in a shaded spot, and was cooled slightly by soft winds off the Choptank River — of which I'd never heard before. After a few hours of being passive participant in a conversation of people twenty years older than myself, and not eager to become the entertainment committee for the youngsters, I wandered off the porch toward the short dock where a small flat bottom row boat was tied. A few tired looking cane poles stood leaning against a large oak tree. Beneath them there in the shade was an old soup can holding a few cigar-like pieces of bait.

Well, two of my uncles had boats at their cottages on little lakes up in Wisconsin. I could row a boat like this. And I liked fishing. It had been a long time since I'd rowed a boat or been fishing. So I said to myself, "Why not?"

I couldn't come up with a good reason, but realizing I was here as a guest, and not willing to do anything more to cast doubts on my competence or trustworthiness, I slipped back inside to tell Pastor Weber of my tempting discovery. He grinned broadly, and revealing full confidence in me (which, of course, up to this moment he had no reason at all to possess!), he advised, "Go for it!"

I felt good, pushing off from dock, and I was fairly impressed with the stroke of each dip of my oars. The smell of the water and the cool breeze combined to make it a wonderful day. As I rowed farther out I was still able to discern the distinguishing marks of the cottage and decided that this might be a good place to stop to drop my line, while I'd still be able to get my bearings for the return to shore. I lifted the cement anchor and lowered it over the side. I removed the oars from their sockets and set myself to do some fishing. I baited the hook and threw it into the water. I had no idea what kinds of fish were in these waters. Not that I really had any serious expectations of catching anything, because I usually didn't anyway.

I kept staring at the end of the pole, as I presume skilled fishermen have done through the ages, reciting to myself the words with which I have so often comforted myself, "It's a beautiful day for fishing even if I don't catch any."

Suddenly the top of the pole dipped into the water. This had to be a big one. My pulse started pounding as I pulled the straining pole up to keep the line taut. I knew I was tugging away at a fish to be reckoned with. I brought him to the side of the boat. He was flailing angrily about, not enjoying the idea of being captured one bit. Neither fish nor fisher could be sure who would win. I said aloud to myself, "Now don't blow it, Karl!" I was sure the pole would break or the line would snap, but surprisingly, I pulled the creature over the side and he fell off the hook to the bottom of the boat. The fish was about two and a half feet long with a large girth and it flopped wildly as I tried to contain it — with relatively little success — between my legs. This was too good a fish story to end with its escape.

I reached for the anchor and as I pulled it up I realized that it had not been lodged in the bottom of the river at all. I'd been focusing all my attention on that small radius of water immediately around my fishing pole and hadn't noticed that I'd been drifting far out in the deeper waters. I was to find out later, I was in Chesapeake Bay!

The cottages and the trees surrounding them had all been reduced to tiny indistinguishable specks in a small thin line of darkness at the distant edge of the waters.

Still wanting to control the squirming fish, and not a little frightened by the groaning growl he grunted at me, I managed to take a quick look at the open waters I wanted to leave. I gasped and became totally unglued. Here bearing down on me from the starboard side, was a convoy of a dozen or more naval ships. These were World War II days and I'm not sure it wasn't in the interest of the fleet nor national security that I should be floating around a hundred yards from their path, maybe fewer, maybe more. I didn't take time to measure.

I grabbed those oars, put them in their locks, and rowed frantically, like a survivor of the Titanic. Of course, these were the days that saw people cavalierly dismiss any idea of safety devices such as seatbelts, motorcycle helmets, or lifejackets. There I was in my skimpy soaked T-shirt, sweaty and splashed. And the waves were high.

Somehow, amazingly, I found my way directly to the cottage. I tied the boat at the dock, and tried to assume an air of nonchalance, of being in full control, as I climbed the steps of the cottage. I held my noisy tired fish out while the friends all looked on with surprise and disbelief. They identified the fish as a croaker named for its vocal outbursts. I didn't bother filling in the details of my adventure, lest they get some hints of this new intern's weirdness.

When I slipped into bed that night and I thought of what might have happened, I simply could not be falling off to sleep without an inventory of the day, and a sobering prayer of thanksgiving.

I can't swim.

The temperature cooled a bit after the weekend. That phrase is a Baltimore euphemism for "the temperature hovered in the nineties."

Our rides to the hospitals each day were a significant part of my internship experience. Each trip took no less than a half-hour — and these were learning sessions for me. Though he invited me to call him by his first name, I held him in such high regard — make that "awe" — I couldn't do that. He insisted, "We're colleagues in this ministry!" We agreed after mutually reluctant compromise that I would call him a less-than-reverent "Rev."

I was really looking forward to hearing Rev preach. "In this first week," he said, "I'll not be conducting services, but I'll make the rounds with you to the wards and the rooms to introduce you to staff persons and residents and to help you find your way around."

I was impressed with the way he made special effort to respect the staff and personnel in each institution we'd visit. He explained, "These are wonderful people who are taking care of those whose families are no longer able to give them adequate care. These hospital personnel have lives of their own — families, responsibilities, and troubles too — that they have to deal with. Yet they come here and attempt to help all kinds of people with all kinds of personalities, and all kinds of problems and all kinds of dispositions and moods. And very often these workers go about their tasks unthanked. Even though they are paid to do their work, they get tired. If you and I can encourage them and affirm them, we help them to serve well. And we do a favor to the residents whom they serve. So these uniformed people are to be recipients of our ministry too, as we bring them our Lord's love by the way we treat them. In a sense they are partners of ours."

He would hardly have entered the room before he already would have assessed the status of a patient to be visited. He would quickly determine whether the person was in pain or discomfort, sleepy, in a jovial mood, depressed, or eager to tell stories — both the heavily disturbing ones or the happier kind. And Rev would respond appropriately.

He'd be careful not to cut off a visit when a patient needed more time. He wanted not to appear rushed, lest the person visited would feel of lesser importance. But he also knew how to bring a conversation to a quick close when the needs of the patient called for brevity. The people we visited not only respected him — they loved him.

As we moved from corridor to corridor and room to room, he introduced me as his new partner — not as a student assistant, but as a pastor.

He knew them by name and if they were new to him, he'd learn and remember their names. He would often talk with them about their families, but he'd never become unduly familiar. He respected their privacy and their dignity, never calling adults by their first names, but he would always prefix an appropriate title.

I was eager to observe him as he conducted a worship service in one of the wards or in the hospital chapel. He said, "I'd like to see each patient at least once a week, and, since there are so many patients, there just isn't enough time to visit with them all. That's why you're here. While I'll be conducting services and making visits, I expect you to be doing so also in different buildings or corridors or wards."

I knew it had been the custom with young seminarians that they submit to an ordained minister their sermon manuscripts before actually preaching. So I asked what arrangements he anticipated for my submitting my sermons for review.

Rev explained I would be preaching probably six or seven times a week. He chuckled, "I really don't see in my schedule time to be your homiletics professor too." He was altogether serious when he said that three years' study of theology and sermon construction should surely have equipped me to put all I'd learned into practice. He reminded me that in our travel to and from the institutions each day we would be finding ample time to discuss Scriptures, the needs of our audiences, as well as other areas of our ministering. He had confidence that I would work diligently in sermon preparation, and if I loved the people I'd be addressing and loved my Lord whose message I was to bring them, I would do effective preaching.

Then he warned me, "You'll of course be using a sermon more than once, or you'd simply never be well enough prepared to preach as often as you're expected. But don't use the same sermon more than four times or it will become boring for you — and what you preach must always have a message for you yourself. If what you preach fails to engage your own interest it is doubtful that your message will be useful to your hearers. And remember, some people in your audience may be hearing their very last sermon. It ought to be the most meaningful, most helpful sermon they ever will have heard — and it needn't be the longest."

That first introductory week was my clue that the days would be busy and long. And it was very clear that my nights and weekends would be devoted to sermon preparation.

Something else happened that week. People in institutions for the most part have relinquished their independence and have been separated quite dramatically from their prior day to day routines. These people would be sharing with us their stories, entrusting to us their private feelings and their deep inner thoughts. I was beginning to learn that sharing in such personal and intimate conversations causes one to absorb into one's own self some of the discomforts, the fears, and the heartaches of others. And I discovered that such ministry of listening is emotionally fatiguing. The weekend was welcome.

One morning, shortly after I arrived in Baltimore I came to the Weber home a full 45 minutes before we were to leave for our hospital rounds. I filled my brief case with tracts and devotional booklets Rev had set out for me to be distributed in my hospital visits so I read a magazine while waiting for him to complete his own preparations.

When he finally appeared he was holding a small black box, explaining, "This is a gift from Wanda and me."

I opened it to find inside three tiny glasses, a frosted glass flask filled with red wine, and a silver box whose cover was for use as a tray — a paten — with which to serve the unleavened wafers stored in the container.

Normally, persons not yet ordained did not administer the celebration of the Lord's Supper in Lutheran circles. Pastor Weber had a word to say about this.

"In this ministry we are Lutherans who are not seeking to enlist members for the Lutheran Church, but we come to people who are experiencing some of the most trying days of their lives. It is our task to assure them that God cares about them and loves them in Jesus Christ. Some of them will be Lutherans, some Baptists, some Methodists, some Presbyterians, some Catholics, some who've stayed away from churches for years, and some who never belonged anywhere.

"Our assignment is to show them that Christ invites them to come to him in the time of trouble. We have the Lord's Supper in which Christ invites people to 'Take eat; all of you drink!' When, after we explain what the Supper is, someone asks to receive it, it may be that person's final day of life, we ought not to stand in the way. This is after all, not *our* Supper. This is not the *Lutherans'* Supper. This is the *Lord's* Supper. That's why we offer such persons this gift, with our prayers and our blessing."

I'd really never had a teacher like this one.

Busy as he was as pastor, Rev was very much a husband and father. The two little ones would be out on the front steps waiting when we'd come home in the evening and run down the sidewalk when the car arrived at the curb mid their happy squeals, "Daddy,

Daddy!" Except of course when it would be raining and they'd be inside in the front room, noses pressed flat against the window as they anticipated our coming.

After the initial smothering with welcoming hugs, Rev would make his way into the kitchen to lavish affection on Wanda, to help in the final stages of setting out the dinner, and to share reports on the events of each other's day.

Meanwhile, Barb and Grace and I would curl up in a chair for story telling. And I usually also found my way over to the piano.

The Chaplain
II.
Assignment: Prison

---

clanking prison doors impede traffic

Through the years my mother had proved herself a near wizard in managing household finances, exhibiting great skills in her thrifty utilization of our family's limited resources.

But her record became flawed during my childhood. For six years, she paid Mrs. DeSchmidt fifty cents each Thursday to teach me piano. I wince at recalling the torments that good woman endured week after week, forced to listen to my performance. When that six-year period of instruction finally came to its end, I had ("mastered" would be too strong a word) familiarized myself (and anyone else within hearing range) with a piece named "The March of the Hollyhocks." One might say I immortalized this composition, if by that is meant that I did it to death!

Nonetheless, I liked wandering about on a keyboard, and would do so whenever opportunity arose. One evening when I was at the piano, Rev came to my side and said he was glad I could play the piano, because the following Sunday he would be gone and I would be leading the worship service for the inmates at the prison at nearby Jessop. In addition to preaching, I would also have to accompany the singing of hymns because the man who normally played for the services would be absent too.

I backed away from the assignment quickly. No way was I of sufficient competence to accompany a congregation in singing. Rev understood. However he said I'd have to lead the service, and if I didn't play the piano, I'd have to lead the group in singing unaccompanied.

I could imagine that a room full of 400 tough convicts would hardly resemble the Mormon Tabernacle Choir, were I to stand before them as their conductor! So I agreed reluctantly to play three familiar hymns for the event, and all week, with almost fiendish intensity I worked on "Holy, Holy, Holy," "Just as I am," and "What a Friend We Have in Jesus," frightened half to death in anticipation of my debut as church musician.

Rev had left his car for me to drive that morning. I missed him. He always would have some words for me that gave me new insights — and new confidence and readiness to take on new challenges.

This time I would be on my own. Had he been with me, he surely would have reminded me that my Lord was with me. But that didn't lessen my feeling of total incompetence. The idea of having something worthwhile to say to an assembly of hardened criminals was itself intimidating. Exposing them to my musical prowess seemed utter folly.

This was my first time at a prison. Signing in, being frisked, the clanking of metal locks, slamming of steel doors, and hollow echoing of footsteps marching down the gangways proved to be slightly unnerving.

A guard led me to a stage where a lectern and a small institutional piano were waiting for me like lions awaited the Christians' arrival in the arenas of early Rome.

Armed guards who had brought in and seated the last wave of inmates took their posts in the rear rows. The house was rather evenly divided, about 200 or so white prisoners on the right side of the center aisle and about the same number of minority background on the left.

I was told that attendance was voluntary. I didn't detect a boundless expression of spiritual commitment. Undoubtedly some were glad just to get out of their cells for an hour. I closed my eyes as I invited them to join their hearts with mine. It wasn't that I ordinarily closed my eyes when praying. There was a bit of concern lurking within me about "what's going on out there anyway" and I didn't want to see it!

When I'd said *amen* and opened my eyes again, all the people were still sitting there, looking at me and wondering what I would do next. I gave them the appropriate number in their hymnals and told them we were all going to sing "Holy, Holy, Holy." What I really meant was that I *hoped* we were all going to sing "Holy, Holy, Holy."

I walked over to the piano. My fingers were cold and stiff. I put the hymnal up on the stand and the page kept turning rather than staying in place. But I really didn't need the music. I had practiced the hymn over and over and over. I could play it blindfolded. Well, enough people started along with me, and by the fourth stanza at least half of them were singing along and I was feeling so

93

good about it I could have even played stanzas five and six if there had been that many.

I gained a bit of composure and possibly even a bit of confidence as the hour wore on. After the third hymn I spoke the benediction almost, as I recall, with a tone of triumph. We did it — the guards, the inmates, the piano — all of us.

I expected them to rise and be led out by the guards, but one in the audience waved his arm and said, "Revrun, the other revrun always lets us pick our favorite hymns after the service and we sing for a little while. Can't we sing some more?" I wasn't about to admit that my repertory consisted of three hymns and that was it.

Explaining that I really had to leave, I promised that we'd sing one of their favorites next week. Did they have a favorite? Several shouted, 'Leaning'! and there were echoes, "Yeah, 'Leaning'!"

That next week I poured all available time and energy into "Leaning on the Everlasting Arms."

And then there were four.

```
┌─────────────────────────────┐
│                             │
│        The Chaplain         │
│            III.             │
│        Douglas Boggs        │
│                             │
└─────────────────────────────┘
```

a revolving door can afford shelter from wild storms

Long before coming to Baltimore, Leslie Weber had been an institutional chaplain up in Buffalo. Earlier, he had served as Pastor of Our Savior Lutheran Church in that city's African American community. He had much to tell me of his experiences as white minister serving in an almost entirely black community.

He told how difficult it was to present to a black neighborhood a ministry sponsored by an almost totally white church body, by people who somewhat romantically idealized such ministry in almost the same manner as they supported foreign missions.

Without explicitly formulating such a statement, the stance communicated loudly and clearly to African Americans: "We want you all to go to heaven, but we'd rather you didn't sit next to us in our churches. That's why we establish 'separate-but-equal' churches for you."

It became then the responsibility of the pastors in those parishes and the small nuclei of members they served to communicate a different message, one that would be faithful to the Gospel of Jesus Christ.

This, Rev insisted, called for cultivating a genuine care for people. Christ never intended for ministry to be selective, exclusive, or conducted with shows of favoritism. This, he said, would be basic for us also, as he and I were to do our ministry together with people we'd be meeting. Most of these were not Lutheran and had no pastor of their own visiting them regularly. This would be especially true when we would be visiting with people of color.

The year was 1943, almost eleven years before the historic Supreme Court decision aimed at ending segregation in the schools. That accounted for the special separated seating arrangement at the prison facilities at Jessop. That's why black patients we visited in the state mental hospitals were lodged in different quarters from those occupied by whites. Maryland was "South" — segregation was legal.

And that's why in Henryton the patient population was composed entirely of African Americans. It was said to be the largest such "TB Sanatorium for Negroes" in the world.

At this time the medical world was still struggling with tuberculosis. The different treatments were long, tedious, often painful.

If a patient's stay was less than six months, it was usually because the patient died. Sometimes the prescribed remedy would call for long periods of resting the infected lung in elevated, mountainous settings. In other instances a lung was collapsed by air pressure, so that healing might take place. And in certain cases surgeons would remove portions of an infected lung, sometimes the entire lung. Three other TB hospitals we visited carried rosters of patients who were white.

It seems hardly possible that the medical world has in recent years made such dramatic strides that have virtually eliminated tuberculosis and have made this kind of special hospital unnecessary in America.

In the forties, however, the African American population seemed particularly vulnerable to the scourge of this deadly disease, in large part because not enough hospital beds were available to them in the earlier stages of the malady.

Even though Henryton was relatively large, not many patients referred there for hospitalization would be admitted without a lengthy period of delay. Because of the long waiting list, very often only those patients most critically ill would be accepted. Henryton was a grim place. A nurse once told us that the hospital experienced nine deaths per week. From my very earliest days on the scene, I could see that Thursday was an especially important day for the chaplain. He loved going there. And it soon became one of my favorite places to visit.

A continuing stream of conversation between Rev and me usually marked our daily trips together. But not on Thursdays.

There was something sobering about our experiences at Henryton. I had never before been confronted by the reality of imminent death. Of course I knew everybody eventually dies. However, my visits with sick people always had been tempered by a latent expectancy of recovery from a hospital experience. That possibility appeared remote for so many patients here.

When we'd be on our return trip home, Rev and I finally would break out of our initial silence and we'd invariably talk about some of the personal experiences and private reflections that these patients would share with us in their stories.

There were of course some patients who survived. Douglas Boggs was one of these. He was a handsome man, probably in his forties. He had a sharp mind and was well informed on a host of issues. He possessed a winsome personality. He welcomed me enthusiastically when I first met him. I'd introduced myself as Lutheran and he immediately responded, "Lutheran? When I was a kid we always used to meet and roller-skate on the steps of St. Martini Lutheran Church! That was one of the few places in the neighborhood where they didn't holler at us, 'You little colored kids, get outta here and go home!' "

The man didn't seem to have many visitors and when I would drop by he'd always urge me to stay. He had more stories for me than I could ever hope to remember. They were always fascinating and he found me a ready audience.

He told me he owned a nightclub in Baltimore. He'd been prosperous. He had traveled frequently and extensively. He was an avid sports enthusiast, and apparently he enjoyed the respect of people in the front offices of the American League's Washington Senators baseball team. He told how they engaged his services to scout for new talent for the Senators. He mentioned the names of some whom he'd recommended and who had made the team. These were white players of course, because these were the days before Jackie Robinson, Roy Campanella, and such had dismantled the color bars that for so many years had prevented non-whites from playing in the "big leagues."

Of course I was thrilled for him when the doctor's word came down, announcing that his tuberculosis had been arrested and he was to be released. In the weeks that followed I missed him. I had always looked forward to my visits with him — and his expressions of appreciation of our conversations and our prayers together were a gratifying affirmation of my ministry.

Some six months or so later I was making my rounds at Henryton and upon entering the room was surprised to see Douglas Boggs in the bed. "Shocked" might be the more appropriate word. I was hardly able to recognize him. His condition had deteriorated so greatly that his face was drawn and appeared almost shrunken. His complexion was ashen. This was a very, very sick man.

"Hello, my friend," he said in a very thin, tired voice. "Sit down. I have much to tell you."

I sat. He talked — for almost a half-hour without my interrupting.

He told how in his earlier stay at Henryton he had prayed so earnestly and constantly that God would restore his former health and permit him to pick up again his life where he had left it.

It was great to be back home, he said. The old gang, the parties, the late hours — breaking away from all the restrictions of hospital life he had endured. It was almost too much enjoyment to last. And it didn't. He became horribly ill, and since he had been a patient at Henryton before, they admitted him again.

Then he made a strange proclamation. "You know, when I was in here the first time I prayed desperately that the Lord would heal me and restore me to my home again. I know now that I cannot trust myself to such a state where I would turn away from God again. This time I pray that I will not recover, so that I can stay close to God and never turn my back on God again. It's simply not worth it!"

Through all my years to this very day I've never heard anyone speak such words again.

```
┌─────────────────────────────────┐
│                                 │
│         The Chaplain            │
│             IV.                 │
│    Young People at Henryton     │
│                                 │
└─────────────────────────────────┘
```

exit doors are often heaviest

Probably the most disturbing of my visits were those I would make with patients who were of my age at the time. Particularly Jeannie and Margean. Jeannie had been in college, and Margean had been gradated two years earlier from Hampton in Virginia. She had taught in elementary classrooms for two years when she became ill.

I could hardly believe they were sick. They looked so well, so strong. They appeared robust and altogether healthy. But the sneaky disease had attacked their lungs and they were in trouble.

They were well aware of the seriousness of their condition. They had both submitted to the extremely uncomfortable treatment of having one lung at a time deflated by injected air pressure. This rendered the lung inactive in hopes of inducing rest for it and ultimately healing. They were able to — and did — speak frankly and realistically about the various scenarios that might play out in the days and years ahead. There was a distinct aura of hope around them.

Margean told of her eagerness to get back in a classroom of shiny nosed kids. Jeannie still wasn't sure what she wanted to do career wise. She had selected no major thus far in college. She was extraordinarily attractive and apparently already had been interviewed for modeling.

Our conversations were very special — we compared notes on our college experiences, about issues on the news reports, about popular songs, about sports, about a wide range of topics that people in their early twenties might talk about anywhere. We talked too about where God fits into human lives, and especially in their own immediate circumstances and at this place called Henryton.

Their honesty, their sense of hope, their reverence for life, and their trust in God in the face of all they were experiencing were hardly what I might have expected, and made my every visit with them a time of great personal enrichment for me.

Quite suddenly the health of each of these two wonderful young women worsened, and shortly after, I learned that they both had died.

Boyd was a young man too — and just as the two women, same approximate age as I was.

He was in an advanced stage of tuberculosis and therefore confined to his bed for the most part. He appeared to have been a strong man in earlier days.

It was not easy for Boyd to speak. He had a delightful sense of humor, but even his gentlest laughter would sometimes induce a coughing spell that would make his talking even more difficult.

He truly became a friend. It seemed that the things I shared with him about faith were especially appropriate and meaningful to him and he was generous in expressing his appreciation for our praying and worshipping together.

He was obviously interested in getting to know me better and he wanted to know all about my home in Wisconsin, my family, my life at the Seminary and, of course — did I have a girl friend. I lamented to him at length about Seminary rules that prohibited students from even becoming engaged before we were graduated. But I told him, however, I'd nonetheless agreed with Esther to be married (of course we referred to it as agreement rather than engagement). We'd made those plans already two years ago and we had only one more year to wait now, and then we could and would be wed.

Boyd was both amused and captivated by such romantic intrigue. Each time I would visit him he'd want me to tell him more about Esther.

He told me too how he had had several friends — young women — of whom he'd been very fond. Once they had learned that he had TB, however, he hadn't received any calls, letters, or any word from them at all. Recognizing the seriousness of his own condition — and with tears seeping from the corners of his eyes — he told how he knew he could never look forward to recovery, let alone marriage and having a family, and that's why he became so very interested in those possibilities in my own future.

Boyd had a wide smile on his tired face when I visited him in late April. He asked me to reach into his little bedside cabinet to retrieve a white paper bag lying on the shelf. I handed it to him, and then he held it out for me to take. I really didn't understand

103

what he had in mind. I opened the bag slowly, reached in, and drew out a tiny pair of infant booties he'd asked one of the nurses to buy for him. He said in a low voice, "I won't be able to be there when you marry Esther, and I'll never get to see your children. But, when the first one comes, put these on his little feet and tell him they come from Boyd."

I had had no idea that my intern year would bring me such a friendship. My bond with Boyd was strong. We went far beyond discussion of my future and together did some deep probings of what probably lay ahead for him. He told of his profound lonesomeness and how much it meant to talk about a loving hand of God. We spoke the Shepherd Psalm together before I left him.

On the following Thursday when I stopped by Boyd's room a new patient lay there and I felt a great emptiness.

Someone new was waiting for my company, for prayers, and for friendship.

Two years later, when Peter Charles Lutze had arrived, Esther and I slipped those booties over his tiny feet and remembered Boyd.

I remember a letter from one of my sisters that winter. She asked, "Isn't working with people in such extremities horribly depressing?"

The thought hadn't even occurred to me. Surely, there were situations I encountered that would tear at anyone's heart. I remember a young man I'd visited in one of the mental hospitals. He had suffered some sort of dementia during his service in the armed forces as a paratrooper. Each time I saw him he was struggling to escape from a heavy wooden chair to which he had been fastened. An orderly informed me that when not restrained he would often climb on filing cabinets or any tall piece of furniture and leap, head first. Bruises on his face and head and an incessant stream of wild mumbling were only hints of the deeply troubled person within that young frame. Other patients withdrew — and hospital personnel only came to his side in his extremest needs. He was pathetic to look at. It seemed everyone felt pity for this hero-returned-home, but no one knew quite what to say or do. I doubt that he heard my greetings, let alone the brief prayers I would speak. I would feel so helpless, so useless. It was as if I were miles away and he in a distant land.

And at night when I'd switch off my light, in the quiet darkness I'd often remember him and imagine him in his night. My sister had been right. Often enough there were moments that were deeply disturbing and depressing.

One thing about this ministry in which Rev and I were engaged: there was much healing going on — surely the medical/surgical teams did splendidly effective work. I'm referring, however, to healing of distressed spirits. We worked with patients under long term care; others who seemed never to have visitors or any contact "back home"; some who learned that their condition called for much longer hospital stay; others whose doctors had told them they would not survive; and the list of problems seemed endless.

An easily overlooked healing, however, was the healing of our own troubled spirits. Often enough Rev and I would climb into the car for our trips home emotionally exhausted. The days usually passed by swiftly, but they were so filled with confrontation with people's heavily burdened lives. What these patients were having to endure couldn't be brushed off as insignificant or unimportant. If our ministry was to be bringing the compassion of God to troubled lives, Rev would say, then we should be expecting that our assignment would call for more than just "making with the words." The very word *compassion* calls for feeling passionately with the one who is the object of our ministry. Rev made it clear that to serve effectively is to identify with the person served — to try to grasp what pain and fear and loneliness and burdens people encounter, so that then we might make an appropriate response.

So he and I would talk about our visits and empathize with each other and encourage and affirm each other. We both experienced healing for ourselves as we reflected on where Jesus Christ fit into all this.

———————

Often enough books read during seminary days, and sheaves of notes taken in class, and lectures spoken by learned professors are never retrieved as useful once the graduate becomes a pastor. But whoever was responsible for the incorporating of an internship should be remembered with celebration. What happened to me during my year at Baltimore had to be more than they could possibly have envisioned. But then they didn't have any idea of who Leslie F. Weber was at the time or what he would be and do.

For me he was the best teacher I'd ever had, his the best course I could possibly have taken. And to this day I draw on what I've learned from him.

Part Three: *The Oklahoma Years*

Felix Christopher

where a door leads is often unclear

I never really got to know Felix Christopher well. His home was four long blocks from the church (in which we had our home). When I would visit him, there'd be an almost overwhelming welcome. Mrs. Christopher, a slight but very strong woman, clearly a dozen or more years younger than her husband, would answer the door and call to him, "Mr. Christopher, your pastor is here!"

This was 1945, and in the world outside their community no dignity of title was accorded these people. Among themselves, however, husband and wife often would call each other mister or missus — and in the churches and in formal or even in casual meetings at the market, they would address one another that way. And of course they were pleased that the pastor and his family regarded them with that same kind of dignity.

Mrs. Christopher belonged to another church, so she did not stay in the room long when I'd come by. She'd regularly peek back in to make sure that neither the lemonade nor the cookies she'd brought out were in short supply.

Mr. Christopher was overjoyed when I would visit. He would reach out his giant hand and bury my hand in its firm grasp. He would say, "I'm proud you came to see me, Pastor." And I believe it was not merely my clergy status that pleased him. White people just didn't come to his — or other houses in the neighborhood.

His name, Felix, was appropriate. He always manifested a "happy" spirit. He had in his early days been deprived of a decent education. He could only read a very few words — and those very slowly. Mrs. Christopher did most of their reading.

He did not share much about himself. He was close to ninety years old. He owned his own home. The weather, his garden, the church — these were items that interested him most, and of course he always wanted a report on the homefront and he'd ask, "How are Mrs. Lutze and that little boy?"

Felix Christopher must have measured near the six-and-one-half foot mark. He stood erect. His closely trimmed white hair crowned a face that suggested long arduous hours of work, and volumes of personal history seemed stored behind his dark, warm, smiling countenance.

Long limbed, his feet carrying mammoth shoes, he would walk slowly, in a sort of shuffle — as if those feet were hurting and each step painful. His voice was soft and low pitched, and his sentences were slow tempo and short. And few.

He did not spend much time visiting with other members when he'd come to church, but would regularly find a place in the front row of chairs, immediately in front of the pulpit. He'd stretch out his long limbs, settle back on his seat, as if he'd been waiting for this moment all week long. He'd thumb his way into the hymnal and when the music began, he would join in, mumbling the hymns, attempting to keep up with the words in the hymnal. When the singing stopped, he'd lay down his book and stretch an arm to the chairs on either side, awaiting the sermon. Occasionally, the children of the Sunday School would have rehearsed some songs that they might sing during the service. Oblivious of the traditional restrained worship decorum for which Lutherans are noted, Mr. Christopher would uninhibitedly applaud, clapping those giant hands together, while the other worshippers nervously fidgeted, half embarrassed by the spontaneous outburst and half wishing they had the courage to join him. And, always, very soon after worship, he would make his way down South Sixth Street to his home.

Once, on a week day, I rose from my desk where I'd been working to retrieve a book from a shelf across the room, and glancing out the window, I noticed Mr. Christopher making his way up the front walk. He was wearing his Sunday clothes and carrying a suitcase. I invited him in.

He said he couldn't stay; he was hurrying to the bus depot (some five blocks farther). He explained that he was "going to Arkansas to visit relatives there for a short spell." He was asking me to tend the large tan bag for him in his absence and keep it safe for him until he would return. He indicated that its contents were precious and very valuable to him and he didn't trust anyone else with it.

I promised him I'd care for it. A few days passed and he had not yet returned. I began to be both puzzled and troubled. Upon calling Mrs. Christopher I found she didn't know when he would return either. He had trusted me with the bag. He'd not forbidden me to look inside. If I did, I thought I might just find something that would be very important for his safety and well being. And then again perhaps my curiosity simply was too great. I decided to open the suitcase. It was not really heavy. I laid it across a chair and unbuckled the thick leather straps, pressed down the clasp release, and slowly lifted the lid. I coughed slightly as a musty odor rose when I opened the case wide.

Inside, in considerable disarray, he had assembled an assortment of papers — copies of a church periodical, service folders from Sunday worship, letters inviting people to participate in special events at this church, along with a few unrelated newsclippings. Nothing more.

Shortly thereafter he returned from his travels and came by to retrieve his suitcase. I told him I had opened it while he was gone and we opened it again together and he felt reassured that all was intact. It was sad to see him take up this piece that was so precious to him and trudge slowly towards his home.

Only a few days later I came in from outside to answer an insistent and impatient ringing of the telephone. It was Mrs. Christopher and she sounded both excited and frightened. "Will you please come right away!"

We had no car back then and I ran, not knowing what might be happening. I hardly expected to see what was there: two sheriff patrol cars with lights whirling atop, and a crowd of two dozen or more neighbors in a sort of semi-circle across the street from the Christopher house. Mrs. Christopher, totally distraught, stood in the middle and two officers at her side. Completely puzzled by the situation I asked, "Mrs. Christopher, are you all right?"

"It's Mr. Christopher up there," she said. And I looked over my shoulder and saw him barefooted wearing only his overalls. He was standing, somewhat menacingly, behind an ironing board. He had before him five old type irons used for pressing clothes all lined up in a row. "Pastor, he's all upset and he won't let anyone up in the house — even up on the porch — or he'll throw an iron at them. He won't even let me come into the house, he says everyone is trying to kill him. He's been like this since yesterday. He's been out there all night and didn't sleep at all. He wouldn't eat anything for three days — afraid people are trying to poison him — even me, and I'm his wife!"

The police were baffled by the situation. They were reluctant to take rash action. They didn't want to risk anyone getting hurt.

So they'd been waiting things out, considering all the options, and concluding, apparently, that doing nothing might be better than doing the wrong thing.

I turned and walked toward the middle of the street and one of the officers called out, "Preacher, don't go up there — that old man is crazy, he's out of his head!"

I cupped my hands at my mouth and shouted, "Mr. Christopher, this is your pastor. May I come up to see you?" He paused. Then he slowly told me to come up, making it very clear that no one else was to come along.

Disheveled and fatigued by the ordeal, yet wide eyed — almost wild eyed, the old gentleman agreed to sit down so we might talk. He explained how certain he was that no one could be trusted — everyone was trying to take his life. I asked if he might not want to go inside the house with me. He was most reluctant, lest the people across the street would be coming up the steps to attack him. He relented, however, when I called out to the small crowd that they were to stay right there and not approach the house.

Once inside (I was to stay close to the door watching, so I could see any who might come close) he relaxed a bit. The poor man was so weary and welcomed my washing his face with a cool cloth. I gave him a glass of water to sip, which he accepted, only on my assurance that it was not poisoned. The house, which normally was spotlessly clean and enviably neat, looked like a disaster area. I asked him if, now, Mrs. Christopher might be allowed to come back in. He wasn't quite sure of her, but if I would stay, he would agree. So I called out and asked her to return. She immediately started to straighten things a bit. I asked her if she had some food she might serve him. He immediately insisted that all food might be poisoned and he wouldn't eat any of it.

I persuaded him to let me go out for only a few minutes to get some food that we'd be sure was not contaminated. I dashed across the street to the little neighborhood grocery where the crowd had been standing, giving the officers an update on what was happening inside. I purchased a can of chicken soup and ran back up into the house. I assured Mr. Christopher that this can had not been tampered with and read to him the contents as printed on the label.

Then I cooked soup for him and personally fed him. And as I did, I realized how weak he was in his near exhausted state. After finishing his bowl of soup he became very sleepy, and, together, Mrs. Christopher and I helped the tired gentleman to his freshly made bed. We tucked him in, I held his huge right hand in both of mine and prayed with him. He mumbled along as we prayed the Lord's Prayer. He fell asleep. His wife breathed a deep sigh as we laid our plans for the morning. I left, the patrol cars slipped away, and the neighbors returned to their homes.

I knew the next day would be difficult. And it was.

It was obvious that our friend was in deep need. It was imperative that he receive psychiatric help. However, procedures for applying for public health services and facilities seem always tediously stretched out over longer time periods. This was 1946, when public as well as private institutions in the South were segregated. "Negroes" (that was the acceptable term then) were surely not expecting preferential treatment in seeking public services. And, anyway, back then systems for dealing with mental health issues were not nearly as enlightened as they are in many instances today.

Delays would not be helpful and at least in this instance relocation would be required. We were advised that the quickest way to effect the kind of transition that was so obviously necessary here was to have the patient voluntarily sign papers requesting hospitalization.

So Mrs. Christopher and her relatives and the family doctor all urged me to explain the entire situation to our friend and try to persuade him to agree to "sign himself in."

The judge before whom the transaction took place was gentle and kind, and indicated that he found no duress or undue force or pressure to get the patient to agree to the procedure.

Before he signed he looked at me and asked, "Is this what I should do, Pastor?" I nodded. He wrote on the sheet carefully, deliberately, "Felix Christopher." His hand engulfed mine in one final greeting as he left with hospital attendants.

It was only a few weeks later that he died.

And I swallow hard as I remember and repeat the name, Felix Christopher.

The Moanings

some doors open wide

In January, 1945, when I arrived in Muskogee, mine was seventeenth name on the Hope Lutheran Church's membership list. With my parsonage provided, plus a $105 monthly salary, I was by far the most prosperous of all the members. Mrs. Lloyd, Mrs. Lowe, Mrs. Martin, Mr. Christopher, Mrs. Johnson, Mr. and Mrs. Hooper, and Mr. and Mrs. Moaning. These members were all in their senior years — all but two of them were over eighty — and all their lives they had been very poor. Yet, somehow or other they with financial wizardry and sheer pluck managed to survive. The few younger church members found themselves submerged in a town whose segregated style and disproportionate economy had little room for any young blacks who stayed at home and had not moved on to the war-generated, booming industrial cities farther north.

In my early visits to their homes I already began to grasp what impoverished circumstances were theirs. Drops that oozed through leaks in the roof would "ping" in appropriately distributed pans and large coffee cans positioned to catch the water — or would fall on the pot belly stove in the center of the house and disappear in a sizzle of steam.

The Pope himself could not have received a warmer, more generous, more genuine welcome than these people bestowed on this young white neophyte who had come to be their pastor.

Mr. Moaning came by during one of those early weeks. This was before Esther and I had married. He informed me that the members wished to invite me to be their guest at dinner the following Sunday. I eagerly accepted, not quite sure how their plans would unfold.

After I'd greeted folks at the door following the service, five of the members retreated to my study for the weekly ritual of counting the money (normally about $19.00 each Sunday). When that was completed Mr. Moaning, Mrs. Moaning, Mrs. Martin (well over ninety, Hope's oldest member), and I walked out to the Missouri, Kansas, and Texas (the Katy Line) tracks that lay some 150 feet from the church's rear door.

With Mr. Moaning leading, the pace was deliberate, walking the path along the railroad bed and occasionally stepping up to walk the ties where the ground was muddy.

116

Some seventeen city blocks farther we left the tracks and walked a graveled road to a two-story structure. Mr. Moaning, the retired carpenter, had built this to provide rental income from the garage space below. The three rooms above served as the Moanings' home.

We mounted the stairs and Mr. Moaning presented me with an elaborately detailed and tremendously helpful briefing of what it had been for him to be living in Muskogee. Meanwhile, Mrs. Martin joined Mrs. Moaning in the kitchen, obviously preparing a dinner.

We had arrived at nearly one o'clock. Now, as it was getting on toward four, and the aroma from the kitchen came floating in on us, I for one was more than ready when Mrs. Moaning brought food to the table. The word "lavish" is hardly adequate. A steaming pork roast; a platter of fried chicken; a huge ham oozing with sweet juices; mashed potatoes; egg plant dipped in batter and fried; creamed peas; creamed brussel sprouts; fresh sliced tomatoes; sweet corn on the cob; a fruit jello salad; and as if that weren't enough, pickles, olives, celery, carrot slices, and cranberry relish. And the desserts: lemon meringue pie, strawberry short cake, sweet potato pie, and an apple pie, and an angel food cake smothered in chocolate icing!

Mr. Moaning explained that all the members had contributed to the dinner and that Mrs. Martin had been selected to represent them because she was oldest and the Moanings were asked to serve because Mrs. Moaning had the largest kitchen. Then he spoke a prayer of thanks — for the church that meant so much to them, for all the fellow members, for the food and all the gifts of life, and for sending Hope its new pastor. AMEN. And the ladies and I added our AMEN.

Then, in arresting simplicity, Mrs. Moaning distributed to us paper napkins and our dinnerware. I was given the only dinner plate, slightly cracked, a large green translucent, chipped drinking glass, a knife whose mother-of-pearl handle was half broken, a slightly twisted fork, and a somewhat bent teaspoon. Mr. Moaning's serving set was a weary and well used pyrex pie plate, a measuring cup, a more badly twisted fork, a paring knife, and a bent tablespoon. Mrs. Martin was given a large soup bowl, a soup spoon, and also a paring knife. Mrs. Moaning kept for herself a quart-sized aluminum cooking pot and a serving spoon as a very utilitarian utensil.

And we ate. Besides the tempting quality of the festive buffet, I began to hear Mrs. Moaning call off different items as gifts from this parishioner or another. I had visions of these people asking later, "How did the pastor like the ham — or the sweet potato pie?" And I was eager to prevent anyone from being offended by what might appear to be ingratitude. So I ate. And I ate. Long after my companions had stepped away from the table, I was still sampling each morsel.

It was marvelous. But it was much!

That very afternoon, when the discomfort of surfeiting had subsided and before the sun was setting, he took me walking again. A long walk — well over three miles. He had another purpose in mind.

Mr. Moaning was so proud of his church and proud that the Lutherans were simply not going to be participating in the racist patterns of the day. To be sure, there was a "white Lutheran church" in town; and there were very likely a lot of other places where Lutherans might not prove to be much different in their attitudes and actions from their white, non-Lutheran neighbors. But at least at Hope Church race didn't become an issue. This was his church and he wanted to tell as many as possible about his experience, and to invite others to come and join.

He wanted me to meet the president of his community's First Baptist Church. A difficult visit, it was at the tiny twenty-bed Provident Hospital and the man was hardly in a position to match Mr. Moaning's enthusiasm. Seems Mr. Marshall had been riding in a Model A Ford in less-than-good repair when the spring in the seat uncoiled in ruthless assault. In spite of this man's discomfort, Mr. Moaning's intention that this man meet me was very strong. I recall my squirming discomfort as I tried to say a pastoral word that might be appropriate. And poor Mr. Marshall graciously tolerated our visit.

Still another visit took us to the Smith Tire Shop, which also served as the office of the editor of the Oklahoma Independent. Mr. M. C. Simmons was light skinned and, as I remember, a man of insight, wisdom, and courage, quite willing to write stories that would never appear in the local white press. Almost assigning to it the stature of a battle scar, Mr. Moaning had beforehand asked me to take note of a place on his ear that had been bitten off by someone angered by his forthright journalism. Ever after that initial meeting, Mr. Simmons was both encouraging and generous in affording me space for reporting any activities occurring at Hope Church. He too felt something unusual was going on in the kind of ministry we wanted to exercise and demonstrate in our church.

There was not only *one* set of tracks bordering on the property where Hope's church and parsonage were located. There were *five*. I can't remember that we ever experienced traffic on all five at once. But aside from one or the other line stopping with a long line of freight cars and blocking the paths of cars and pedestrians for long intervals, there was a particular nuisance with which we learned to cope.

In addition to being less than affluent (my salary was increased by the Mission Board by $10/month when Esther and I married) we also found ourselves experiencing some of the constraints that came with wartime.

No wash machines were available while the energies of industry were devoted to military production. From our modest financial reservoir, we purchased a shiny wash board so Esther could do our laundry in the bathtub. When she would call, I'd emerge from my study to wring out, by hand, the sheets, towels, and such. Together we'd head for the washline to let them blow dry in the sun.

Problem: Fifty yards to the east, on track five, the Frisco Railway maintained a water tower where switch engines would fill their giant tanks from time to time. When ready to move on, they'd produce a thunderous rumble, a raucous blast of the whistle, and begin their roar down the track.

On washdays this would serve as a piercing alarm to us. If the wind were blowing from that direction, we would dive from the house and gather everything from the lines before a huge cloud of

119

black soot could cover Esther's handiwork with a thick film of ugly particles of coal dust. We didn't always win our race to the clothesline.

———————

Every Sunday morning, every Thursday evening (for Bible study), and every Wednesday evening of the Advent and Lenten seasons, we'd see the Moanings come into sight. They loved their Lord. They loved their church.

Esther and I walked everywhere. There were no cars to purchase during those war years either. And when our firstborn arrived we did more and more walking, pushing Peter's little cart before us. We managed to visit all of our nearer-by members frequently enough, but Esther had never gotten out to visit the Moanings.

By 1948 the limitations of wartime had relaxed significantly. We got a wash machine. With the generous help of a friend we were able to locate — and purchase — a used, four cylinder Jeep station wagon. No member of the congregation had a car, and the members were every bit as thrilled as we that the pastor had a car!

It was a Thursday that we bought it, and that night after our session in the church everyone came out to adore the vehicle with appropriate oohs and aahs. Mrs. Moaning said, "Well, now, Mrs. Lutze, you can finally come out and see where we live!"

Esther was quick to reply, "That's right, and we'll come out to see you this week!"

Mr. Moaning at once interjected, "No, Mrs. Lutze, if God wills, you will come out and see us!" Always having things in proper perspective, he would of course have said just that — no surprise! And we waved goodbye as they left for their trek home, silhouetted against the red sun.

———————

It was about two-thirty in the night when our jangling phone woke us. She didn't identify herself — didn't need to. No one had a voice quite as soft and high as Anna Belle's: "Pastor Lutze, the Moanings' house burned down, and they burned up." And in uncontrolled sobbing she hung up.

Travelers on the highway a block away had seen the flames and stopped to try to rouse the occupants. They threw gravel at the windows, to no avail. The firemen found the two lying next to each other in their bed. They'd never even awakened.

Their son and daughter came in from California. It was Hope's first funeral — and mine too. A double funeral.

And a double loss.

Gentle, loving folk.

Two Who Soared

some doors are stubborn

I don't really know much about Taft, Oklahoma, and its beginnings. I do know that Oklahoma was still a very young state when I moved there in 1945 and that its days as "Indian Territory" were remembered by some of the folks still living there when I arrived.

I know too that Oklahoma, though regarded a "border state," was very much a southern state, below the Mason-Dixon Line, and therefore patterns of segregation were woven deeply into the cultural and legal fabric.

Accordingly, when the state sought to exercise its responsibility towards the mentally ill, its orphans, and children with severe vision and hearing impairments, it established "a separate" — and supposedly — "equal program and facility for Negroes."

So a little community, some eight miles or so west of Muskogee, was selected. High on the hill north of the highway were the red brick buildings that housed the institution that served "the deaf, blind, and orphans." Across the highway to the south were more red brick structures — these for the mentally ill.

I have no idea how or why the town received its name, nor how many people had been living there before the state's facilities were installed there. I do know, however, that there was a considerable population pocket that had developed there through the years. Since these state institutions were established as segregated — "for Negroes" — the situation provided unique employment opportunities for African Americans, as administrators, staff, and service workers. Most of these became residents there. So Taft had become quite a town with churches, a few stores, and schools as well.

There were small farms nearby, and families living there attached themselves to the town of Taft and community life there. One such family was the Hamilton household. I first met them when I performed my very first marriage, when their son Homer and our church pianist, Dorthy Hooper, were wed. I never did learn where or how they met, but they were both in their twenties, very much in love, and a joy to be with and to have as members in our small church.

One could hardly regard the couple as financially prosperous. Dorthy was an employee of a dry cleaning establishment, and had been providing a major share of the income for her father's household, consisting of her father and mother, her sister, a high schooler nephew, and his younger sister — and herself. They crowded together in a four and one-half room rent house, one that had seen better days.

Homer had recently returned from overseas where he had served with the army's motor pools. He had had experience driving the heavy military vehicles over the treacherously narrow mountain roads of Italy, and had not only become a seasoned operator of motorized equipment, but he'd also learned mechanical skills and was equipped to do repair work on vehicles and other engines.

In making plans to marry Dorthy, Homer decided to move in to Muskogee and found a job with a local car dealer. In spite of his experience and skills — because of his race — he was hired only to do menial work — washing and waxing cars, changing oil and doing grease jobs, and serving as janitor. The mechanics and others who worked there regarded him as a sort of "errand boy." However, not infrequently, cars with complicated troubles rolled in, and, when the problems challenged the mechanics beyond their experience or competence, they'd call, "Homer, come over here and look at this!" He always welcomed the opportunity to demonstrate his capabilities and he relished the opportunities to be working with engines. But I sensed that he chafed a bit when there was no recognition of his performance. There was never a hint of a possible promotion to a higher position or increased compensation for his productivity.

The time came when there was a cutback in the number of persons this dealer had in his employ, and Homer Hamilton was one of the first to lose his job.

Homer and Dorthy had scraped and saved and by this time had been able to find a new home for themselves — a modest three room house about a mile and a half from the church. There was nothing very cheering about their situation, but both remained faithful in their participation in church life and were an inspiration to me.

It was about that time that I got to know Nathan Sams. He too had completed his term of service with the military, having been one of the first flight instructors for our country. Overcoming a long held prejudice that African Americans could not possibly qualify as flight officers, the government developed a program specifically "for Negroes" in Tuskegee, Alabama. Nathan Sams had excelled as a pilot and was chosen to be one who would train others for flight.

When World War II came to an end, ever so many white flyers upon leaving military service would apply for positions with the commercial airlines and were eagerly snatched up because of their skills and experience. However, employment patterns in the air transportation industry were no exception to the practices observable almost everywhere else in commercial America — north and south: "If you're white, all right; if you're black, step back!"

So there were no openings for Nathan Sams. He was a bright and resourceful young man and with pertinacity and ingenuity obtained a franchise to sell General Electric appliances. He set up an outlet store in Taft. The market for his product was decidedly limited in that small and financially strapped community, so he kept his eyes open for other opportunities. And one such surfaced.

Hatbox Field had represented Muskogee's bid to be involved in the widening era of aviation. However, dreams and promises of those who had originally espoused the venture did not materialize. For a while the city received reimbursement — sort of like parking fees — as the air force left some of its surplus retired planes in a ring around the field. These were ultimately dismantled and moved away. The field fell into virtual disuse and was no longer a source for government funds.

Nathan Sams had not abandoned his love for flying when he came out of uniform. He owned a plane of his own and decided to approach the city fathers, offering on a dollar-per-year basis to manage and maintain and operate the airport and thus keep it accessible and viable. They agreed to the arrangement.

Entrepreneur that he was, the young flyer approached several prominent and prosperous citizens of nearby Tulsa to interest them in flying. Unless one had racially prejudicial hang-ups, flight instructors with Nathan Sams' credentials didn't come along every day. So a few signed up — and some of them invited friends to do the same. Not only did he teach them and help them to become licensed flyers; he also sold them their own airplanes, built by Cessna, the company that had awarded him a sales franchise.

As his clientele grew and his business expanded, the operation was in need of more personnel. Nathan Sams knew Homer Hamilton. They'd attended high school together. And Nathan knew Homer's knack for mechanics. He had much confidence in his character and respect for his skills, so he invited him to work with him. In his new setting, not only did this new employee learn all about aircraft engines and structure under his boss's tutelage, he also learned to fly. In a short time Homer was awarded his pilot's license.

———————

The Hamiltons were a warm-humored, unexcitable, caring couple who would surely have made wonderful parents. Although they were remarkably fond of children — and children loved them — they were not blessed with children of their own.

In his later years, Homer's Dorthy became seriously ill with a malady that required amputation of both legs. Those days became occasion for him to devote special time and care to his burdened mate — and occasion for both of them to reflect on the gift of companionship and support their life together had given them. Theirs had been a marriage that had endured so many difficulties, that found them both grateful for the presence of their Lord in their days and hours together. Homer has died too. I think of them often and miss them.

———————

And Nathan? He didn't join Hope Church while I was still its pastor. However, he and his lovely wife Carolyn and their two children began attending our services. They were much loved, and their participation was enriching to the entire congregation. This young man had risen from their midst and was a model of courage and resourcefulness. Although he had long been denied the hero status he deserved in the service of his country, he had stood tall in the face of what seemed insurmountable hurdles to become an exemplary community leader. And, by the way, an active member and leader in Hope Congregation.

At age 81 he lives alone now. Carolyn had died in 1991. Their children still check in with their dad regularly. His daughter, Natalie, is now a flight attendant for United Airlines, out of Seattle. His son, Clarence Felton, works with NASA's space program in Houston and his wife is an astronaut. Another generation of people who soar!

Nathan and I have managed to stay in touch through the years. He remains a dear friend and an inspiration to me.

```
┌─────────────────────────────────┐
│                                 │
│     Three from Reeves            │
│          I.                      │
│     A Boy Named Floyd            │
│                                 │
└─────────────────────────────────┘
```

opening locked doors

In my mind I envisioned Muskogee to be laid out something like a wall clock. White residents populated most of the face of the clock. A small pocket of African Americans lived at twelve o'clock and some at six o'clock. At the ten o'clock point were Honor Heights Park and the Veterans' Hospital. There was a small black neighborhood tucked in there as well.

Like the shaft of the clock's pendulum, South Third Street stretched downward, a long walking distance, with Reeves Addition becoming the sphere at its end.

Reeves was regarded as a community of its own and might probably have been categorized as semi-rural. The pavement ended at Reeves. This was the turnaround place for the bus that was used primarily by people who would have to travel cross-town to find household and other menial jobs in the white community.

When I first began my term of service at Hope Church (up near the forehead part of town), I found the records left behind by my predecessors to be both brief and few. Among the items was a short list of names of children whom they had involved in church activities. Some of these young people still attended our services, a few had moved away, and some seemed simply to have disappeared.

The name of one was listed simply as:

Henderson, Floyd — Reeves Addition

Members of the congregation had either only the slightest or no recollection at all of such a lad. No age was mentioned, no further address, no telephone number.

The day was pleasant enough, so I walked, and walked, and at last arrived at the pavement's end. This was Reeves. I decided to try first visiting some houses off to my left. People were gracious enough, but I sensed a sort of guardedness when I began to ask about Floyd Henderson. Whether I would inquire at someone's front door or stop to talk with someone I would meet along the way, one after the other would answer me politely but consistently with a shrug of the shoulder, a shaking of the head, or a simple, "No, we don't know anyone by that name."

130

Whatever direction I would walk — and probably I inquired of a couple dozen people — the results were the same.

The roads were dusty and the sun was hot, and I was getting nowhere. So I returned home. I knew that I had at least given finding young Floyd a valiant try, and I was now ready to regard my search as hopeless and to dismiss him from my mind.

From our earliest beginnings in Oklahoma, Esther and I wanted to get acquainted with more and more of the people among whom we'd come to serve. Because the patterns of segregation were so deeply imbedded into Muskogee's social life, we found attending events held in the segregated schools an effective way to get into the community to be with people without being ushered into special separate seating areas. We must surely have been a bit conspicuous. We were usually the only white people present. What was no less important, we got in on some excellent and engaging programs and we'd especially enjoy the athletic events.

High School Coach Walter Cox managed to come up with exciting seasons each year, both in basketball and football. There was one exceptionally talented player whom everyone knew as "Polly" — Polly Henderson. For a good long time it didn't even occur to me that he might be the "missing" Floyd Henderson I'd been looking for.

When the realization finally came to me, I dropped in at the high school gym one evening after practice and asked him if his was the name in our files. In awkward embarrassment he nodded and explained that indeed he had attended Hope in earlier days. It turned out that he had been living with his grandmother (probably in one of the very houses I'd visited in Reeves). Obviously all the people were being honest in telling me then that they didn't know anyone by the name of Floyd Henderson — everyone knew him as *Polly* Henderson. More important, they were manifesting solidarity. They had no idea who I was — whether I was a bill collector, a salesman, a government employee or officer — and they weren't

131

about to expose this young neighbor to anything or anyone that might endanger his well-being or might jeopardize his future.

Floyd told how his family often found it difficult to scrape enough money together for busfare, so he had discontinued coming to Hope. And by the time he had grown older and was in a position to get about on his own, he felt awkward and maybe a bit ashamed about returning. We chuckled, chatted more, and our friendship took root. The very next Sunday he was with us for worship and he became regular in his visits to our church.

Floyd was the kind of fellow any mother would have loved to claim — modest, courteous, considerate, dependable, congenial, bright. All these and more.

He surprised me one day with an afterschool visit to my office, acknowledging his indecision as to how to respond to mail he'd been receiving. Four or five of the larger universities and colleges in the North had invited him to play football, and each offer carried an attractive scholarship assistance proposal, were he to accept.

He was sure, he said, that he could readily compete with players from the kind of teams that his high school had faced. All those schools were segregated and of relatively small enrollment. He did not know, however, how he might measure up against players from larger schools and better teams. He liked playing football, he explained, but he didn't want to be enrolled at a school where teammates were of such higher caliber that he'd be sitting on the bench most of the time.

I had almost no acquaintance with any colleges or universities anywhere and was a bit overwhelmed by his asking me to offer help in making his decision. I told him that I knew some of the personnel at Valparaiso University, a relatively small Lutheran university in Indiana, and if he'd want me to, I'd send for information.

In a remarkably short time Floyd returned, wearing a broad smile and waving a letter in his hand. Valparaiso had offered him an attractive athletic scholarship and he had decided that was the school he wanted to attend.

As he was readying himself for his new experience, he asked whether he might become a Lutheran. I told him how much his commitment meant to me. I suggested, however, that he might do well to withhold making a decision till later. It would be helpful for him to learn more about the Lutheran faith with other pastors as well. And, besides, it was important that everyone understood that his receiving a scholarship from this Lutheran university was not contingent upon his first becoming a Lutheran.

Floyd was the first African American at Valpo to engage in intercollegiate athletics. Valparaiso was an all-white city then and only a handful of black students had enrolled at the school and he was among the first of these.

His teammates and the football cheering section loved him. Small wonder. In his first game he ran back a punt almost seventy yards. The sports page of the University's *Torch,* in describing the play, told how almost everyone on the opposing team got a hand on him, but none had been able to bring him down on his touchdown sprint.

During his freshman year he attended Lutheran services in Valparaiso, and he did become a Lutheran. The following summer he spent with his father who lived in Flint, Michigan. Floyd was able to find employment there, a tremendous help to him in meeting additional living expenses at the University.

In spite of his busy schedule, Floyd would find time to write us an occasional letter to apprise us of happenings in his new world. We always looked forward to hearing from him.

In one that he wrote, shortly before he left for his summer in Michigan, he requested my recommendation of some Lutheran church he might attend while in Flint. I was unacquainted with the church scene in Flint, so I copied the names and addresses of four or five listed in a church directory and sent them to him.

When I spotted a response from him in the following Tuesday's mail, I quickly opened it with my usual happy anticipation. But his words abruptly dispelled any happy mood I'd been in.

I kept no copy of that letter, but I read it and reread it and after all these years I remember almost each word he wrote.

In his letter Floyd told how he'd discovered one of the churches I'd named was only a few steps away from where he was staying. He'd gone by on Saturday evening to read the church's bulletin board to check on the time of the next day's worship services. He was pleased that the church was so close.

On Sunday morning, dressed for church and ready for worship, he returned. He greeted a man standing there at the foot of the outside stairs, who rather abruptly informed him that this was a Lutheran church.

With his large smile, Floyd had proudly responded, "I'm a Lutheran!"

The man persisted, "You don't understand; we don't have any Lutheran churches for colored here in Flint."

Floyd's letter told how he had just returned home and was sitting on the side of his bed. He apologized for crying. He said he never cried. He was so deeply hurt and confused. He didn't know Lutherans were like this. Hadn't he learned from the Lutherans that God excludes no one from His grace and that in Christ all are one, and that we shouldn't abandon "the assembling of ourselves together"?

I was angry — I was furious! For the first time I really understood what St. Paul meant, when — at his pastoral best — he had written: "Who [among my congregation] is caused to stumble and I burn not!"

I didn't wait even a minute before phoning the pastor of that church to vent my feelings. And I was surprised — and gratified — that in his response he seemed almost as angry as I.

This pastor called for an immediate assembling of his Church Council to inform them of what had happened. They too were dismayed. He later reported to me that together they had vigorously attempted to identify the person who had taken upon himself the role of one-man unwelcoming committee. None of the members had any idea who it might have been. And in fact all of them seemed genuinely affronted that this sort of happening could occur at their church.

And yet they all realized that regardless of how deeply the majority might have resented such behavior, as long as one person could and did do this, the act was as effective as if the entire church membership had been armlocked together *en masse* on the steps of the church saying "You cannot come in here if you are black!"

The elders and pastors paid Floyd a personal visit, apologizing to him, begging his forgiveness, and earnestly inviting him to make theirs his church home.

Eventually Floyd was graduated from Valparaiso, where he'd met Susan, his lovely wife. He later pursued graduate studies in library science and became head librarian for the United States Department of Forestry in the Twin Cities.

Almost thirty years later, I was conducting a workshop for churches in metropolitan neighborhoods experiencing racial change. A delegation participated from Immanuel Church in Minneapolis. Floyd was one of that parish's leaders present, helping to make his congregation an inclusive, welcoming church.

It was a gratifying reunion and I was honored to learn that among the Henderson children, Scott, the eldest was given a middle name Karl — spelled with a K.

I chill to think what would have happened had Floyd walked away from the Flint church and had not written of his experience so that we could finally work through the troubled moment, the emotional distress, and were able to gain new perspective and renewed vision.

Three from Reeves
II.
The Lowes

peeking into doors slightly open

Years later, when serving with the Lutheran Human Relations Association of America, I would be speaking to a group of Lutheran church women at St. Peter's on Chicago's far South Side. I was commending the stand of a man I had only met once, but admired greatly. He had been principal of First Immanuel Lutheran Elementary School on Chicago's near West Side and had played a vital role in persuading that congregation to welcome children of African American descent into their school.

It happened that one of those young children died.

The congregation maintained its own cemetery for use by those who belonged to the church and members of their families. At the proposal that the child be buried there, a dispute arose, and, in a special meeting of Immanuel's members, the child's family was denied the right to bury their little son with the white Lutherans. The issue clearly was a matter of race.

Mr. Krenz, the principal, was indignant. Demonstrating his deep distress and opposition to the congregation's decision, he resigned from his post. With clear conscience he could not and would not affirm the church's attitude and action by remaining in his position of leadership at First Immanuel.

In closing my presentation to the group, I observed that his was a powerful and effective witness to what the Christian faith and life are all about.

Later, when I returned to my seat and the group took to coffee and cookies, a woman came towards me from a far corner of the room. In a soft, low voice she said, "The story you told was true. That was my little boy, and because of Mr. Krenz and what he did, I am a member of the Lutheran Church today."

This was my first confrontation with segregation of the dead in the North. However, I had learned to expect such arrangement in the South.

On the far, far south side of Reeves Addition lay Lowe's Cemetery, an alternative to the larger cemeteries for whites, and marked by gravestones far more modest than the large ornate, sculptured counterparts "'cross town."

138

It hadn't occurred to me till I'd lived there a few years that there was any connection between the name of the cemetery and one of our members, Ms. Eva Shawnee Lowe. Mr. Lowe and she had been married at one time and were parents of three girls and a boy, all, by this time, in their thirties. The senior Lowes had been separated for some time.

Mrs. Lowe was a sweet, home loving, industrious, motherly person, a faithful and loyal church member. A bright woman, she had attended Hampton in West Virginia and Oberlin College in Ohio. She spent many years commuting each weekday to work as an employee of the state's Institution for the Deaf, Blind, and Orphans, just a few blocks up the hill from the mental hospitals in the all African American town called Taft, some eight miles west of Muskogee. And of course all these institutions were intended as alternate to their counterpart institutions operating for the white citizenry at other sites across the state.

I never got to know Mr. Lowe well. Mrs. Lowe did not mention him to me, nor did he ever refer to her in my visits with him.

I liked him already the first time I met him. He did not appear to be at all the stay-at-home type. And he surely would not have fit any preconceived stereotype of what a cemetery manager and attendant might be. He was a very literate man and an enjoyable, stimulating conversationalist. He possessed an undeniable charm, and a mischievous sort of humor. This was apparent in the column he would submit occasionally to the *Oklahoma Independent,* a weekly published for an African American readership reaching to a range of more than thirty miles of Muskogee. In these pieces he would reveal his impatience with churches, institutionalized religion, and almost any kind of formal but phony piety. Yet he tolerated my clergy status and was always respectful of my ministry and me, and with polite persistency declined my invitations to worship with us at Hope Church.

It was hardly surprising then that these two exceptionally gifted people were not together and that I didn't initially tie their names together. These were two very different persons, each altogether unique.

I did get to know Mrs. Lowe well. She was immersed in her faith and devoted in her faithfulness. She would attend church, Sunday after Sunday — and often in between. When we first met she was in her seventies. In her later years she experienced severe difficulties with her leg, so I'd often visit with her in her home.

It was a neat home. And a very busy home. Her daughter Myra Jeanne lived with her. Myra was a beautician. An addition to the north side of her house served as her shop. As her mother's condition worsened and the diseased leg had to be removed, Myra was there to fill the role of caregiver. Her mother was grateful.

I remember a phone call from Myra. She was laughing so hard she could hardly speak. She said she simply couldn't wait to pass on to me a comment her mother had made: "Myra, that was a marvelous dinner, I'd like to lie down now. And if you could play some soft music and I could hear one of the pastor's fine sermons I'd fall asleep right now." And we both chuckled.

Mrs. Lowe had not had an easy life and, especially in her years of illness, she experienced more than her share of discomfort and unrelenting pain. While none begrudged the ultimate respite and relief that came with her death, all who had known Eva Shawnee Lowe acknowledged the passing of a dear, kind, and altogether gracious lady.

In earlier days, if my visits to the Lowe home happened to fall between her appointments or a customer would be sitting under a dryer, Myra would come out to the front room where I'd be chatting with her mother. Our conversations often turned to church and religion. I would invite her to attend Hope's services again and again. The most reasonable of her excuses cited the large volume of appointments women would make for Saturdays, presumably so they'd be at their prettiest for church the next morning. Myra's services were not only skilled but considerate and accommodating, and therefore she'd be working late, often till one or two o'clock on Sunday mornings.

One Sunday, either wearied or worn down (I'd rather think "persuaded!") by my repeated invitations, Myra finally came to church with her mother. She attended Bible study hour. I was impressed with her comments and thoughtful questions. She returned and kept coming and acknowledged that she really liked the church. It was then that she confided that she had a serious drinking problem.

Other ministers had told her they'd like to have her join their churches, but each of them had made her turning away from alcohol a prerequisite to membership. She had tried, she said, but the urge to drink always proved too strong. So since the churches had given up on her, she had given up on the churches.

In my seminary experience alcoholism had been given only the scantiest attention. Because my acquaintance with the subject was so decidedly limited, I was hardly prepared to deal with the issue. However, I was to get some tutoring in the matter from Myra. She spelled out for me in lucid and gripping terms her addiction and her desire to turn the corner to a life of sobriety.

Her long working hours were tedious and stressful. Coming to church was one of her first respite experiences she'd had for months and months. In my visits I had never found her to have been drinking. She told me that after long days of work, and after her mother was already asleep, she would regularly resort to some relaxation — and her beverage of choice. And on some occasions the final customer would stay on to imbibe with her.

I had suggested that she seek out Alcoholics Anonymous for help. We found out that the local presence of AA offered service only to whites. These were the 1940s and there was no such resource for people of color here in the South.

My reasoning with her was simple. "The Gospel's message is not 'If you change your selfish ways and are perfect, God will welcome you.' That's hardly 'good news' when you are struggling with destructive impulses — and losing." I assured her that the good news of the Gospel informs us that we are welcome immediately to a dependable and faithful God who supplies strength to counter those powerful urges that do damage to our lives.

She wept. And she said she deeply desired that kind of relationship with God. She said too that she wanted to be a part of Hope Church's community of folk who shared a devotion to such a

Gospel. She desperately wanted help to put aside her past dependence on alcohol and begin a life of service to God and to neighbor.

Hope's membership roster listed fewer than three dozen. There was room for lay ministers. Myra was gifted and Myra was ready. She became a Sunday School teacher, a leader with the youth group, and was quick to participate in any volunteer activity that we needed. I could always depend on her — and she obviously began to depend on the church and its pastor.

One night in particular this became evident. It was very, very late and our phone rang. She told me that she felt terribly tense and had placed an order for some liquor. (Oklahoma was a "dry state." There were no liquor stores and one could not buy liquor in taverns. Yet we regularly received post cards in the mail, addressed to "occupant," providing a number to call for home delivery, listing the prices of different brands of whiskey and such.)

I drove to her home quickly. She opened the door and stood there in the white uniform she always wore when at work. Her eyes were heavy and sad, her face almost expressionless. It had obviously been a wearing day. She looked totally exhausted — frazzled.

As I was about to enter, the deliveryman stepped up on the porch with his package. I stood aside as she paid him. He left.

Neither of us spoke a word as I followed her inside. We sat opposite each other at the kitchen table, the parcel between us.

She began to pour out her experiences of what had been a particularly menacing day. I listened, and when, finally, in a flood of tears, she came to the end of her story, I opened the Bible I'd brought with me and began to read to her verses I thought appropriate for the moment. Quite suddenly she lifted the package from the table. She separated the bottle from its wrappings and walked to the sink. There she unscrewed the cap from the flask and poured its contents down the drain. Then she held the bottle under the faucet to rinse it clean. She set it to the side as if its emptiness were some sort of trophy. Then, turning to me she said, "Thank you, pastor. Now will you say a prayer?"

My prayer was short, and together we spoke the Lord's Prayer. Once more she thanked me and said, "I'll be able to sleep now." And I left.

One Sunday morning Myra brought a fine looking young man along to church. She informed me that they would be married. He was polite and friendly. I was impressed and I could surely understand why she had been impressed.

Muskogee was hardly the land of opportunity for any young African American seeking a career of any kind. Jobs were scarce. So Myra continued her work in her shop in her home. Before too long she announced that a child was on its way. After the months of excited waiting beautiful little Guinevere was born. And then an unexpected and a most unwanted development occurred. Myra's new husband left her, taking with him financial booty and leaving behind an array of debts. And an expectant Myra.

Myra remained faithful in her church life and was a loving mother — a very caring person.

It wasn't a bit surprising then that I found a stranger in her home one day. "Pastor, this is Uncle Matt," she said. The old man was sitting there, rocking little Guinevere in his arms as they swayed back and forth on the porch swing. He was short of stature and looked every one of those 94 years he claimed to be.

When we had stepped inside I said, "Myra, I didn't know you had any living uncles or aunts!"

"I don't," she replied and then unfolded for me what had happened two weeks earlier.

This man, a total stranger, had appeared on her doorstep, knocked gently (he didn't appear to have the strength to do more than a tap) and asked if Myra might lend him fifty cents. He explained he had some kinfolk in Arkansas and needed money for the bus fare. She informed him that fifty cents was hardly enough for such a ticket. He hadn't eaten anything all day, she discovered, so she invited him to sit on the porch swing while she readied a sandwich for him. She had to leave him there while she attended to one of her customers.

When she returned, she found him fast asleep there on the swing. He looked so utterly exhausted that she left him there to continue his nap. She returned awhile later determined to wake him and send him on his way again. She asked him to wait long enough, however, so she could provide him with a little sustenance for the way.

Minutes later, when she came back with his bowl of soup, she found he had picked up a broom from the corner and was sweeping both the sidewalk and the front porch.

"He looked so grateful — and pitiful!" Myra said. She laid out a blanket on the floor for him and told him he could stay till morning. Next morning when she woke she heard him outside raking together leaves in the yard. "He's just stayed on and he helps a bit and takes care of Guinevere."

Uncle Matt simply had become a member of the family. It was only a short time later that Guinevere's little brother was born.

Myra had a great sense of humor. After her little Thaddaeus was born she delighted in telling how one of her customers came by to see the infant. She apparently took one look and said, "Myra, I knew that Uncle Matt was up to no good around here. This baby looks just like him — he's all wrinkled up, he's bald — not a hair on his head and he doesn't have a tooth in his mouth!"

None of our members seemed as altogether sorrowful when we left Muskogee as Myra. And we were sad too. The memories of her and her loved ones that I still carry have been rich and gratifying. I even had a little bit of special pleasure in knowing I filled a role in her bout with alcoholism. Years later, however, word came to me that she had moved from Muskogee to New York and once more succumbed to the devastating allure of liquor.

How little I really knew about that dreadful malady. I had had a part in relieving her of her dependence on alcohol, but unwittingly I had very likely become a new object of her dependency. Once I was gone, she reverted to the old dependency.

I look back with a muted joy, recalling that, at least, there were years of sobriety for her, especially in her early days of mothering. But I am sobered and saddened as I realize my own inadequacy.

replacing fallen doors

On the outskirts of Muskogee there were many unattended fields and smaller lots that grew high with wild weeds and grasses. Beautiful in their greenery as they swayed in gentle winds of summer, they were frighteningly treacherous as they changed from gold in autumn to brown in winter.

There were nights I would sit up in my bed when I would hear the siren's wailing screams. I learned early on how errant sparks and glowing embers or carelessly flipped cigarettes could ignite such quiet fields, transforming them into roaring carpets of leaping flames. And so the fire engines would race to combat the hungry fires before they might spread and swallow in their blaze the tiny fragile houses in their paths.

And sometimes when the temperatures were freezing, people in such little homes would overstock their tiny stoves with fuel, generating heat that would tax the tired smokestacks beyond their strength, and first the roof, and moments later, the entire house would be wrapped in fire.

Every year such homes would burn. And often people would die in those fires. And those who lived in those little houses were very poor. Like the Eikners.

Henry Eikner was a short man. I never did learn his age. Mr. Eikner could have been sixty — or eighty. His youngish face masked his many years. Jobs were hard to come by in Muskogee in those days, especially for older men. His advanced age, however, made him eligible for a meager assistance check from the state, but that was hardly enough for him to provide adequately for his small family.

Mrs. Eikner was much younger. Her face was that of a woman of courage and strength, a hard working woman, fiercely loyal to her family, unwaveringly faithful to her God. She regularly brought her two daughters with her to attend worship services, but their father never would come the more-than-walking distance from Reeves by bus. Although the bus fare was quite low, transportation costs taxed their tight financial means, since Corrine (her mom called her "Peaches"), a fifth grader, and her younger sister, "Dumplings," a third grader, would have to travel by bus each weekday to attend our church's one room elementary school. Their mother did

146

domestic service to help bolster the family's limited and strained economy.

Once I came to know Mr. Eikner, I found time spent with him rewarding, as he would share stories of his youth — days of warm humor and often desperate survival. When he discovered that I liked to fish, he invited me to join him. We'd walk from his home over to Lowe's Cemetery. It was a good place to fish — few people frequent such places after dark. We'd often sit there far into the night, flashlights beaming towards the pond to check whether our bobbers were being bothered by the catfish. In soft voice, so as not to disturb the fish, he would tell me his stories. Of course we caught fish — not big ones. But then, these pond side hours were serious — the fish we caught were intended for the Eikner table where the fare was always healthful but the helpings were often sparse.

Though by almost any standard this family's circumstances would have to be regarded as "below poverty level," I could never conceive of the Eikners as poor. There was an abundance of care and love for each other, and one never heard a whimper or whisper of complaint.

I was shocked into a realization of their neediness, however, when a phone call alerted me, reporting that one of those dreaded fires engulfed their little house. The family barely escaped with the clothes they were wearing, and their every earthly possession was consumed in the inferno. When I arrived on the scene, the fire fighters had soaked the last glowing ashes, and Mr. Eikner was poking about in the black gooey rubble, finally realizing that nothing could be salvaged.

His wife and their two children stood to the side, wrapped in a blanket some thoughtful neighbor had provided. Almost emotionless, she looked at me and said, "Everything's gone, pastor; I've no more tears; we're all cried out."

Neighbors in their already too small houses offered to give them shelter for the moment. Members of our congregation — almost all of them poor themselves — did what they could. There were no agencies prepared to give any kind of relief. And of course they'd not been insured. All these people had was that little plot of ground, now littered with charred boards, broken glass, and ashes, and a few crumbled cement blocks.

Mrs. Eikner asked "What do we do, Pastor?" And the members of the church asked the same. And I asked myself too. My seminary education had never prepared me for this. The situation called for social work skills, for financial management, for construction experience. And I really had no credentials in any of these categories. If I had never realized it before, I certainly had to acknowledge my inadequacy now.

I was also certain that all this did not give me license to walk away from this situation, and with whatever resources I might muster I had to respond as quickly and helpfully as possible.

When I had first arrived in Muskogee I met Mr. Croisant. He was an unusual man — casual in his appearance, a man with unusual practical skills. He was very helpful and considerate. I remember him bringing bags of peaches and, later in the season, apples from his orchards. He seemed genuinely appreciative that through Hope Church we were serving the African American community. He also seemed particularly solicitous of the personal needs and well-being of this young, innocent, and naïve young couple from up north, and in our ministry, and in the people among whom we were serving.

He was a member of the "other church across town" — the one the white Lutherans attended — yet he and a handful of other members of First Lutheran were conspicuously present on my first Sunday at Hope, the day of my ordination. Whenever we would schedule some special festive Sunday afternoon worship event, Mr. Croisant would be present. Otherwise he would be attending his own church. He never would be absent from any service there.

Esther would have him join us for dinner occasionally. He was a man of few words, congenial, but a passive conversationalist.

He would drop by to fix some leaking plumbing in our somewhat antiquated residence (which also served as our church), or to attend to any other repair needs we might have. And he'd do the work himself.

Mr. Croisant owned the cotton gin in town. He also owned a farm implement sales and repair company. And, of course, the orchards. And there was also a small oil well on one end of the orchards. One would have hardly guessed him to be so prosperous. He usually drove a modest pick up truck (no name on the door). He was unassuming, modest, and reserved.

He had dozens of employees, but, almost always, he himself would arrive unaccompanied when he'd drop by to lend a hand.

So I called on Mr. Croisant and told him what had happened. In virtually no time at all, he came by to drive me out to Reeves to see the place in shambles. I could tell he was moved when he saw the chaos and as I introduced him to the Eikners. He said very simply, "We'll see!"

With tape measure in hand he began tapping pegs into the ground and stretching strings. He lifted two shovels from the rear of his truck so that Mr. Eikner and a neighbor could immediately begin to dig trenches within the lines he'd marked off. He would be back that afternoon.

By sunset, men he'd dispatched to the scene from the cotton gin had laid a foundation, and before the week had passed, a neat, modest, four room, shingle sided house was in place, interior unfinished, but ready for occupancy.

We told others about the magnificent transformation, and suddenly we were helping to move beds and blankets and mattresses and cooking ware and chairs and a table and lamps and a few pieces of carpeting and even curtains that some people asked us to pick up and deliver.

And of course Mr. Croisant sent no bill.

And the Eikners, and the neighbors, and the members of Hope, and the people at the cotton gin, and the cross-town Lutherans — and Esther and the boys and I — and Mr. Croisant all learned a little more about being in the Christian family.

Jno. F. Schultz

installing larger doors

True enough, Oklahoma probably had its share of people who didn't take God seriously. And there were certainly lots more who didn't attend church every Sunday — or at all. But to hear the Reverend John F. Schultz describe the situation, the entire and focused stance of the churches to all our neighbors ought to be one of immediate and total urgency.

The district of our church body included 65 congregations, and at least two dozen of these were subsidized "mission stations." And all these small churches and their pastors served under the supervision of the Oklahoma District Mission Board and its administrator who was *Jno. F. Schultz*. That's the way he signed his name, in a large flamboyant scrawl. He was a large man, with a large voice. Had he been in the theatre, he could have filled the role of Julius Caesar or a police precinct sergeant. Everything about him was large. His signature even seemed to leap from the page and say, "I am a large man!"

When he would gather all of "his men" together at our conferences, he made it very clear that we had a job cut out for us. We out here in "frontier country" were here on behalf of our Lord and the Lutheran Church (but, clearly, in that order!). Our assigned task was to connect the fallen, the forgetful, the wayward, and those preoccupied with a host of distractions to the God who wanted them back in his embrace.

He told us we were accountable for what we did — and for what we didn't do. Of course we all had known that we were accountable to God, but he made it clear we were accountable as well to Jno. F. Schultz. There were reports to fill out: how much time spent on sermons, on deskwork, on visits — to members and non-members. Especially non-members. "Pastors spend far too much time visiting their own members," he would say. "It's no compliment to long-time church members when you keep going to their houses and spoon-feed them as if they were babies; let them take care of themselves and one another. You've got to attend to the immature in faith and those who are outside the church's door, hungry and undernourished."

When we'd come out of such meetings we were fired up, ready to do a Billy Graham job on the nation. He didn't strike fear in our hearts; it was sheer awe. We were inspired.

Well, maybe a little bit of fear.

I'd only been a pastor for a few weeks. The Sunday morning service had just begun and I was up in front, facing the altar as we ended the singing of the first hymn. I turned around to face the little congregation.

I looked up from the service book. Panic!

There they were in the fourth row, center. Large Jno. F. Schultz and his wife had slipped in and were sitting there among our parishioners. I don't doubt that they wanted to worship with us, but it was clear enough also that this was an occasion for checking how things were going with Hope Lutheran Church in Muskogee and its new pastor. Maybe the appropriate word to describe my status at that moment is intimidation, or utter inadequacy.

As I recall, however, no one walked out on the sermon. Nor had there been a thunderous applause or standing ovation — by Jno F. Schultz. Or anybody else, for that matter.

I cannot remember whether or not he even commented on the experience. I do remember, however, a warm feeling of having been affirmed. He was truly an ally.

And I learned more and more how he became a champion of the pastors entrusted to his charge. One of these "mission congregations" was an older one in a rural setting. The people had arranged for a new pastor to come and were discussing his coming with Jno. F. Schultz, who had dropped in to see whether things were in readiness for their new leader's arrival. They took him into a rather antiquated parsonage, which they had tidied a bit and here and there had touched up with a few brush strokes of paint.

The big man walked into the living room and noticed a crack in the wallpaper. He stepped closer, slipped his big hand into a loose spot, and, eventually, reaching behind with his entire arm buried, he tore down a yard-wide strip of old paper. With their eyes opened wide and in an almost audible chorus of gulps the parishioners watched him continue to tear down more and still more. And with his loud voice he chided the welcoming committee, "Your

153

new pastor has just married a new wife and this is to be her wedding present — a new home with tattered wallpaper?" And of course they were obliged to do it right.

I'm not sure everyone loved the large man with the large frame and the large voice. But if there were such, they had not been able to discern behind all that largeness a large heart.

Some two or three years later we learned that he'd been traveling along the west border of Arkansas and taken ill. A colleague from nearby joined me to visit our "bishop" in the hospital. Even there, though pale and weakened by the ordeal, his voice boomed out a large welcome and then he pontificated, "The lesson to be learned is that you never should delay when your body tells you it is time to use the bathroom." And of all the many things he taught us, his hospital words still evoke an appreciative smile from me.

And, indeed, though I barely knew him — and only for a brief time before his far-too-early death, I have come to regard him as one of God's very special gifts to enrich my ministry.

Carolyn and Clark

danger of swinging doors

Carolyn was one of the first people I met after my initial arrival in Oklahoma. She was a second grader, a winsome, cheerful child. She was bright, well mannered, always neatly dressed. Other children found Carolyn a favorite playmate. Adults enjoyed having her with them — she was altogether lovable. She was an eager learner and a teacher's delight. She became a capable pianist and in her early years already began playing hymns for our worship services.

While living in the segregated South was surely a confining experience for people of African American descent, their community provided a sort of place of refuge. Here all members could return and find welcome, support, affirmation, and encouragement from others who themselves knew and had experienced the humiliating and repressive status of being black in the midst of a white majority.

Like countless other young black men and women leaving their more sheltered and protective environs to find a place in the larger world, Carolyn left home to accept a scholarship offer from Valparaiso University in Indiana. Here, among almost 3000 students, she — and the two other students of color enrolled with her — already began early to experience the subtleties of racial discrimination.

Her roommate at the time, Lou Jeanne Bray (now Walton, who heads Valparaiso University's Department of Social Work) tells how their attending Sunday service at Valparaiso's Immanuel Church had proved so humiliating to them. Some worshippers chose not to participate in the Lord's Supper and hurried out of the church when they saw Carolyn and Lou Jeanne step toward the altar.

Carolyn maintained her membership at Hope Church in Muskogee. It was after I had become pastor in Tulsa that Esther and I received a phone call from Carolyn announcing her intent to be married, and inviting me to perform the ceremony. We were delighted and were eager to learn all about the man she intended to marry. And she was equally eager to tell us all about him.

His name was Clark Shephard — spelled with an "a" instead of an "e." He was in the armed forces and stationed in Wichita, and a wonderful person. She was, of course, far more expansive in her

156

description of him and far more lavish in listing his attributes. We were as persuaded he was the right choice for a husband for her as we were convinced he couldn't have found a more wonderful wife.

The time passed swiftly toward the day of the nuptial event. We met together, laid all the plans for the ceremony, and spent time in prewedding conversations.

Clark became a real person to us, no longer just a name. Although we surely had known Carolyn for a far longer period of time, we felt very close to Clark, now that he was to be Carolyn's husband. We talked about him often and would refer to him by his first name as though we'd known him all his life.

We anticipated the wedding day with excitement and I particularly wanted my brief address to be something they would remember. I had decided to show the significance of their Lord's role in their new life together and prepared my homily, drawing on the Twenty Third Psalm. This would surely mean much to Carolyn and Clark.

Because their families might not be able to be present for their wedding — and because Carolyn and Clark were so very special to us, we thought it might be meaningful to present them with a picture for their new home; if possible, one that in the years to come would remind them of their nuptial day.

Esther was in full agreement and, after shopping about, she selected a lovely picture, portraying Jesus in the role of the Good Shepherd. It was large and bright colored, well-suited for eventual hanging in their living room.

On the celebration day we carefully placed the beautifully wrapped gift in the car and left for the sixty-mile drive to Muskogee. I had performed fewer than a handful of marriages up to that point and since Clark and Carolyn were both such dear people, I was eager to "do this one right!"

And it was a lovely wedding. The bride was beautiful and teary-eyed, the groom was handsome and attentive to her every need, and all the worshippers were obviously pleased that these two fine young people had found each other and were beginning a new life together with the Lord.

It was late as we began our return trip to Tulsa. Of course, we rehearsed all that had happened and we were both immersed in a sort of euphoric gratification about how well things had gone. When suddenly I gasped, "Esther, do you realize what I did! Clark's last name is Shephard and my sermon theme was "Take the Good Shepherd into your Home." And Esther added, "And the picture will always be there to remind them!"

When the young couple returned from their wedding trip a few days later I was able to call Carolyn and blushingly explain. And Carolyn, full of grace, simply said, "I liked it — I thought it was a clever play on words and that you did it intentionally."

The details escape me, but I do remember Clark and Carolyn taking up residence in Wichita, Kansas. Wichita had experienced dramatic changes during the war years. Boeing Aircraft was called on to supply planes for the military arsenal. Pressures for increased production in manufacturing and assembling placed unprecedented demands upon Boeing's various operating divisions. This called for around-the-clock, three shift employment patterns. Because of the need for workers, people crowded into Wichita from everywhere. Some rooming houses were renting out their bedroom space on an eight-hour interval basis. If you worked an eight a.m. to four p.m. shift, you were to lock your belongings in a drawer provided and another roomer would get your bed upon completing his shift, and he in turn was to vacate the room for the man who came in from the third shift for his eight hours.

The Korean War had dragged on so slowly that it almost seemed a surprise when it did come to an end. Clark was no longer in military uniform.

With the end of the war, the need for military aircraft ended with equal suddenness. The layoffs began and the number of jobs available diminished at a frightening pace and the crowds of jobless people mushroomed.

It was into this stark situation Clark had come, wanting to meet his responsibility as a husband to the wife he loved so dearly and

158

who only a short time before had given birth to a precious daughter. Wherever he applied for work he encountered rejection. He and Carolyn had depleted all their reserves and there was simply nowhere to turn to find help to meet the rent on their modest quarters or to supply food for their table.

It was after a day of such futile search that Clark returned to their apartment. Carolyn had left briefly with their small daughter and arrived shortly after he had. She found him curled on the floor, unconscious — and on the table nearby, a half-eaten piece of bread covered with peanut butter and rat poison! At once Carolyn called for emergency medical help and the rescue unit revived him. After some anxious hours of care, he recovered and was with his family again.

Clark had reasoned that, having exhausted all other resources, he was able still to convert his military insurance into an asset that would benefit his wife and child upon his death.

Surely, some would censure him for not trusting God or produce some other reason for condemning his decision. I choose to remember our Lord's words that aver, "No greater love does a man have than to lay down his life for his friend."

That's the kind of person — that's the kind of husband — Clark was. And I am awed to remember that I had a role in the founding of this family.

The pastor and some of the members of the Lutheran congregation which the Shephards had joined proved to be helpful friends to them in those difficult days. And the church afforded community to the young family and provided them with focus for their lives.

While Clark still expended valiant efforts to find employment that would supply sufficient income to meet their needs, Carolyn became increasingly involved in volunteer activities at the church. People recognized quickly her talents and willingness to serve, and she accepted the challenges offered her. She became particularly active in the congregation's educational program, and when it

159

appeared that her participation might be limited because the Shephards had no car, one of the members offered to drive her to meetings and return her to her home again.

That kind of friendly support meant much to Clark and Carolyn. They felt sure that they could not have found anywhere a truer experience of Christian care.

Until — until one evening when this exemplary church member frightened Carolyn with romantic words and improper physical overtures. More than disillusioned, and offended, both Carolyn and Clark were deeply hurt and angry.

They realized that the humiliating experience was really the fault of one man, and not a sin in which the rest of the congregation participated or which they would ever condone. But that the incident occurred in the context of churchly activity left the young couple with many thoughts and feelings to be sorted out.

Wichita did not hold good memories.

Clark moved on ahead to an East Coast metropolis in hopes of establishing himself there and setting things up so the rest of his little family might join him there.

He was eager to find a church home in his new environs because he had found the church to be very important in their lives — in spite of the devastating experience they'd had in Wichita.

He'd asked his pastor what church he might recommend in the city he had chosen and received from him a list of names and addresses of Lutheran congregations there. He selected one near the apartment he had found and already was renting, and went to visit the pastor.

Pastors don't normally sit in their studies waiting for strangers to drop in and ask to join the church. So this minister, of course, was pleased to welcome this prospective member. And when he learned that Clark's family would be coming later, he was likely even more pleased.

Since Clark was at this point still living by himself, the pastor explained that he too was a bachelor and would be able to spend more time with Clark in his getting settled. Clark was grateful for such hospitable and solicitous care.

Until — until, unbelievably, the clergyman made homosexual advances. Clark was crushed. And when he informed Carolyn of what had happened, she too was disillusioned. Obviously, turning to a church when one tries to find one's moorings and bearings for living one's life does not always guarantee favorable results.

In later years Carolyn traveled to Cleveland for lunch with me at the airport as I stopped there between flights. They had now been living in nearby Oberlin.

No longer Lutherans, Carolyn and Clark and their daughters (there were three now) had relocated. They had been found and welcomed by a fine Christian congregation that surrounded them with a community of loving care.

Carolyn was a librarian at the college; Clark had established himself as a portrait photographer and had a studio of his own; and their three daughters had completed college.

Our brief reunion provided a gratifying updated report on how these two had beaten the adversities and had fashioned a wonderful home and life together.

Our two families did a slightly better job of keeping in touch in later years. Carolyn was only a little more than fifty, and therefore it was distressingly disturbing to learn that she was found to have a serious cancer. She manifested great courage through the ordeal and found her Clark to be at her side through it all with strong support.

Surprisingly the malady's vicious persistence abated and she reached a plateau of relative wellbeing. In spring of 1992 we invited Carolyn and Clark to join us for a special family celebration and both came. It was a happy, nostalgic event, and their being there contributed significantly to its specialness. She, delicate, lovely, charming, and warm-humored, in spite of her recent ordeal — and Clark gently and devotedly attending her.

The remission could not last. Months later, Esther and I visited Oberlin, where we met Clark who told us of the days that marked the close of a beautiful marriage. He described the tenderness of her daughters at her bedside, the warm and caring presence of her stepsister, and the preciousness of the last days and hours he had with his dear Carolyn.

We walked the soft, green lawn to her grave. And with moist eyes we remembered.

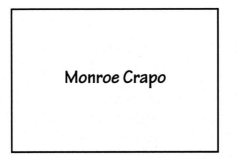

Monroe Crapo

_____

side doors

_____

It must have been precisely fifty years ago that I met Monroe Crapo (they pronounced it "kray-po"). Today a letter came from his wife Naomi. Monroe died. And the memories keep seeping down like rivulets from melting snow. And they are warming memories.

I was serving Hope Congregation in Muskogee then, and "Uncle Jno. F." Schultz, the somewhat awesome, autocratic Secretary of Missions, to whom I was accountable, tacked an additional assignment to my agenda, asking me to revive a mission station in McAlester, some sixty miles down the road to the south.

Seems that a half dozen or so years earlier the leaders of the financially strapped Oklahoma District, trying to save money, conceived a style of operation that anticipated the ingenious concept that would come into vogue in the 1990s among the moguls of world commerce, then to be called down-sizing.

So these leaders, desperately hoping to keep the organization afloat, simply shut down the efforts of several struggling little groups across the state who were earnestly trying to establish themselves as viable congregations. Uncle Jno. F. was decidedly not of that mind; he didn't think a church body would grow by snuffing out little beginnings.

I climbed aboard the bus to McAlester and, as I had been instructed, began to look up some people whose names were given me on index cards as the only records of what Lutheranism had once been in McAlester.

As I remember, several of the people had now become Presbyterians, and they were not about to be ducking back and forth under different denominational umbrellas. They didn't at all appreciate that the church had once abandoned them, and they were altogether unwilling to rejoin such a tentative regrouping that really held no sure promise of surviving anyway. No building, no pastor of their own, no membership core — this was hardly an attractive venture.

After a few visits to homes, a lot of walking about, some short notices in the newspaper, we began holding services in makeshift arrangements in sundry residences and halls. We finally negotiated with the pastor of McAlester's First Presbyterian Church, who graciously presented our cause to his laity. They in turn gave us permission to use their very worshipful, burgundy carpeted chapel, replete with a little organ and oak pews. The facilities would be ours every Sunday afternoon at four o'clock without cost.

It was somewhere in that period that the Crapos came to worship. Norma — Monroe called her "Nim" — had belonged to the Lutheran Indian Mission in northern Wisconsin, somewhat to the north and west of the Menomonee Reservation. She herself was a Stockbridge Indian and when she apprised me of this, I probed further and discovered that as a child I had worshipped in that church and still remembered the now dismantled school building that had stood next to the church, the mission school she herself had attended. Further conversation revealed that on one occasion in the early 1930s, her father had led my own father and my uncle on a fishing trip in that region.

Monroe, of Cherokee derivation, was a strong quiet man when I met him. And he was very pleasant, but a man of few words; his sentences were usually short, terse. He came to all the services, but was somewhat reticent about his participation, until in one of our conversations he revealed that he had never been baptized.

He held a profound respect for the Sacrament of Baptism, but expressed a reluctance to be baptized, primarily because he felt an unworthiness to experience the holy ritual. This prompted long conversations between us, and offered wonderful opportunity to note the awesome gift aspect of Baptism, how it effects for the recipient identity with the crucifixion and resurrection events of Christ, and bestows adoption into God's family, into membership in the body of Christ. When he saw that the blessings of Baptism are not bestowed upon the one baptized by virtue of that one's wholesomeness, but rather in spite of unworthiness, frailty, and imperfection, he was ready. I had never before baptized an adult. It was a moment of awe and all in our little group were deeply moved.

Nim's letter prompted more rememberings of earlier contacts with the Crapos.

Two years ago a package had come from McAlester. Enclosed was a Book of Celebration, tracing over fifty years of Trinity Congregation's history. It made gratifying reading — and all the more so because its content had been researched, written, organized, and edited by Monroe. The 65-page booklet tells the stories of faithful beginnings and persevering efforts that culminated in a sturdy little congregation with its own church and pastor and an excitement for ministry.

During those years more than 45 pastors have served them for longer or shorter periods. And now an important event occurs in Trinity's life — the parting of Monroe Crapo — to stir up rememberings and to prompt songs of thanksgiving.

The passing of years has erased, for me, the names of many of those people of Trinity, but not their faces. One woman I particularly remember. She was tall, pale, and her eyes were red and very tired from too much crying. She explained in a soft voice that her child had arrived prematurely, stillborn. She asked, would I accompany her and her husband to the graveside to conduct the infant's burial service. We agreed to meet at the cemetery two hours later.

I'd never participated in such a service before, let alone led one. All my books about how to conduct services for special occasions — weddings, funerals, and such — were on the shelf next to my desk sixty miles away. There was no experienced colleague around to consult. I was on my own. In the intervening minutes I selected a few passages from the Psalms and composed some short prayers. And I whispered a few panicky prayers of my own that I might have the appropriate words to provide perspective and courage to this young couple.

The mortician was there with the tiny white casket covered with a spray of red roses. Together we all walked across the soft lawn to the open grave. Before I even opened the Bible in my hand, the young mother asked, "Will our child who has never opened her eyes on this earth really be in heaven?"

I conceded that, to my knowledge, the Scriptures had little to say on the matter. I told her, though, that there were ever so many instances when Jesus expressed his very special kind of fondness and affection for little ones. And time and again the Scriptures speak of the close bond between mother and child. And then it occurred to me that the account of very pregnant Elizabeth's visit with the newly pregnant mother of our Lord was itself pregnant with implications for all expectant mothers of all times.

Quite obviously the fetal child derives all its nourishment and development through the umbilical cord from its mother. The responsible mother-to-be therefore eats healthful food, drinks uncontaminated liquids, breathes clean air. The child is helplessly and entirely dependent upon its mother in all those prenatal days. So much for the physical.

How is it that, in the story of these two expectant mothers, Elizabeth's little unborn, who cannot yet see or hear, leaps for joy when the mother is confronted by Mary and is able to perceive that the Savior of the world is in this visitor's womb? Can it be that until her infant's birth, the mother's umbilical tie to the unborn child indicates its spiritual dependence and involvement with the mother in her spiritual life? And all of us who stood there derived comfort from the thought.

It was a meaningful and worshipful ending of the day.

Mr. Courage

doors not clearly marked

I shall call this man Mr. Courage. I didn't know him well. I had not gotten to visit with him often or for longer conversations. As best I could learn, his roots were in a small rural community in Arkansas. His mother had died when he was still a child — though the oldest of several little ones. His father had not married again and for the most part this eldest son was left to fill the role of home-maker.

His unrelenting responsibilities kept him from attending school, so he never did learn to read or to write. The burdens of house-keeper and surrogate parent proved heavy and in his early teens he left home.

A small framed man, his strength was seriously impaired by some internal injury incurred on a job that strained him beyond his capacity. This left him incapable of lifting anything even moder-ately heavy, and there were other unpleasant side affects that at-tended his ill health. He was in no position to afford medical/surgi-cal help that might have corrected or at least alleviated his condi-tion. And at the time there were no public health and medical ser-vices for which he might have been eligible. This state of dimin-ished well-being, coupled with his inexperience in work situations, rendered him virtually unemployable.

Somewhere in his later teens he met a young woman, also from his native Arkansas, whose earlier years remarkably resembled his.

When she too was still a mere child, her mother died an early death, leaving the widowed husband with five tiny children. She as eldest had to learn about caring for the family, missed out on school, and found herself swept into a role of adult responsibility before she had even lived out her childhood.

She too left home in her midteens and by chance met, fell in love with, and became married to Mr. Courage. They brought with them to the marriage little beyond the love they had for each other and a strong commitment to achieve a good marriage. When I first met them, they had already been married a dozen years and at least nine children had been born to them. Really, the love and loyalty of the members of that household were strong and admirable.

Mr. and Mrs. Courage had few trophies to show for their per-severance. There were the children, of course; and the names they gave them, as each would arrive on the scene revealed the high and noble hopes the parents had for these little ones. All were called after strong leaders and folk heroes. These children were this young couple's prize, their achievement, the ones who would embrace them and give them respect and affection and dignity and identity and purpose. All that was in short supply outside the family.

Yet their living circumstances were all but intolerable. Mind you, this was in Tulsa, the city that hailed itself as the Oil Capital of the World.

The place they rented was on a short unpaved street that became impossibly impassable when the rains came. Cars would become mired in mud down to their axles. And the building was hardly vintage housing. It had no running water — they drew from an outdoor spigot on their next-door neighbor's house. Their light was from an oil lamp. A two burner, oil-fed little range was for cooking. As I remember, there were only three rooms — and a path to outback "facilities."

Wherever he was able, the father took "by the hour" little jobs, and the mother did some laundry, and one of the boys had a paper route. They pulled together but their resources were so few. The children and their mother would come to our church with admirable regularity. But the couple seemed to have virtually no friends and often appeared to be overwhelmed and fatigued by the burden they carried.

And then came the Christmas season.

Dodee Brockhoff, wife of the pastor of Our Redeemer Congregation on Tulsa's far southwest side phoned one day, and with appropriate preChristmas cheeriness (which Dodee managed to maintain all year round!) she informed me of a plan their members had proposed for this particular Christmas. "Instead of filling a random number of baskets with goodies and giving them to the poor, we'd like to remember one particular family with special needs. Do you have a family in your parish that has particular needs at this time?" And I assured her I did.

When she asked me to describe the family, providing their ages, and the sort of information that might help them in buying appropriate gifts, I began: "There are four children in the family — all boys; their mother does volunteer work and cares for the household; the father seems to be hard-working and is quite underpaid. Then I explained the oldest of the boys was in fifth grade, the next in second, the third in kindergarten, and the fourth in highchair stage."

"Oh," she replied, " that sounds just wonderful! Can you give me the names of the boys so we can put them on their gifts?"

"Surely — the oldest is Peter; the next, Steve; the third, Tom; and the youngest is Mark." Before I could even finish the sentence she realized I was naming our four Lutze boys, and, after reprimanding me appropriately, she asked that I get serious and be helpful. Then I mentioned to her the Courage family, supplying the names and ages of all of the Courage children.

On Christmas Eve, after the festival worship, and before beginning the celebration of our own household, I drove over to the Courage home — trunk and backseat loaded with boxes and bags. The people of Our Redeemer had been lavishly generous and the packages were wrapped beautifully. I came to the door and brought in all the gifts. The children stood politely to the side in a row, obviously coached to be quiet and yet unable to conceal their excited expectations.

There were shirts, trousers, blouses, skirts, dresses, coats, caps, mittens, an ample supply of Christmas dinner makings and sweet tooth cravings — and a toy for each child. There was a new dress for their mother and a new suit, shirt, and tie for Mr. Courage. Such happiness! The children laughing and chattering excitedly, and tugging at my sleeves — and tears on the cheeks of Mrs. Courage. I don't know if I had ever experienced such a gratifying feeling of having done something right — just the way it should have been.

And having wished them a loud "Merry Christmas!" I walked toward the door, which Mr. Courage was holding open for me. With his arm lifted slightly to shake my hand, with a face almost empty of any message whatever, he said very simply, almost in a whisper, "Thank you, Pastor; do you think you could find me a job?"

Suddenly, as though gallons of cold water had been poured on my head, I realized what I had just done! I had snatched away from this man the role of father, which he so desperately wanted for himself. I had "out-fathered" him! I had reduced and diminished him — before his own family — to be less the father, less the man that he wanted to be.

It was not a good Christmas for me.

———————

Weeks later I dropped by the Courage home one evening. Mrs. Courage asked me in. I inquired about her husband and she confided in me that he had left her. I was shocked, and not a little angered. As if this poor woman didn't have a heavy enough load, but she should be left to carry it herself! My righteous wrath was spilling all over the place.

I began slowly to realize, however, that without a husband in the household, Mrs. Courage would suddenly be eligible to receive public assistance denied to her as long as she had a husband in her home. I helped her make the appropriate applications and in a very short time there was financial relief for her. The amount was hardly lavish, but it certainly proved to be more than had been seen in that household for a long, long time — possibly ever.

This obviously became a substantial benefit to compensate for the absence of a father. Things seemed to be looking up; the morale seemed significantly improved.

I would visit at somewhat regular intervals to make sure that matters were going well for the family. Then, to my great surprise and joy, one evening when I dropped by, Mr. Courage was sitting in the room. I shook his hand enthusiastically and told him how pleased I was that he had chosen to return.

Then quietly — so the children would not overhear him — he asked whether I might walk with him to our church office two blocks away, so he could talk with me in private.

We went quickly, and as soon as we sat down he confessed the secret of his heart. He told how he could never stay away from the family he so loved; but he knew, after trying so desperately and futilely to find regular, consistent work, that his best hope for his family's security and survival would be his departure from the residence. He decided indeed not to abandon his family, hiding or concealing his presence from authorities or from neighbors who might report him.

I kept his trust — and the secret. And the family continued to receive assistance needed.

A few months later Mr. Courage died. But not my memory of him, ever.

```
┌─────────────────────────────────┐
│                                 │
│    Mentor and Colleague         │
│           I.                    │
│    Birth of a Church            │
│                                 │
└─────────────────────────────────┘
```

some doors open to friendship

I had been pastor of Hope Lutheran Congregation in Muskogee, Oklahoma, for about five years when I received an invitation to speak in Tulsa, some sixty miles away. I was to address a group of men who belonged to some of the Lutheran churches there. They wanted to hear a report on whether or not the ministry of the Lutheran Church in Muskogee's African American community had been at all "successful."

They were pleased to hear that in just the short time I'd been serving there (my predecessors had served there only on a part time basis), attendance at worship had tripled, as had the adult membership. I was happy to report that our facilities proved too confining, and that we had been able to purchase and move to our new location a U. S. Army chapel from nearby Camp Gruber which was being shut down. I described our surprising enrollment of children — nearing the 100 mark — in our Summer Vacation Bible School program. Obviously, the people in our community welcomed this ministry.

Comparing the two cities, I pointed out that in Muskogee the non-white population represented twenty percent of the total number, while in Tulsa, the non-white group accounted for ten percent. However, since Tulsa was the larger city, the *number* of non-white people was far larger, reaching 25,000 in contrast to Muskogee's 8,000.

As I recall, the men in my audience represented a half dozen different Tulsa area churches. I told them how I had seen their congregations' announcements of services in the papers and was familiar with their signs that stated "Everybody welcome!" I told them, too, I had no reason to doubt the sincerity of any of such invitations. Then, alluding to the obvious, I had to say, "In all my years as your nearby neighbor, I've not yet heard even of an isolated occasion when an African American has visited any of your churches. They nodded their reluctant acknowledgment that had such an event happened, word most likely would have gotten around. Then I somewhat mischievously chided them, "Is it possible your signs aren't effective, or that people of color don't really believe the invitation is genuine?"

There was a lot of blushing, but during the short time that followed, as we were coffeeing together, the conversation continued and prompted some thoughtful questions and comments. The group expressed a genuine appreciation for our evening of serious discussion. I felt that maybe we had at least started some people thinking in new and different ways.

I was hardly expecting what happened the following week. Charles Irsch, who had chaired the meeting, called. He had gathered some of the group together. They decided to ask me to conduct a feasibility study to determine whether or not — and how — an effective Lutheran ministry to people of color might be developed in Tulsa.

Before a week had elapsed, I went to learn what I could about Tulsa. After a brief and limited bit of investigating I returned to Mr. Irsch's committee with my initial report.

As a first step I had discovered that a sort of peninsula reached out to the north from the center of the community where most of the African American residency and activity were concentrated. In this somewhat recently developed area, the city had erected a handsome new high school. This was intended to be a sort of "last ditch stand" in the city's resistance to desegregation. The new building was intended to communicate the message, "Look, you have the newest and nicest high school in town. Why would you ever want your youth to be going to one of our old all-white schools?"

The closest Lutheran church in Tulsa at that time was two miles away — and hardly qualified as a neighborhood church. I had learned that there was then only one church within a mile of this new Booker T. Washington High School, St. Philip Episcopal, three blocks to the west. The larger community did have a high number of churches of many denominations, but none had yet located in this area. I was to learn later that the Roman Catholics were contemplating possibilities of locating a new St. Augustine Church two blocks north of the school.

I had interviewed various leaders in the community: High School Principal Henry Whitlow and his wife Thelma, executive director of the North Tulsa YWCA; Attorneys Primus Wade, Amos Hall, Waldo Jones, and Benjamin Franklin; pharmacists Roberts,

Williams, and Tollie Harris; hospital manager, businessman, and former high school teacher J. T. A. West; merchants like the Manns and Latimers; physicians Norvel Coots and Charles Bate; and other randomly selected homeowners who lived near the high school.

Probably most helpful of all my interviews was with the Reverend Ben Hill. Several of my previous interviewees recommended my meeting with him because of his insights and wisdom. I had already known him a year or two earlier when he had been pastor of Ward Chapel African Methodist Episcopal Church in Muskogee. I had met him only briefly then, but I remembered how highly he was respected by his members there and by other members of the community.

Now he was pastor of large and prestigious Vernon AME Church in Tulsa on Greenwood, the hub of North Tulsa's activity. He would have winced at hearing his parish called prestigious. But the church did indeed have that kind of reputation. I remember Marion Taylor telling me that when he arrived in Tulsa to become the first Executive Director of the Tulsa Urban League, several people advised him to join either First Baptist or Vernon AME. Those were the two churches to which the real community leaders belonged — the kind he'd surely want to enlist for his programs.

Ben Hill was the embodiment of warmth. He welcomed me into his study. As I walked in, I could not help but notice a complete set of the writings of Dr. Martin Luther on his "Methodist shelves." I recognized them immediately because I owned such a set. He was very proud of these books and explained that he had ordered them at a special pre-publication price. They had been shipped as they came from the press, a volume at a time, until the book that completed the set was produced. I had purchased my set under the same arrangement. Sometimes the copies would arrive after only a short interval of time and I would get to read only a chapter or two of each volume. Ben, on the other hand, told me he had read everything in them and said he had been tremendously enriched by his readings.

We talked a good deal about Luther and he told how many of the theological insights of Luther would be useful for community life today. He would truly welcome in North Tulsa's religious community a theological influence that really had its roots in the things that Luther wrote and stood for, because of Luther's strong and insistent regard for the Scriptures and the Christian Gospel.

(In later years, I often teased him that he sounded more like a Lutheran parson than a Methodist. He'd respond, "Maybe so!")

Then Ben described the situation of his community. He lauded its rightfully proud spirit that helped it rise from the ashes of Tulsa's bitter and violent race riot of 1921.

> *Later when I had moved to Tulsa, Attorney Benjamin Franklin (father of the noted historian, John Hope Franklin) told me how he, almost forty years earlier had, from his hiding place in a culvert, been an eye witness to what had happened. I could tell how deeply he was moved as he described for me the terrifying event which had left the area in a charred rubble and after which "they stopped counting the dead when the number reached one hundred."*

Ben named people who had begun their own independent businesses and told of the large number of people who had built and purchased their own homes. He talked of the high caliber of professional persons, and he described the performance of the dedicated cadre of teachers as valiant. For, he explained, there was another side of the community, a lamentable side. And the teachers found themselves dealing with this each day. They served in difficult situations, for at that time unemployment was disturbingly high, and many of the people who did have employment received scanty wages. There were still places, he said, as near as two blocks away from his church, where people lived in "crowded shanties, without plumbing, some with animals in the back yards, amid vacant, dilapidated houses."

He said, kindly but firmly, that North Tulsa did not need any more churches that had to expend all their members' and community's energies and resources for survival and maintenance of facilities. However, he added, there was always room for any kind of institution or people or program that cared about the people and their children and would be a contribution rather than mere

179

baggage or a drain on the community. "If a church is to be faithful to God, then it must be faithful in its performance, in its genuine care for God's people, even those who are not members."

Ben Hill became my friend at once. As time passed on he became more and more my mentor.

I was ready to make a preliminary report to those who had commissioned my assignment.

I suggested that because in a sense this new neighborhood was quite "underchurched," the Lutherans might well consider bringing their ministry to this place.

I also reminded these men that, normally, a congregation's beginning stems from a small group of people banding together and they become a nucleus for the new venture. They would in all likelihood ask a parent church body's regional administrators for assistance in developing a program and providing facilities and whatever other help might be needed to ensure a sound future for their new church.

No one from this North Tulsa community was inviting Lutherans "in." The only valid justification for Lutherans to establish a congregation here would be a desire to share what good things Lutherans have and to enrich this community. It would be absurd and disastrous were these people to get the impression that we were saying, "Here we are, you lucky people!" The idea of planting church facilities in this place and subsequently suggesting that the community be saddled with the responsibility of paying for it, would be discourteous at least, and, at worst, insulting. Entering this community would require a discernible posture and style that would clearly communicate that we recognized that our franchise for being there was a genuine commitment to service to this community and the people who lived there. Any other approach would be seriously flawed.

Furthermore the enterprise must be able to convey to its new neighbors a message like this:

> *We Lutherans have found in our heritage resources that have proved of great value in our personal, our family, and our community life. We are*

eager to share this with you. We have not adequately shared this with you before and we wish to make amends for that now by establishing a church in your midst.

We are not asking you to join the church, or become its members. We wish primarily to share with you its services, pastoral counseling, visits to the home-bound, programs for helping your children, and many other benefits. They will be at your disposal to use as much or as little as you choose — and without cost.

It is understood that this is not to be a sort of "mission outpost" of the larger church, nor is it to be a segregated "Negro church." It is to be a **Lutheran** *church. It is to provide you with a convenient place to participate in the good things we wish to share with you. Should any of you wish to participate in such sharing at any of the Lutheran churches in other locations of the city, we promise you will be welcome among us.*

The Lutheran pastors of Tulsa, all of whom proved tremendously helpful and supportive of my ministry, were present for this meeting too. In the discussion that followed, my report and recommendation received thorough scrutiny, deep reflection, and serious discussion. After several hours of intense conversation, their unanimous acceptance prompted another assignment. They asked me to explore the availability of property to see whether such an idea could actually materialize into reality.

I discovered a generous sized lot for sale, only one-half block from Peoria Avenue, and three blocks from the high school. Peoria was a main artery that carried traffic from the city's extreme north end to its far south side. The lot would need to be rezoned, but, I had been assured, if agreeable to the immediate neighbors, this would be a simple matter.

That very week I began making visits to all the residences on adjacent lots, and a few more down the street. Once I had explained the likelihood of the building of a new church on this corner, I found these neighbors receptive to the idea and some even registered an enthusiasm for it.

So with petitions in hand, signed by neighbors who supported our coming, I again met with those who had commissioned my study and relayed to them my findings and recommendations.

Weeks and months followed in which the committee and their pastors attended to all the necessary negotiations that made possible the purchase of the property, its rezoning, and ultimately engaging of an architect. Having heard our intentions, he and his staff developed and presented to us plans for what would become an English-Gothic little brick and stone chapel. It would be an aesthetic and serviceable contribution to the already attractive neighborhood.

As construction got under way, the community saw something not usually seen at larger building sites. As specified by the new tenants, the architect agreed to secure bids of contractors and subcontractors only from minority firms. Plumbers, electricians, and other workers were people from the larger North Tulsa community. People passing by were able to see that we intended to make sure that, as much as possible, monies spent during construction would go to North Tulsa businesses.

Erecting of the building wasn't completed in a day. Even before the first trenches were dug or the first concrete poured, we arranged to have a children's program and Sunday services in a temporary trailer chapel. We attempted to serve the community at once as best we could. Members from Hope Congregation in Muskogee would travel to Tulsa on Sundays to help out with music and youth instruction.

When the blueprinted plans began to materialize into concrete and brick and stones, we'd arrived at the appropriate moment to lay a cornerstone for the new structure to be named the Lutheran Church of the Prince of Peace.

Well, of course, the committee members would be there. And their pastors. And a few of their members. What would passers by or people who would attend really see — and what kind of statement might we unwittingly be making? This was likely to look like everything we didn't want it to look like — a program of white people launching a white project.

I was sure we didn't need some white clergyman to be speaker for the occasion — no matter how eloquent he might be. I went to see Ben Hill. He said he was delighted we had decided to accept the challenge and establish a church here. I at once asked him if he would speak at the laying of our cornerstone. He said he would be honored.

I asked his advice then, how we might be able to develop the event to include participation of people of the community. Pastor Hill at once helped arrange for a meeting with Ms. Carrie Pearson Neeley, choral director at Booker T. Washington High School. She seemed pleased that we asked her and promised to prepare and bring with her to the event an octet of students. They would provide music for the occasion.

When the day of celebration arrived, a small group of neighbors and some of the leaders I had earlier interviewed were on hand. A car-full of members from our Muskogee congregation had come. And of course the committee that started all this, their pastors and a few of their members were present. The weather was pleasant and we needed no shelter. The selection of music was superb and the singers' voices were clear and fresh.

Pastor Ben Hill's message was stirring and proved to be both affirmation of what this ministry envisioned and a benediction upon our efforts. It was a great day, and one in which we tried to communicate our purpose to the community.

When the Tulsa project was initially conceived, my work there would be temporary on a part-time basis. I was still serving as pastor in the Muskogee parish and it was not intended that I should leave Hope Church. The work at Hope had been prospering so gratifyingly. I was quite surprised, then, when the regional officers of the church, who had originally assigned me to my Muskogee post, had decided that I should now be assigned to serve at the new Tulsa church.

My wife and children and I were the only members of the church. We were quite resigned to the reality that we'd not be gaining members by transfer. There simply weren't enough African Americans who were Lutheran moving to Tulsa from anywhere else anyway.

If we were to manifest genuineness in our presence, then this new Lutheran Church of the Prince of Peace would have to be demonstrating its concern for the well being of the community. Since Esther and I were the only adult members, we, of course, were the ones that became involved. So I joined the North Tulsa YMCA and served on their annual fundraising committee. I became a board member of the Tulsa NAACP. I became a member of the Greenwood Chamber of Commerce (the downtown Chamber of Commerce did not accept African American memberships). My wife Esther participated in the North Tulsa YWCA's programs.

Together we'd attend concerts, athletic contests, and other events sponsored by the different North Tulsa schools. Our very first programs at the church were geared to care for the well being of the children while parents worked. And we would do much visiting with those parents.

All this took a great deal of time. And I didn't really have time to see Ben Hill very often. He was a very busy man, and rarely, except in meetings we'd both happen to be attending, did we have much time for conversation together. And meetings don't usually lend themselves to lengthier discussion periods. I truly wished there might be more occasions to tune in on his unique perceptions, perspectives, and wisdom.

Mentor and Colleague
II.
Brotherhood

---

some doors admit two

Fortunately the Dean of the School of Religion at Langston University, halfway across the state, asked me to participate as a speaker in a Religious Emphasis Week he'd be leading at the University. The opportunity to be working with young college students was very attractive to me — and even more so when in his effort to elicit my acceptance he mentioned that the Reverend Ben Hill would also be on the program. Not pausing for a second, I accepted, asking whether I might be lodged with Ben Hill as my roommate.

From the moment we arrived in Langston, Ben and I were together in conversation for the better part of the evening and after the hostess had served us a tasty snack we prepared for retiring. We were still talking at three in the morning, when we finally and mutually agreed to get in a little slumbering lest we'd have difficulty staying awake during the next day's program. Those late night visits continued throughout the week. Before we left, the Dean asked if we might be able to return for next year's event.

Pointing at me, Ben said, "I'll come again, if he comes again, and if you'll put us in the same quarters again." I enthusiastically concurred, and for three successive years we enjoyed the kind of visits we never were able to arrange back in Tulsa.

I was a bit embarrassed that some of the first members to join Prince of Peace had been inactive members of Vernon AME. Why couldn't they have belonged to another church! I did not want to indulge in the practice that clergy folk often referred to as "sheep stealing." How ever would I go about informing him of their decision? It was an awkward moment.

Ben initiated the discussion by saying, "They're certainly listed as sheep of our fold, but they surely have been wandering a distance from our flock, and it doesn't appear they regarded me as a very helpful shepherd. If you're able to lead them beside the still waters of God's care, then I am glad indeed you are here for them. If they are not going to be served at our church, I cannot think of another church I'd rather they turn to for pastoral care and guidance."

Then, smiling broadly, he added a thought that my seminary professor, Dr. Theo. Graebner, had first taught us, "If someone accuses you of sheep stealing, always respond, quickly, 'Whose sheep are they, anyway?' "

In one of our late hour sessions he told of a figure, a familiar street character who always appeared a bit shoddy. In winter he would wear an oversized olive drab army coat that reached to within inches of the ground. The sight of him was familiar to anyone who transacted business or happened to be traversing through the lower Greenwood area. He'd be checking the parking meters and coin return cups of vendor machines and pay-telephones, hoping to find small change. He'd often accost people on the street, asking for handouts. His behavior was always a bit extraordinary and sometimes bordered on rudeness. He was not a very responsible person. People didn't seem to know much about him because they probably didn't care to get involved with him at all. He was a "street person" and it was neither strange nor unusual to see him about.

However, Ben reported, one Sunday he wandered into Vernon AME Church, walked down the center aisle to the front pew and seated himself. "Now, *that* was strange and unusual," he said.

Everyone in the congregation took notice — every choir member, every child, every usher, every worshipper — and of course the pastor. The air was filled with uncertainty and a nervous expectancy hung over the congregation. No one gave any signal that some usher should ask him to leave or to escort him from the church, although the idea surely must have occurred to some.

Every eye was on this man as he shifted restlessly in his seat during the announcements, prayers, and readings with which the service was begun. He gained some composure however when the choir sang its anthem and upon its completion he applauded loudly. The pastor stepped forward to take his place at the pulpit. The visitor also rose, and before the preacher could speak a word, the man walked to the front, put a coin in the offering plate. He turned and in silence he left just as he had come into the church, returning by the center aisle.

The congregation, somewhat stunned, was very quiet.

Ben Hill put aside the sermon he prepared. After a long pause, he told the congregation that the sermon for the day had already been delivered. He asked the congregation whether they felt more comfortable, now that this man was no longer there with them. He recounted for them that this visitor in his simpleness had presented himself for worship. He had listened to the songs that describe and assure us of God's love. He had responded with praise. He had left an offering to our generous God and now was returning to the world into which God sends us all. Then he asked, "Is not this the very essence of what our worship is to be?" Then he told his congregation that this may well have been the clearest visit of God in their midst that they had ever seen or ever would see. With only a few more words Pastor Hill ended what was probably one of his shortest and most powerful sermons.

This man could take the simplest events and illustrations and shape them into tiny sermons one could never forget. I recall the time he addressed a fund raising committee, and he asked them, "Don't you know what the Scriptures say about giving, that you should cast your bread upon the waters? — and you know you'll find it coming back to you with butter on it. And the Bible doesn't exactly say it this way, but if you cast your cake upon the water, it will come back with frosting on it!"

In our times together, we often made excursions into the Scriptures, finding new meanings and implications together that we probably would never have found by ourselves. Each of us claimed we always learned more from the other than we'd ever taught.

Ben had such a wide background of literature and history and the Scriptures and he spoke with a delightfully simple eloquence that sometimes verged on the poetic.

I had become acquainted with the practices of the AME — after all, Ben was my teacher. Rather than by appointment, bishops of the different regions were chosen for office by an election process, utilizing a campaign system somewhat similar to secular political procedures. I had met a number of AME clergy through the years, but I had never met one with the attributes and credentials that Ben Hill would bring with him. So, one day I said to him, "Ben, churches today have such great need for capable leaders who

188

are both competent and faithful theologians as well as skillful administrators. Have you ever thought of offering your services as bishop? You could really perform well in that role — for your Lord and for your church."

He turned to the side a bit, as if to gather his thoughts and said, "I appreciate what you are saying, and it means much to me that you say it. Yes, I've thought about it, and others have tried to persuade me to run. And I've come up with this dilemma, 'would I rather be a bishop or would I rather go to heaven?' " And then, lest I thought his answer to be merely facetious, he cited ways in which pursuing such a significant administrative position might actually divert one's attention from the real and true responsibilities of the Christian life and ministry. "And," he added, "all pastors must approach their holy calling with the same awe and awareness of such diversions and distractions."

Ben and I were, along with pastors of four or five other churches, sitting in a sort of semi-circle on the stage of Booker T. Washington High School's auditorium stage. The student body had been convened for a kind of pre-graduation assembly, as I remember, honoring the senior class.

The lectern was tall, and Ben, short of stature could barely peek over the top, so he stepped to its side to speak. It was really the first and only time that I ever heard him make mention of his own physical appearance.

He said to his youthful assembly, "Here I can see you all more clearly now. And you can see me too. And you probably don't think this is much to look at. I'm so thin and so short, all bent over and can't straighten up.

"Well, I've lived with this for a long time now. The condition is called curvature of the spine and that's a part of me. But that's not all of me." Then he talked of inner strengths and beauties, the kind a person can't see by looking at or by touching that person. "If you can cultivate these inner strengths you can handle all kinds of other weakness" — and he named a few, like loss of a parent or some other loved one, poverty, impairments, and other difficult burdens.

Then, half in humor, he pointed to the other clergy sitting there, and urged the audience to notice how several of them were rather large across the waist (at which prompting all of us drew in our abdomens as far as they would go). "Now mine is sometimes called a deformity," he continued, "but theirs is never called a deformity. I can't do anything about mine, and they have to figure out what they can do about theirs." A soft chuckle passed through the hall.

Even in that secular setting he told and showed how God had not abandoned him even in his darkest hours, and he was not about to walk out on that loving God who had blessed him in so many other ways. And this is the relationship he was recommending to these seniors and all the students, as they would be reaching new plateaus en route to manhood and womanhood.

Ben's communication skills were so obvious and coveted that the North Tulsa community weekly, *The Oklahoma Eagle*, engaged him to be its editor. His kind of direct and moving style brought vital and thought provoking messages to the readers week after week. They would open to his page first when their copy arrived.

In the days and months that followed my leaving Tulsa, as the sharp lines of segregation more and more were dimmed and in many instances altogether erased, more people outside of North Tulsa got to know this man Hill and came to draw on his giftedness. He was elected a member of the Oklahoma State Assembly and served well.

No small factor contributing to the effectiveness of this unique man was his bright, caring, and loyal wife. Fannie Hill was a precious source of inspiration and encouragement to her husband. He spoke frequently and fondly of her as a special gift to him from God. In her ninety-sixth year we still stay in touch, although her Ben died more than a dozen years ago.

When our family moved from Oklahoma, we were all torn by the reality of leaving behind some of the very dearest people we had ever known.

I was successful in my suggestions that Pastor Hill be invited to be a guest speaker at the 1966 Valparaiso University Institute on Human Relations.

In his address he urged people to look about "where you live" and see the children.

"In the Name of Jesus who himself had been a child and urged us to bring and not hinder the little children, we have been given an agenda, to regard ourselves and all people as God's children, needing to be noticed, understood, and loved."

Through the years I often wondered if ever I were a parish pastor again, could I ask for a better associate in ministry — a partner — than Ben Hill?

For all he has been during his lifetime — and still is — to me, I shall always be grateful. God gives amazing gifts! Ben is one.

The Wise One

a door to new rooms

For Whitney Young the government authorized the publishing of a postage stamp. Vernon Jordan became renowned as an advisor to President Clinton.

Less remembered is yet a third man who also served as Executive Director of the National Urban League, Dr. Lester Granger, who preceded both of them in that office.

It must have been in the mid-fifties — and in his own later fifties — when I first heard him speak.

While the stirrings of change from its segregated patterns and policies became increasingly more vocal and more strident, this country was becoming familiar with the comments of pundits, politicos, and patriots pronouncing prospects for a bright and eventual tomorrow — some day in our future.

On March 17, 1954, the United States Supreme Court had declared that racial segregation must come to an end — beginning in the lives of school children. And the jurists insisted that it be done with all deliberate speed.

With heels dug in, ennui and resistance developed as communities north and south emphasized the deliberating and ignored the speed factor.

A decade later the voice of Malcolm X would chide African Americans who were awaiting the rosy future: Ten years have elapsed since the Supreme Court directed schools to desegregate, and there's been only a ten per cent compliance. Must we wait another ninety years, neglecting generation after generation of little children, before giving our children what the court says is rightfully theirs, right now! And at that very time Dr. King would be preparing to publish his book, *Why We Can't Wait*.

Already in an electrifying address, Lester Granger impatiently proclaimed: Tomorrow is Today — Tomorrow is Now!

In personal conversation he enthusiastically affirmed the confrontational approach of the National Association for the Advancement of Colored People. However, he counseled, that style of approach called for a procedure to complement and thus ensure its effectiveness; he called it conference table communication. And that was the pattern the Urban League had been developing, gathering all people involved in issues of racial disharmony or conflict

194

to talk through all the facets of such differences with a view towards arriving at a constructive solution of problems.

Small wonder then that as interracial turbulence surfaced in the armed forces, the government would call on a man of such insight and experience for help. President Truman and his Secretary of the Navy, Forrestal, engaged Lester Granger to draw up blueprints for the desegregation of the United States Navy. His recommendations, I was told, subsequently also became guidelines for use by other branches of the military.

Tulsa's Greenwood Chamber of Commerce, composed largely of business and professional people, had formed because people of their race were simply excluded from the affairs — and of course meetings — of Tulsa's downtown Chamber of Commerce. Nonetheless, the Greenwood group generously invited me to become its white member.

(Some time later another person, a businessman who operated a small ice cream stand near one of the community's elementary schools, applied for membership in the Greenwood Chamber. Members discussed the matter of whites being admitted to membership. One of the group pointed out that I had joined. A tall, dignified Mr. J. T. A. West, a retired high school teacher and at this time real estate agent and owner of the community's movie theater, brought the discussion to quick resolution saying, "Shoot, that's different — he's one of us." I can recall few moments when I felt more honored or more genuinely welcomed.)

Some of the Greenwood group had become acquainted with the work of the Urban League and brought to the table their proposal that explorations be made for introducing the Urban League program to Tulsa. I was chosen to serve on a committee assigned to pursue that matter. And that's how I got to meet Lester Granger.

He became tremendously interested in Tulsa, self proclaimed Oil Capital of the World. He acknowledged the city's swift growth, its great wealth, its beautiful gardens and its museums, and yet described it as one of the country's most clearly segregated metropolitan centers.

He knew, of course, of the devastating, gruesome racial conflict of 1921 which left more than 150 dead, whose story by

195

consensus of a shamed community had been assigned largely to whispers and a public silence. All this had resulted in a moving-closer-together by the Blacks of Tulsa — and of course, a sort of tacit approval from the white community in seeing these people contained — and ostensibly controlled.

It was normal procedure in constituting local chapters of the Urban League that there be equal representation from both the white and the non-white communities.

With only one white person involved in Tulsa's embryonic planning, Dr. Granger had to tell us we weren't meeting basic requirements. But he had an idea. He would return to New York and recommend to the National Urban League Board that we be assigned the status of National Urban League Project in Tulsa — an obviously altogether new category in Urban League's structure.

We were to be supported with professional staff help in the months ahead and be given one year to get our act together. We would have to come up with a full board, evenly balanced racially. There were other conditions, but this would be our major hurdle.

Before leaving, he placed a sizeable personal check on the table as a show of his own hopes for and confidence in a future for the Tulsa Urban League. And this of course primed the pump and prompted generous financial participation from members of the Greenwood Chamber.

Well, it's another story to remember the Granger assistance in the Tulsa Project's scheduling erstwhile governor of Arkansas, Winthrop Rockefeller, to be our speaker at the first Urban League dinner at a downtown Tulsa hotel. Once it became known that the Urban League was receiving the endorsement of such a prominent member of the Rockefeller oil family, it was easy for us to reserve the Mayo Hotel for the event. And almost effortlessly we were able to sell places at the tables to the officers of local oil related and financially concerned commercial organizations.

Subsequently we got people from the southside to take places on the Urban League's board, and we had garnered sufficient esteem to warrant inclusion for support in Tulsa's United Way budget. And, really, relatively few ever came to realize what an inestimably valuable gift Lester Granger gave to Tulsa in all this.

And I shall never forget what a gift he was to me, personally. Lester Granger was not a little intrigued when I told him about our church in North Tulsa, and how the other Lutheran churches and their pastors not only had become supportive friends as this young congregation got started, but how helpful they were in their own parish ministry, affirming the churches' responsibility with regard to racial matters.

I was amazed, when I attended the National Urban League's meetings, to discover how much energy Lester Granger invested in his work. There were some sixty different Urban Leagues across the country. All of them were up to their earlobes in problems. Local League executives wanted to discuss their problems with him personally. And of course there were board members — national and local — who wanted their moments with him. And there were folks from the news media as well.

I was truly awed by his mini-lectures he was giving to individuals and small groups that would gather around him — such awareness — such insights. He seemed to know what was going on in all the cities, and he was offering suggestions for dealing with testy issues.

And in all his busyness, he would catch my eye and tell me he wanted to speak with me. His schedule for the few days of the meeting was always cluttered even before he would have arrived, and almost any spot that might look like it offered a moment for respite or catching his breath had already been preempted. So on at least two occasions, he had been scheduled to return to his room in the hotel for shave and shower in anticipation of a dinner engagement and presentation he would be giving immediately thereafter. He invited me to meet him there. And from the shower and from his dressing room he would shout out to me his questions and his comments and his counsel. And he was always wanting to know how Prince of Peace Lutheran Church was prospering.

When I left Tulsa and began my ministry with the Lutheran Human Relations Association of America this man was still a mentor to me, and I continued to attend National Urban League Conferences to learn more from this leader and teacher.

In so many respects my work with the churches called for practicing Urban League style. Indeed the strategies of LHRAA's ministry included a confrontational style, as we brought resolutions to church conventions challenging status quo and practices that perpetuated patterns of subordination and exclusion because of racial considerations. In LHRAA's newssheet, the *Vanguard,* we'd expose instances of prejudice, discrimination, and segregation. And we'd visit church leaders to apprise them of such conditions. We were indeed confrontational.

More than once LHRAA board members would retrieve the moss-covered, well worn analogy to remind us that it would be necessary to beat the stubborn mule on the head in order to get his attention.

There was need too, however, in all these confrontational occasions to sit down together, to review and survey honestly the realities in which we found ourselves, and to collaborate in strategizing for genuine constructive change.

So much was Lester Granger supportive of what this ministry was attempting, that, despite his busyness and preoccupation with myriad demands on his energy and time, he agreed to attend and address LHRAA's annual Valparaiso University Institute on Human Relations in the summer of 1960. He understood well what we were about and wanted much to affirm us in the path LHRAA had chosen for its ministry.

We stayed in touch through occasional phone calls in the years that followed, and after his retirement he accepted a teaching assignment at Dillard University in New Orleans. It was while he was there that I last spoke with him.

Once before when we were in conversation I had remarked, "Lester, you always have time for people. You're always willing to find time to be helpful to people."

He responded, "Well, I really want to care for people, and care for them genuinely." Then he added, "But you know I really don't like *every*body. There are two people I do not like. I've tried hard to like them, but I simply cannot." Then he named one of these and explained, "I know very well why I don't like him, and that's because he is mean — he is really a mean person, and that's why I don't like him!"

Then he added, "And the other person," and he spoke his name, "well, I've tried to figure it out, but I can't come up with the reason; I just simply don't like him. That's all."

However, the rest, and I suppose that includes all humanity, Lester Granger apparently liked.

I have many times thought back on that conversation, and that's what made this particular phone call so especially striking.

He said he was glad to be talking with me again and then, almost abruptly, asked, "Karl, you've heard people talk about angry young men and rebels without a cause? Well, you're hearing an angry *old* man, and I have a cause!"

And angry he was. No need for four lettered expletives. This man of dignity, whose speech was always elegantly eloquent and whose choice of words was always precisely articulate, was speaking — a slight quaver in his voice. He was indeed angry.

He spent the rest of the conversation lamenting the state of affairs in the movement towards racial integrity, genuine justice, and equal opportunities in our country. Instead of what he had hoped and worked for, he saw the divisions in the ranks of those who should be struggling side by side, he grieved about infighting and jockeying for positions of leadership and appetite for personal recognition and even self aggrandizement. And he ached, because the people on the edges were being forgotten and he felt so powerless in the face of it all.

Not much later I tried to contact him and I was told he was no longer available.

The work never is finished, Lester Granger. And in old age to be dispassionate about those issues, which absorbed your commitment of earlier days, is to be unfaithful. You still teach, as I — and others, of course — keep remembering.

Part Four: *The Valparaiso Years*

Prophet and Mentor
I.
His Beginnings

groping for doorknobs

He had had enough of it. His father saw little worth in any more education and constantly taunted the young high schooler about his love for study, and intimated, none too subtly, that his basic problem was laziness or fear of work.

Andrew slammed his books on the table as he came home that evening and in anger shouted, "All right, I quit school. Now where do I find a job?"

The senior Schulze was ready. "I talked to the owner of the bakery and you begin working tonight." And young Andrew, no doubt in full pout, stormed off for the first of many long stifling Cincinnati nights before the scorching heat of those great ovens.

He worked long hours and he read when time allowed. There was more about his existence that he found stifling than just the hot kitchens of the bakery.

It was World War I time, and the mixture of restlessness, tedium, boredom, and patriotism prompted his enlisting in the United States Navy.

Andrew never seemed to have much to say about those days. They surely must have helped introduce him to dimensions of life that he'd not experienced in his earlier provincially and parochially bound days. One story I recall.

His ship had been harbored in some English port. It was an ugly, stormy night and many of the sailors took advantage of shore leave. Putting on their large capelike raincoats, they hustled off to the nearby pubs. Less adventurous Andrew stayed behind and climbed into his hammock for the night. He'd hardly fallen asleep, it seems, when he heard the loud chatter of his reveling shipmates — and — were his ears deceiving him — some decidedly female voices!

These young fellows had smuggled some girls onto the ship under their ample rain togs and were bedding down with them a bit. Later, well before dawn, in same fashion, they escorted their guests from the ship. Andrew was learning about life.

Many times in his past the idea of some day becoming a pastor would disturb him. The thought was fascinating — tantalizing. But he felt unworthy. And too old to begin such studies. In his church most students began their pre-seminary studies when they were still boys of thirteen or fourteen. But enroll he did.

As his own pastor had counseled, he attended his church's "second seminary," established to accommodate students who would be studying for the ministry at an advanced age. He noted that a young assistant professor was offering a not-for-credit course in New Testament Greek. This subject was not available in the school's official curriculum. Andrew wanted very much to be as best prepared as he might be, and that's how he met Otto Paul Kretzmann. Years later that young professor would become President of Valparaiso University in Indiana, and would engage his onetime student, Andrew, to become a teacher in his theology department.

I had already heard about Andrew Schulze when I was a seminary student. Almost everyone knew that he and Pastor Pollatz in Detroit were pastors of the two largest Lutheran congregations with primarily African American members. These were both Missouri Synod pastors, but the Missouri Synod had no provision in its structure to receive people of color into their ranks. That meant that their congregations were not really recognized as Missouri Synod Lutheran. The church did collaborate with other smaller Lutheran bodies in preparing students to be ministers and teachers and did certify their readiness for service. However, they formed another organization in which African Americans were expected to function. This meant that their congregations were not really officially Missouri Synod Lutheran.

As harmless and even benevolent as the church's policies may have appeared to most white Lutherans of that day, the attitude of aloofness and condescension was a source of discomfort and even pain to many — especially to African American Lutherans.

Andrew Schulze was labeled as pastor of a "silk stocking congregation" — of "upper class Negroes." True, most African Americans in "the Lutheran fold" had come from rural or grossly oppressed communities in the South, the stronghold of segregation. Among the people at St. Philip Congregation in St. Louis were many who had left the deep South, had gotten a college education, and had begun to assume positions of responsible leadership. Good pastor that he was, Andrew listened to these people speak their hearts and sensed their revulsion at the arrogant and patronizing attitudes and conduct of their white fellow Lutherans.

This pastor would not keep silent about the issues that most church leaders, lay and clergy, seemed to want hushed — or at least tabled. Earlier in his ministry, when he was serving a small parish in Springfield, Illinois, he learned that the administrative church board was paying white pastors like himself, who were serving black congregations, twice as high salaries as pastors of color. He was outraged! He sent back half his salary (or thirty dollars) to that mission board. The resentful and embarrassed board returned his check and forthwith raised the salaries of all pastors to sixty dollars. The pastors who benefited from this service were not told who it was that had prompted the awarding of this "largesse."

Andrew was further challenged. Some who particularly resented his come-uppance suggested that he present a Scripturally based paper to the local pastoral conference, stating his case.

When he described the scene to me in later years, he told of his fright. He had never made any theological presentation before so many clergy persons. Furthermore, he had prepared for the ministry under the abbreviated terms of "the second seminary," and here, sitting before him, in the front row were all the esteemed and revered members of "the number one" Concordia Theological Seminary of St. Louis. These were regarded in the larger church as the ultimate authority in theological orthodoxy. They were here, he was sure, to dissect his manifesto.

The assemblage did not disappoint his worst fears. Time and again, people rose to counter his assertions and quoted Scriptures to quash his positions. He recalled for me, "These were the fathers of the church; these were the learned doctors and teachers; how could I possibly be right and all of them wrong?"

There was one towering, red haired man, a young man among those veteran Seminary teachers, who, after the ordeal, approached the weary victim of battle fatigue. He came and said, "Pastor Schulze, will you come to my office at the Seminary tomorrow?" They agreed on a time of meeting and parted.

It was a heavy night for the pastor. He had no idea how the next day's confrontation might compound the difficulties he was already experiencing.

No less nervous than on the previous day, Andrew found his way down the corridor to the door whose translucent window bore the name, Professor Alfred Rehwinkel. He knocked, and a booming voice urged his entry. The big man reached out, burying Andrew's hand in the strong grasp of his own baseball-glove-sized hand.

The professor could not say enough about his excitement at hearing the previous day's presentation. It was one of the most challenging and timely papers he had ever heard at a pastoral conference. And the reason he had wanted Andrew to come to his office was to encourage him to develop what he had prepared into a book, because what he had presented was a message that church people everywhere should hear. He offered also to be an advisor to him, as he would proceed with the work.

And to work Andrew went, his wife, Margaret, working at his side. While still faithfully attending to his parish responsibilities, Andrew now took to the task of writing and did so with vigor and fervor. With coaching and suggestions from his new friend and mentor, he was soon ready to submit his manuscript for publication, as Dr. Rehwinkel had urged him.

Word about Andrew Schulze and his radical proposals for full welcome and inclusion of non-whites in the community of Lutherans had been buzzed about in Lutheran circles. Employees at Concordia Publishing House had heard about him too. He no sooner entered the large room of writers and secretaries than he was greeted by a heckler's voice, oozing with sarcasm, that cackled, "Behold, the great emancipator!"

He was accorded a somewhat civil, albeit chilly response from the editorial group. In rejecting his manuscript, the committee made it clear that what he had written was unsound theologically and in any case, dangerously inflammatory.

Disappointed and discouraged, the indefatigable pastor sought the counsel of members of his St. Philip congregation, people with whom he'd consulted for input and advice in the writing of the book. These members were as committed to seeing the project through as was their minister. They agreed to put up the necessary funds to get the book printed and published independently.

The little green covered volume, *My Neighbor of Another Color,* came off the press and arrived at the Schulze parsonage in dozens of cartons. Lacking adequate promotion, the books languished in the Schulzes' attic.

Somehow a copy of the book fell into the hands of another Concordia Seminary faculty person, who took sharp exception to the book and in a lengthy and detailed review in the *Lutheran Witness* denounced both book and author.

While the *Witness* hardly merited space on the nation's newsstands, it did find its way into large numbers of Lutheran homes and pastors' studies. Their curiosity tweaked, hundreds and hundreds more wanted to get their hands on this *causa celebre* sort of book that was stirring up so much discussion.

The first edition sold out. Dr. Otto Theiss, Executive Director of the Walther League — the independent but affiliated youth organization of the Missouri Synod — deemed the work so important that he successfully urged the League to publish a second printing of the book, this time in paperback. This edition sold out as well.

Rather than regard the success of his publishing efforts a mark of his own achievement, Andrew saw what had transpired as a nudge from God to venture farther.

There were others who emerged as new, like-minded friends. Encouraged by their comments and indications of support, he organized the St. Louis Lutheran Society for Better Race Relations. Not much later the group led by this enthusiastic leader offered an Institute on Race Relations at St. Matthew, a local Lutheran Church in a predominantly white community.

St. Louis itself was hardly a trailblazer among American cities when it came to removing racial barriers. Not surprisingly, therefore (Andrew learned later), FBI personnel had been posted nearby to take necessary measures, should the occasion become emotionally (or otherwisely) explosive.

```
┌─────────────────────────────┐
│                             │
│      Prophet and Mentor     │
│             II.             │
│       We Team Together      │
│                             │
└─────────────────────────────┘
```

holding the door for each other

At that time I was beginning my ministry in Muskogee, Oklahoma (I was officially ordained and installed at Hope Church on February 4, 1945). I was returning to St. Louis to be married to Esther. There was of course the dizzying busyness of prenuptial plannings and, with limited success, welcoming and making comfortable my parents and sisters who had come in from Wisconsin for the event. Somewhere in all this, Esther and I found time to visit the Schulzes in their home.

They were — as I was to discover later — always the most warmly hospitable people one might visit. The brief session was exciting and inspiring. We left their house, not merely to take on the challenges of a little church in the South, but to move into a pivotal moment of history in which the church would be challenged, as in few other moments in history. Andrew had quoted the words of Mordecai to us — words we would hear from his lips again and again through the years, "Who knows but that thou are come into this place for such a time as this?"

The pace at which Andrew Schulze operated was not only a few notches ahead of almost any of his contemporaries — but probably beyond his own capacity as well.

Margaret with her silky white hair piled on her dainty head, her soft, spotless complexion on a tiny, petite frame, was a striking contrast to her husband. Andrew, of humble bearing, always stood tall, pointed chin, pointed nose, deep set eyes, and long wisps of silver hair whipped from a point on his forehead straight and partless — a little long at the neck. I don't remember him in much other than black. Black tam, black clergy vest, black trousers, black socks, and black shoes, and in winter black scarf, black gloves, and black earmuffs. White clergy collar often and occasionally a blue shirt and sometimes one of a plaid flannel that caused him to look stunningly out of character. He had a bony frame and his personal safety appeared altogether in jeopardy should a brisk wind be stirring. That or any similar assessment would be misleading. Long after he became seventy I would help him lift incredibly heavy objects, and he would always warn me against straining myself, always showing me first how to bend the knees to gain leg leverage, rather than put dangerous stress on the back.

Church leaders in Chicago invited him to implement a strategy for ministry in the burgeoning near-southside. Immigrants from the South were moving by the thousands every month. He worked tirelessly, establishing two congregations, while endeavoring to interpret to the larger Lutheran community, and especially to its leaders, the challenge the new neighbors presented to the church. Long hours, stone walls, and church leaders reneging on promises took their toll. Later he was to tell me how, one day, while driving on the multilane Lake Shore Drive, he blacked out completely and "by God's grace the car found its way to a shoulder and settled there."

Shortly thereafter he saw his doctor to learn what had happened to cause his episode. It was in one of Chicago's tall downtown buildings. He had to wait while other patients were called in. He was still feeling unsteady, unsure of himself, and, as he was to recall years later, "For some unknown reason I made my way to the window and peered out with my hands at the bottom of the frame. Suddenly the receptionist called my name and I turned and followed her into the doctor's office. Karl, I don't know what I was doing at the window; I honestly feel that, had that young woman not called me, at that moment, I might have leaped from that window!"

In the months and years that followed, both he and Margaret adopted a rather austere health regimen. There were no repetitions of the earlier frightening encounters.

Those of us who knew and worked at the side of Andrew Schulze knew his warmth, his gentleness with little children, his genuine, caring concern for people experiencing troubles, his appreciation of what was clever and humorous. To many, however, he appeared rigid and severe.

He was, in fact, intensely serious. There were those who complained that he was able only to focus on racial issues. True enough, at every opportunity he would speak — or write — or meet in order to expose the need for Christian voices to be raised on behalf of justice.

211

Andrew simply threw his entire store of energies into any commitment that was his. He was outraged at the exorbitant charges involved in funerals and he helped form a society that addressed this matter — and did so with significant results. Similarly as he began his work as University teacher, he approached his task with diligence both for theological course content and for classroom performance. And long before gun control enjoyed any significant popular support, Andrew's bumper sticker expressed his unwavering commitment to outlawing handguns.

In his later years he also became deeply involved in nutrition and health matters, and seriously investigated the virtues of the charismatic movement. It was at one such meeting in St. Louis that he demonstrated his interest in concerns other than race. Yet he refused to abandon his prior commitment to another issue in which he had earlier immersed himself.

As he later reported on the St. Louis event, he told of hundreds of charismatics assembled. Following a particularly stirring message the congregants joined in singing "There is a Balm in Gilead." The director of activities then welcomed Andrew, this veteran, venerable churchman, to address the assembly.

Andrew began by reminding his hearers of the comfort that God's gracious balm had been in the days of Gilead. Then he continued, "However, elsewhere, at this very moment there is a place of little comfort, for far away there is a bomb in Vietnam."

When Andrew continued in his reporting on the St. Louis experience, he told in sad disappointment how people started to rise from their seats in droves, emptying the auditorium. Deeply disillusioned, he added, "They could speak of the comfort the Holy Spirit of God can bring, but they could not bring themselves to care for all of God's people."

Andrew Schulze seemed to live for the moments he would be given to speak. They would become occasions for him to teach — really, to share what he had been busy learning. For he was a learner. He was always excitedly learning from people he would be observing, from lectures he would hear, articles he would read, conversations in which he'd be participating. He seemed always to be thinking, contemplating, putting things together in his mind — and he could hardly wait till he could share his insights with anyone who would listen.

So he loved his classroom — even though students there often weren't quite as enthusiastically and emotionally committed to digging more deeply into issues that were so vitally important to him. More opportunities to teach came at meetings of the board of the Lutheran Human Relations Association of America. Those board members were intensely interested particularly in the matter of racial injustice. They not only came to conduct the business of the Association's ministry; they also came to learn from this ready teacher who was the executive director of their organization. And ready he was for them. He'd always come prepared to inform, challenge, and help us to grow. And even the University president would stop in to benefit from that portion of the meeting, as would some other faculty members, like Victor Hoffmann (more about him later).

From high positions in government, from the academic world, from the press, and from secular organizations, voices were being raised to protest the inconsistencies rampant in a nation that prided itself as "the land of the free and the home of the brave," "with liberty and justice for all," yet returned its black veterans of the wars to a status of second class citizenship. Andrew insisted that far worse than America's compromising its basic principles was church people's compromising their Christian principles.

Prodded by Andrew's persuasive presentations, the board, year after year, would prepare and propose resolutions to be submitted to the voting delegates of the Lutheran Church — Missouri Synod in their national conventions. Such proposals ordinarily were assigned to individual committees who would consider — and often alter or refine — the proposed resolutions for formal presentation to the assembly in convention.

To the surprise of convention committee chairs and their members, the LHRAA-sponsored proposals drew unprecedentedly large crowds on hand to hear Andrew Schulze defend the carefully crafted propositions against attempts to reverse, water down, or render completely innocuous these calls for change in Synodical policies and actions. When the resolutions were ultimately presented to the convention for vote, they passed overwhelmingly. That kind of success was heady for all of us involved. Andrew was always quick to remind us that if we'd shown any success in our efforts, it was only the blessing hand of God that had used us to accomplish a divine purpose. And again he would say, "These are exciting days; 'Who knows but that we are come for such a time as this!' "

———————

On one such occasion we were driving back to Valparaiso in the early morning hours. It was one of the rare occasions when his wife Margaret was not along. She usually took responsibility for all his notes and papers being there when he needed them. She'd see to it that copies of our literature were in the trunk and that Andrew's tie was straight before he rose to speak. And she was there as comptroller of his diet, usually supplying appropriate fruit, vegetables, carefully selected vitamins, and sunflower seeds, when pangs of hunger would strike.

This particular night things had gone especially well — so well that, in spite of the hour, we weren't a bit sleepy, but we did need a time-out from the road and a few moments to stretch. We found a somewhat lonely cafe. Once we had warmed up a bit and bent our limbs a little, Andrew nudged me over towards the counter and said, "It's been a good day. Let's celebrate a little and have a snack." I was totally amazed when he put the menu aside and said to the waitress, "I'll have a cup of coffee and a piece of lemon meringue pie," a very un-Margaret sort of choice.

Utterly amazed at this complete and total abandonment of his austere and rigidly disciplined dietary regimen, I made no comment except to the waitress, "The same!"

This was historical — and I near-hysterical! Andrew precluded further discussion. He simply said, "Don't tell Margaret."

Each time Andrew would rise to speak, he appeared like a prophet. Gaunt, silver-maned, his deep-set dark eyes flashed. His long, trembling fingers of both hands meeting like a church steeple to steady themselves, he would first clear his throat — sometimes twice or more. And then in low tones he would begin and sometimes he would surprise his audience and invite them to sing along with him some hymn or spiritual.

And prophet he was — no screamer. For the role of the prophet is to call the people of God back from their idols. Those who feared him had never really come to know Andrew Schulze. This is the one who reveled in the Scriptures, whose prayers were frequent and earnest, whose humility was genuine, who reverently treasured the Holy Supper — who wore his clergy collar, he would tell me, not as a badge of privilege, but as a constant reminder to himself that he was in the service of his Lord.

In his last years Andrew and Margaret became Californians, as their eldest son, Paul, invited them into his home.

There I had my last moments of our long years together. I had agreed to prepare Andrew for his afternoon nap while Paul took his mother for a stroll. We talked about our ministry together. He became very tired. I took him to his bed. He was quite helpless. I undressed him, pulled the covers back and tucked him in. He complained that his head was cold so I covered his forehead with a small towel and then I sang his childhood prayer, "Muede bin ich, geh' zu Ruh' " — "Weary now, I seek your rest...."

I brushed my lips on his cheek, pulled the blanket warm around his shoulders. He was asleep. And then I left. It was a good goodbye, Andrew — teacher, pastor, prophet, precious friend.

Victor Hoffman

doors that never quite close

Earlier in these pages, a statement referred to "people like Victor Hoffmann."

Well, actually there were no people exactly like Victor Hoffmann — nor will there ever be. He was one of God's mavericks.

People often expressed disbelief when they would discover Vic was an ordained Lutheran pastor. He taught in Valparaiso's Political Science Department. When I congratulated him on the occasion of his being awarded his Ph.D. degree, he countered, "Thanks — but it doesn't mean a thing. I'm no different from the way I was before. Only now I can get people off my back who keep dismissing me and what I've said and stood for as if I didn't count, as if I didn't have credentials."

Independent he was — the kind of person who was unafraid of controversy, ready to challenge the status quo, particularly when such status had become hallowed, and even more especially when it didn't make sense. Vic was a people-monger. He cared about people — what they were thinking, what they did, what happened to them.

At his church he taught an adult Bible Class, and would manifest — and generate in his hearers — genuine excitement as he would discover in the Scriptures new insights for people's everyday life.

Long before most Christians were beginning to be troubled by the perpetuation of discriminatory practices which relegated African Americans to subordinate roles in almost every area of life in our country, Vic Hoffmann was already speaking out against racial injustice. It was small wonder then that a strong bond of friendship developed between this young man and the human relations veteran who had come to campus, Dr. Andrew Schulze.

Dr. Hoffmann agreed with his new colleague that there must be a formal communication begun, engaging members of the larger Lutheran community in discussion about these vital issues. The *Vanguard* was born and Victor became the editor of its first issue.

Really, no one who knew either of these strong minded, strong willed, and brilliant men would have expected otherwise, but Vic suggested after the first issue that Andrew take over the editor post, along with his position of executive director of the Lutheran Human Relations Association of America. *Vanguard* was now its official organ. We who were immediately involved chuckled softly as we knew from the very start that each of them would have his own strong — and very likely different conviction about how the paper should look or what its contents should be. Vic withdrew with the same gracious grin he wore so often, nevertheless maintaining his great respect for his senior colleague and continuing his support of LHRAA's ministry. Now, more than forty years later, the *Vanguard* with regularity still serves to keep the church's attention focused on issues of oppression and injustice.

Not yet fifty, Victor and his family moved to Milwaukee where he accepted a position as head of a human relations department in the University of Wisconsin (Milwaukee) Graduate School. He also became associate pastor of Cross Lutheran Church, a thriving inner-city congregation in that city. And the mayor, Frank Zeidler, appointed him chair of Milwaukee's Human Relations Commission.

Back in Valparaiso his absence did not go unnoticed. One colleague who particularly admired him, commented, "The conversations are all kind of dull and drab around here since Vic's gone." And he added, "You know, Vic wouldn't even have been able to discourse dispassionately about a lily petal!"

An area immediately to the west of campus, close to the cemetery, was where some of the city's most impoverished folk lived. Students and profs were stopped as they walked by and were asked by youngsters — and their parents too, "What's happened to Mr. Hoffmann? Has he moved?"

These people had come to know him too. He had often stopped by to chat with them and made himself accessible as a good neighbor, generously offering his counsel and care. And they missed their friend.

Not too many years later, Victor Hoffmann died in a hotel. It was the night after a strenuous day in his role as consultant to United States Senator Vance Hartke.

That evening before retiring Victor, thoughtful, caring, and loving husband and father, penned a personal note to his wife Lucille and to each of their children.

In the days that followed, in a service at Milwaukee's Cross Church, people from everywhere thronged to express their respect and their grief. His closest teaching colleague at Valparaiso, John

Strietelmeier, reminded the worshippers that Victor Hoffmann's was a life that called for gratitude — a gift to many, many people. He urged his audience not to forget that into his fifty-some years, Victor had packed more living and caring than most people who live into far later years.

Nor will hundreds of students who had him as teacher forget him, his spirit, his message.

On one particular night I had gathered some thirty students in the basement of our home for a two-hour presentation on the significance of the Psalms for people experiencing intense personal turbulence. I had barely begun the session when our doorbell rang. It was Victor.

Esther explained that I was just beginning my presentation to a theology class. He said, "Good!" and asked to be shown the stairway. Down he came, and after my brief introduction and invitation to make whatever comments he might wish, Vic launched into what was a magnificent discussion with the students on the very matters I had planned to present. They caught his passion for teaching, his passion for people, his passion for justice, his passionate faith. It was only a few days after that visit to our home that Victor died.

Pages could be — and ought be written about Victor Hoffmann. One more story should be told, though.

As happens from time to time, a student will "step over the line" and the offenses warrant expulsion. On one such occasion the young man was told to leave on "the next train out." In the early hours of the morning the despondent young man was sitting quite alone in the dimmed Pennsy station, awaiting his train. Professor Hoffmann came through the door and walked to the bench where he was, to sit with him till train time. Shamed, the young man was no longer a student. But for Victor Hoffmann he was a person. God's child.

There's no way of knowing what their conversation was about — there was a lot of silence. But, knowing Vic, we were sure he talked about the God who forgives, who gives second chance, who befriends.

Victor knew all about friendship. Victor was a friend.

The Great Man

windowed doors that allow for vision

Every time he spoke it seemed to me a sort of far wind from deep within him carried the words across his throat — even when he spoke more loudly — they had a sort of whispered quality.

He had briefly served as a seminary professor and then became executive director of his church's youth organization, called the Walther League, and then, president of Valparaiso University.

Both of these organizations had close ties with the Lutheran Church — Missouri Synod, and, in fact, each served and was supported primarily by members of that church body. Both, however, were financed and structured and functioned quite independently. Both, largely under this man's leadership, ventured into areas the church body itself was slow to enter.

Although the Lutheran Laymen's League had pioneered in assigning financial and managerial responsibility in the church to laymen, the Walther League and Valparaiso University focused sharply on developing the young laity in the church for responsible participation in church, community, and world affairs.

Banquet speaker, lecturer, writer, Otto Paul Kretzmann became well known in Lutheran circles. True, a conservative church was not hurrying to vote a churchman like him (and it's doubtful there were *any* like him!) into any elected office. His was a prophetic voice, pointing up contemporary issues that called for appropriate response from a church that claimed to be faithful to the Scriptures and to the Lutheran traditions of honoring of God's calling of the laity to assume responsible roles in society. That made many a bit nervous about his perspective as he introduced them to areas they'd not yet themselves explored. However, more and more people came to appreciate and welcome his vision and his voice. The word was out and the name became well known.

And it came to pass in those days that Otto Paul had two sisters and a bunch of brothers. One was an authority on liturgy and church architecture and pastor of a large Chicago congregation. Another was a journalist. Two of them were prominent in the field of foreign missions, one in India, and the other in Africa.

And then there was Norman, eventually to become a clergyman with significant pastorates in Massachusetts and later in Minneapolis — and ultimately a church journal editor. He was youngest of the siblings and enrolled in a seminary at the time that his big brother O. P.'s star was rising.

And it further came to pass that one evening Norman and his friend Joe Ressmeyer were meeting with a set of twins, one of whom was ultimately to become my wife. Joe they had met before, not Norman. When the two seminarians arrived, Joe introduced Norman, explaining that he was "O. P.'s brother."

In total innocence one of them (years later neither of them would acknowledge which one!) asked, "Who's O. P.?"

In later years a friend of mine who knew the story would often whisper to me when Dr. O. P. Kretzmann would be introduced, "That's Norm's brother!"

Chapel services at the University were unusually impressive when the President would be the speaker. And worshippers would be spellbound in their attention to his carefully crafted sermons, the poetry-like phrases, the arresting words, the appeal to all the listener's senses.

Often at night he would find his way to different student residence halls to present a vespers meditation and homily. Regularly clusters of couples would gather outside the women's dormitories in the days of O. P.'s presidency, the fellows all cozying up to their girl friends for a final goodnight before they would duck into their halls for the ten o'clock evening curfew. He would look into the face of none of them, but edge his way through the little crowd with a smile on his face and say, "All right, everybody, break it up — coming through!"

It was not unusual to hear some student tell of an encounter with their President on campus or in one of the halls, "O. P. stopped and talked with me!" And though the experience was common enough, it always was something very special that a person of such importance should find time for a "mere student."

223

His sons were to tell me years later of the trip the family took to Wisconsin, a trip that revealed rather vividly the great man's altogether human-ness.

While traveling along the expressway, they agreed that the next tollstop would provide a good occasion to dispose of a fistful of pennies they had accumulated. By the time they approached the tollgates their father was so preoccupied with his lead role in the conversation, that quite without thinking, he hurled the handful of coins towards the basket, only to hear them all falling to the pavement. He'd not noticed that he had driven up to an attendant's gate and there was no basket.

As I recall, the boys had to get out and gather the strewn coins while their father registered an apologetic and blushing smile for the bewildered and somewhat disgusted man in uniform. Indeed, O.P. was human.

In the days of inner-city turmoil, our Lutheran Human Relations Association, located on Valparaiso University's campus, developed satellite centers in Cleveland and Chicago to provide its ministry with a presence in those troubled cities.

A call from our Chicago Project's director, George Hrbek, brought us an update on his meetings with leaders of some of the "gangs" that had come into prominence there. Leaders of the Blackstone Rangers had contacted him offering him opportunity to demonstrate the genuineness of his offers to effect reconciliation in tension areas. This was their story and proposition:

Years earlier a tradition had begun honoring a mythical hero, Bud Billikin, who himself was supposed to have experienced the hardships of immigration from the rural South to industrial Chicago. He was remembered with an annual mammoth picnic for the African American children of the city. The program featured free refreshments, games, and music. The event had become a highlight of the year for southsiders, and this summer's date was approaching soon — next Saturday!

These leaders told of their fears that the police would be present in droves and would be especially on the lookout for Blackstone Rangers and would not be above provoking some disturbance and giving them reason to "do some head banging. So on Bud Billikin Day we want to be far away from the park. Now, can you find a place for us to have our own picnic?"

They explained that they were chartering busses, and most of the group would be youngsters between six and fourteen. They'd bring along all the food, they'd supervise the kids, and they'd clean up afterwards.

George asked, "Can they come out to Valpo?" I reminded him, "Hey, George, I only work here — but I'll ask O. P."

The President's response was immediate, "Well, of course! Do what you have to do to give them a good welcome."

Saturday was approaching fast. It seemed all the "take charge" kind of people around the University had other plans for the weekend. We were left pretty well to take things in our own hands.

We found the athletic department people very helpful, providing us with bats and softballs, footballs, volleyballs, and basketballs. We had chalking wheels and laid out a few softball diamonds around the east campus. And we set up a few ad hoc volleyball courts and football fields too.

Saturday came and so did the Rangers. They poured out of the busses like the interminable parade of clowns emerging from the tiny cars at a circus — unbelievably many. They were wild with their new spacious freedom. Yet the stern voiced, no-nonsense leaders shepherded them in firm discipline to places where they were given their briefing and assignments for play.

Fortunately for this very hot day the athletic department had also located some student swimmers to supervise groupings of forty that would take to the pool in shifts. (In one of these periods a lifeguard had to fish a youngster out — he hadn't ever been swimming before and jumped in at the deep end. Later in the day the same frightening thing happened, and — surprise! — it was the same boy who'd been rescued in the morning!) Other than that, there were no anxious moments.

225

When it was mealtime we gathered at the bleachers of Brown Field (named for Valparaiso's sixth president — who by the way strongly opposed the idea of intercollegiate athletics). The guest leaders spread out their sumptuous fare, and the University's food services had prepared gallons of lemonade. And next to the dispenser were O. P., greeting the young visitors, one at a time, and his dear wife, Flora, filling their paper beverage cups.

There were some city police cars passing by rather frequently during the afternoon. The chief complained the next week that we hadn't apprised him of the happening. I don't recall exactly how we answered him, but O. P. dismissed the matter in his accustomed wry way, "They probably hadn't noticed that we didn't need any help."

And the visitors picked up all the scraps of paper napkins and cups and wrappers, mounted their busses, and ended an unforgettable experience that many have forgotten, and some people never even knew about.

Long before the Blackstone Rangers visited Valparaiso, President Kretzmann wanted to make it patently clear that the idea of racial discrimination and segregation were simply incompatible with the Christian faith.

Not surprisingly then, when the first voices were raised in the church, calling for an end to positions, policies, and practices that excluded racial minorities from full exercise of their rights and their God given status as complete children of God, O. P. Kretzmann lent his support.

He insisted that the forum for dealing with these issues be at Valparaiso University, seeking to be faithful to the University's motto, "In Your light we see light." Annually the University would host an *LHRAA Institute on Human Relations* inviting prominent national figures as speakers and viewing contemporary racial issues in the light of Scriptures and the Christian faith. And O. P. and Mrs. Kretzmann were always in attendance, eager to be identified with the cause.

Cooperating with the Lutheran Human Relations Association in these concerns, he also invited the organization to have its meetings on campus. He would also sit in on these, including its board meetings.

It was O. P. who initiated the decision of the *LHRAA* board to engage an executive director. Knowing full well the improverished status of the Association's finances, he suggested that the person selected should also, upon approval of the University, be engaged to teach in Valpo's theology department part-time, thus ensuring half of the salary requirements. And as further contribution, he invited the Association to take up residence on campus, with office space, utilities, and custodial service supplied by the University.

Years before, after World War I, at the time when Valparaiso University's fortunes had fallen on hard times — as excellent as its earlier reputation had been, it had failed to become an accredited school and enrollment had plummeted to about 900 from its glory days of 5,000-plus. The school was up for sale. An announcement reported that the successful bidder was the Ku Klux Klan.

Apparently the community did not go into shock and there seemed to be not a ripple of anxious concern, let alone word of protest. Most students had found lodging and meals in neighboring residences that had (often outrageously, architecturally speaking!) tacked on lean-to additions, and pushed out their walls to widest possible use. Now in the absence of students, landlords in their enlarged shells were relieved at the idea of *any* newcomers filling their vacant rooms.

On the day the deal was to be closed no representative of the Klan was present. The organizations' leaders were squabbling among themselves, freezing its funds. The Klan forfeited its transaction for purchase of the university. Two years later the school was purchased by an association of Lutherans in the north Midwest, organized for the primary purpose of preparing the laity for responsible roles in church and community.

These Lutherans now owned a school that had fallen on severely hard times. They had assumed the responsibility for restoring its reputation. Their challenge: to develop a quality institution of higher learning that would win the respect of the academic world and gain the esteem and support of its Lutheran constituency.

In the months that followed the Klan's reputation diminished considerably and ultimately suffered a serious blow in a scandal involving its leader in a horrid and well-publicized felony.

However the Valparaiso community had not been averse to the original plans of the Klan to own and revive the University. One can understand then that no African Americans lived in Valparaiso.

At long last Inez Parker of Philadelphia enrolled and four years later became the first of her race to graduate from a four-year liberal arts program at the University. Far from naive, Otto Paul Kretzmann was well aware that the decision to enroll this student was flying in the face of custom, and he knew what kind of resentment she might encounter in her new setting.

Learning of her time of arrival, he went to the Pennsy Station to meet her train. He went afoot leaving his car at his home. When the train had screeched to its halt, he helped her from the coach. Instead of going directly on a diagonal route to the campus, they went a block to the north to Lincolnway Avenue, and together, Inez Parker and Otto Paul Kretzmann walked down the city's main street. Peeking from behind curtains, and in some instances stepping outside their little shops, all could see this much-respected President of Valparaiso University, carrying her suitcase, personally welcoming her. He had made his statement and the message was clear.

When the occasion called for standing up to be counted, O. P. was there. But this was no "show-boating."

Before my colleague Andrew Schulze (at that time Executive Director of Lutheran Human Relations) went to Albany, Georgia, in response to Martin Luther King's call for support in an early demonstration there, O. P. called to make sure we would be participating in the event, encouraging our involvement.

Subsequently Andrew was arrested and in jail for several days. O. P. took it upon himself to wire both President John Kennedy and Attorney General Robert Kennedy, calling for them to respond to the situation in a way appropriate to their respective positions. And when my colleague was about to be released I received a call from So Heidbrink, secretary to Dr. Kretzmann, asking me to come to the office. When I arrived, she explained that Dr. Kretzmann was gone from the city but had called her that morning instructing her to call me. She then lifted her desk blotter and took from beneath it ten twenty dollar bills. I was to use these to pay for Andrew Schulze's bail and release from jail.

That was the same kind of concern evident when he called me one morning to tell me he had learned that forty Valpo students had driven down to Montgomery, Alabama, to participate in the culminating of Dr. Martin Luther King's historic March from Selma to Montgomery. "I'd feel better if I knew someone from the University were with them. Will you go?" And I said "yes." When I would know what kind of answer he wanted, that's the only kind of answer appropriate.

And so I went. There were no reservations for Montgomery available on any kind of public carrier, but I found a group of priests and nuns who had chartered two antiquated DC3s to fly out of St. Louis for the March and they made room for me.

Amazingly, in that immense spread of marchers, six abreast, that stretched for more blocks than I could count, I found all forty students. When I reported on the experience, O. P. said, "I would hope the parents know that we care about their sons and daughters too and that we affirm their standing with the victims of injustice."

I wasn't surprised then that he asked (make that "ordered"!) me to negotiate for, direct, and teach in an exchange semester with Miles College (member of the Negro College Fund) in Birmingham, Alabama. He was enthusiastically supportive in my carrying out the program. He wanted Miles and its students to reap positive benefits from the arrangement and he was eager that students from his own university have the kind of enriching experience that he felt this program could provide.

Nor did he care only about the children of other parents. He called another time to ask whether I intended to participate in Martin Luther King's March on Washington. And when I said I was going, he asked, "Would you take Jody along with you?" Jody learned well from his father. Long after Jody's high school days, he was also to be at my side here in Valparaiso. We were walking by twos in a demonstration welcoming black citizens of Gary who had received death threats when they planned to come to redress a grievance in the case of a racial hatred murder. The Great Man's penchant for justice and compassion was a legacy transmitted to each of his three sons.

If one were to differentiate between "vision" and "dream" by defining vision as a clear, achievable goal and dream as a hoped for eventuality unbounded by impediments of reality, one might be inclined to regard Otto Paul Kretzmann more the dreamer. And dreams he had! But the development of a great university and producing thousands of graduates through the years who made and still make rich contributions with their lives wherever they are gives testimony to his being a visionary.

And when he died, a cloud of sorrowful rememberings covered the campus.

His body lay in state in a dark brown wooden casket at the foot of the thirteen-stepped nave of the towering Chapel of the Resurrection that had been erected during his day. Robed in clergy garb with pendant cross lying on his chest he still exuded the familiar presidential dignity. The somber bells tolled and the great organ voiced the hopes of Easter chorales.

On the steps, strewn in random echelon, lay all the hoods of honor this revered leader had received through the years in recognition of his giftedness. The scene was near breathtaking — at the foot of the tall Christus Victor cross above the altar — the Great Man had come to the end of his journey here — a statement made in his death about casting all our trophies aside when coming into God's presence.

And I remembered a line from a sermon he had preached, "When you have gathered all of life's glories and discover they are dust in your hand and ashes on your lips...." He was urging us to get our priorities straight. His funeral was an *amen* to that sermon.

And, outside, a young student was going about to all the stop signs at intersections around the campus area. With her little brush and white paint, she raised her memorial, inserting two periods so that against the bright red the letters spelled:

"ST. O. P."

The Pastor from
New York
I
Shaping of a Pastor

cutting doors in walls

In the early 1900s career prospects for young African Americans were decidedly limited. Especially in the Deep South. And of course one couldn't go much deeper than Louisiana where Clemonce Sabourin lived.

He learned carpentry, and he was good at it. But young Clem was a thinker, and he was bright, and his busy mind entertained thoughts of other career possibilities.

He was Lutheran. A serious Lutheran. He loved his church, yet he saw its weaknesses and inconsistencies. He was able to discern the devotion that led this denomination to contribute considerable sums of money to include African Americans in their number, and he could appreciate that. It confused him, however, that the church maintained the segregating patterns so deeply imbedded in southern life that relentlessly and uncompromisingly assigned African Americans to subordinate status. Clem himself would describe it this way: "White Lutherans really want to embrace us — but at arm's length!"

Clem had a great respect for Lutheran ministers — most of whom he observed were white. He was impressed with their dedication and commitment. It disturbed him, of course, to see that they were privileged in their whiteness, and that outside of their churchly activities they quite easily accommodated themselves to the segregation policies and practices that attended living in the South.

Yet, Clem set his heart on becoming a pastor.

For years Lutherans had maintained preministerial academies and seminaries in many places across the country. Assuming, and with a degree of accuracy, that the South had been favoring white children and had under-served and sometimes simply neglected the others, church education leaders felt their own "white" institutions would not serve this new constituency well and therefore established what became known as "Immanuel Lutheran College and Seminary for Negroes" in Greensboro, North Carolina.

234

Loose translation — and common conceptions — of the above: "Educationally, young Negroes just aren't capable of measuring up to the quality of young people in the white world, and therefore we won't have such high expectations and rigorous demands for proficiency." It would not take a giant step, then, to build on that premise as rationale for the practice that would prevail, thoughts like these:

> *It's appropriate for white "missionaries" and teachers to serve black communities.*
>
> *Better yet, let's find black workers to serve black congregations — because they don't require the highly trained professionals that these white workers are.*
>
> *And of course the young black pastors and teachers would not be adequate to hold such positions in white Lutheran churches and schools.*

Obviously such patronizing, condescending, haughty posturing could not survive close scrutiny and for that reason was not *formally* articulated.

Some of the seminaries began to experience the awkwardness of having no African Americans on their roster of students. When challenged and asked why they didn't intentionally recruit students of color, they would lamely explain that they did not wish to compete with Immanuel in its enrollment efforts.

It probably really never occurred to people that if Clemonce Sabourin was going to be a pastor that he would apply for admission in any school other than Immanuel. And so, Clem went to Greensboro.

Years later, Clem, conceding that his seminary education had hardly been the best, nonetheless had appreciative words for those who taught and served there. One man whom he particularly remembered with fondness was Dr. Henry Nau, Immanuel's President. Dr. Nau was especially impressed with his "three S men" — Sabourin, Smallwood and Sorrell. (In later years Dr. Smallwood would be on the University of Maryland's faculty and Pastor Sorrell would serve parishes in Houston and Baltimore.)

Recognizing the extraordinary talents of these three, Dr. Nau spent much personal time with them, challenging them with extra-curricular studies that helped them to become exceptional graduates of Immanuel.

Upon graduation, young Sabourin was ordained and installed as a pastor of Grace Lutheran Congregation in Greensboro, where he maintained his ties with Dr. Nau and became an inspiring pastor to Immanuel students.

The word about this young, handsome minister and his excellent preaching got around, and more and more visitors found their way to his services. Years later, with a large smile across his face, he'd recall to us how he had been particularly intrigued by the presence of two young women from town who would attend. At the close of service, it was his custom to hurry to the front door of the church to greet those who had come to worship. He was repeatedly disappointed to find that the two strangers would always have slipped out of church before he could meet and greet them.

Ultimately he learned where these attractive young women lived. He paid them a visit, ostensibly to assure them of their welcome at the church and to offer his pastoral services if ever needed. They were both teachers, and the one named Glenice quickly became his heart's desire. Initially, she was not interested in any kind of social relations with a preacher. As the story unfolded, however, the reciprocal fondness blossomed into a beautiful marriage.

The Pastor from New York
II.
A Church Grows in Harlem

---

building entrance doors that are marked "welcome"

I first met Clem when he was pastor in New York's Harlem. Only a few blocks away from his Mount Zion Lutheran Church was the famous Abyssinian Baptist Church. Newspapers unreservedly described its pastor, Congressman Adam Clayton Powell, Jr., as rascal, maverick, and a public shame. Clem Sabourin, however, would cite the man's resourcefulness and the exemplary compassionate concern this congregation down the street showed for the needy in the neighborhood. This, he observed, was what won for Powell the loyalty — and the votes — of his community supporters.

One time, I recall, we were walking together in his neighborhood and Clem pointed out a beauty shop owned by the wife of Joe Louis. Not far in the other direction stood the building where, years later, Malcolm X would be assassinated. This was the heart of Harlem.

When Glenice and Clem first arrived, they came accepting the invitation of the regional offices of his church body. To receive subsidy to maintain the church's program called for submitting to certain conditions, like adopting procedural practices and programs that were already in place in other Northeastern parishes. Clem appreciated the support promised his ministry, but he was hardly enamored of the requirements imposed, since he was convinced that in his situation some of the proposed programs were simply inappropriate, if not ill advised.

Determined to serve his community and eager not to be shackled by the conditions imposed by the arrangement with their district, Clem and Glenice set themselves to the dual task of developing a program of ministry of their own design and to help the congregation become self sustaining as very soon as possible.

The setting of Mt. Zion and the parochial school it conducted was hardly like anything the young pastor had ever experienced in the South. The church itself was attractive and lent itself well to an atmosphere of worship. Clem intended Mount Zion to be useful for people who might drop in at the church for personal prayer.

On my first visit there, when I entered the church, what caught my eye was a jukebox close to the front entrance. Before I could even ask the question, "What is this," Clem answered that no coins were required; people who would stop in to worship needed only to press a button and make their choices from a wide variety of hymn selections offered by the record player.

Mt. Zion won a reputation in the community as a care center for people who lived in or frequented the neighborhood. A five storied building was attached to the church. The bottom three floors provided pastoral and school offices, classroom space, dining facilities, and a small gymnasium. The fourth floor at first was used for storage and the fifth served as the Sabourin parsonage. Obviously there were significant expenses involved in maintaining so large a complex.

In a relatively short time the Sabourins, together with a talented, dedicated, and loyal membership had expanded the school's role. The School on the Hill, as it was called, started to serve as a place for parents to drop off their children on the way to work in the early morning hours, earlier than the first class of the school day began. Similarly, an after-school program provided supervised care for students till their parents returned from their work. With the purchase of a school bus, the program expanded to provide pick up and delivery for such children. Of course, parents found such service highly attractive. They appreciated the Christian tone of the curriculum, the skilled faculty, the caring atmosphere, and they gladly reimbursed Mt. Zion for such a program.

With careful management of both school and church business, Glenice Sabourin proved a superb administrator, and with Clem quite literally spelling out the Church's message through his personal involvement in the community, Mt. Zion became self-sustaining and quite independent of governance or financial subsidy of the parent church body.

Held in such high regard in the community, Mt. Zion was approached to collaborate with a local mental health program. Utilizing the fourth floor of the parish building, the group conducted a program involving patients in dramatic and musical activities. The facilities lent themselves well for instruction, rehearsals, and, ultimately, from time to time, actual presentations. Famous drama and music personalities of the day participated in these and evoked even more plaudits and support from the community for Mt. Zion.

All these developments required ever so much remodeling and adapting of facilities to make such innovations possible. And the young preacher would put on his working clothes and, wielding all his carpentry tools and skills, he would keep such costs to a minimum by doing almost all of this work himself.

```
┌─────────────────────────────────┐
│                                 │
│       The Pastor from           │
│         New York                │
│           III.                  │
│      A Larger Audience          │
│                                 │
└─────────────────────────────────┘
```

clearing the doorways

In his devotion to the development of his Harlem parish, however, Clem never lost sight of his responsibilities towards the rest
of God's people beyond the walls of Mt. Zion. Clemonce Sabourin
was a warm and welcoming person, gentle and caring. But
Clemonce Sabourin was also an angry man. He bristled at the inconsistencies of a church that claimed itself faithful to Jesus Christ
and his redemptive Gospel of reconciliation and unity and justice.
Wasn't it obvious that tolerating the policies and practice of white
superiority and subordination of non-whites, not only in the secular world, but especially as this spilled over into the life of the
church, was an affront to God! In the interest of a false peace and a
superficial calm, in accepting these repressive practices, the church
and its leaders were accommodating themselves and their programs
to evil practices that diminished the lives of African Americans.
People claiming to be Christians were actually aiding and abetting
those who promoted and maintained this evil system! And, for the
most part, white Lutherans would intentionally look the other way.
In anguish Clem would ask, "How can this go on?"

People who heard about Clem Sabourin or got to know him
wanted to hear more. Increasingly, pastors attending meetings or
conferences at which he would speak were moved by his arresting
and challenging comments. Laymen and women's groups would
invite him to speak and those in attendance would be stirred by his
message. (I recall one such engagement. I was sitting towards the
rear and, while this young and very handsome pastor stopped in
his presentation to sip some water, a woman sitting near me whispered to the woman next to her, "Isn't he wonderful? For him I
could revise my views on interracial marriage!")

Meanwhile, Dr. Andrew Schulze, first in St. Louis, later in Chicago, was speaking the same message, criticisms that church leaders did not really want to be hearing. The two "prophets" were
delighted and encouraged to hear what the other was saying. They
developed a warm partnership. Andrew, who now had become
Executive Director of the Lutheran Human Relations Association of America, provided new audiences to hear the Sabourin
message.

Clem's first appearance on Valparaiso University's campus at LHRAA's annual summer Institute won him more friends. This is where I got to meet Clem too. Subsequently the University bestowed on the young pastor an honorary doctorate. And LHRAA members were so thoroughly impressed with him that they named him the Association's president.

To have found an organization of Lutherans so committed to addressing the problems of racial disharmony was more than young Sabourin had ever hoped for.

Encouraged by the support of his new allies, Pastor Sabourin took pen in hand and wrote an autobiographical piece, an account of his revisit to his native South with his son, Clemonce, Jr. He described the pain he experienced in attempting to relate and interpret to the young boy the story of his life and the lives of his people. With moving earnestness he brought his message to a close, praying that God give courage to Christians — particularly preachers — that they might speak out boldly against the sins of racial segregation and subordination. He ended, with the words he also gave as name to his book, *Let the Righteous Speak!*

He often expressed his appreciation for LHRAA and for the new companions he found in the cause he embraced. When the first printing of his book had completely sold out, he permitted the Association to do a second printing, with the understanding that profits from its sale would go to LHRAA's ministry.

Wanting to serve more than only as president in name, Pastor Sabourin assumed an active role, accepting many assignments to speak at workshops, conferences, and in church services on behalf of the Association. He frequently wrote articles both for LHRAA's paper *The Vanguard* and other church periodicals.

On one occasion when the work of the Association was under severe financial duress, I received a letter from Clem to find enclosed a check for $1,500. His congregation had presented this to him so that he and his wife Glenice might have a vacation in Europe. The Sabourins simply decided to forego their travels and sent the check as a gift for LHRAA.

Such a decision could not have been a casual one. The very nature of their work and its setting and the location of their home there combined to make their lives quite confined. This was especially true for Mrs. Sabourin. Her husband could regularly take to the streets to do his work, while she was for the most part to be found in the school office or tending to home management responsibilities in their living quarters.

I recall, on one of my visits, after one of Glenice's delicious meals, Clem had to step out for a short time, so I chatted with her in the kitchen. She was leaning over the sink. I was drying dishes while she was washing them. Suddenly a little sparrow, hardly beautiful, as birds go, settled on the windowsill. She interrupted our conversation and promptly addressed her little visitor, chiding him, "You silly little bird! You can fly all the way up here to this window — why don't you use those wings and fly to some place where you'll find green lawns and trees and flowers!"

Surely, the members of Mt. Zion had understood how highly desirable some travel respite might be for this hard working team, and it was their sensitivity and love that no doubt had prompted their gift. I had known, of course, how much the Sabourins loved LHRAA, but this particular generous expression brought home to me how deep and self-sacrificing that love truly was.

Whatever things I was learning from my readings — or from my own experiences, whenever I'd share them with Clem, he always seemed already to have worked through those issues himself. I always felt my meetings with him were "catch-up" sessions, because he always seemed about five years ahead of me — regardless of the subject — political corruption, systematic delays in justice, legal circumventions, racial and ethnic migration. He invariably proved himself informed and wise.

Every trip I would make to the east, it seemed, would include a stopover with Clem Sabourin. He was a favorite resource, an encouraging and invaluable mentor and teacher. He would have places to take me, sights to show me, stories to tell me, perspectives to share with me. I'd follow him about if he was doing maintenance work on his facilities and I'd hang on his every word. We'd sit for hours talking. Or we'd walk the streets while he'd interpret what we were experiencing as we walked.

I recall one occasion when, on foot, we made our way through a neighborhood reputed to be particularly dangerous. It was midday, and yet policemen walking their beats walked in teams of four. In the course of only a few blocks we encountered three such teams. In spite of Clem's knowing well the brittle nature of the situation at that particular time, there was nothing "different" about his conduct, and any one observing him would have concluded he was entirely oblivious of what was going on about him.

Not so! Alert and aware, he moved about with a composure that manifested self-confidence and competence. He knew his community. And the community knew Clemonce Sabourin.

———————

In 1974, in the thirtieth of his thirty-two years of ministry at this church in Manhattan, members of Mt. Zion planned an elaborate program with which to honor their pastor to celebrate his years of service among them. They honored me by asking me to be speaker for the occasion, probably not because of my close ties of friendship with their pastor as much as their awareness of his high regard for the Lutheran Human Relations Association. He had been one of its founders and its second president, and I now happened to be its executive director.

An elegant event it was — the small church was crowded. Community leaders and church officials spoke words of tribute. Colleagues in ministry from Philadelphia and Long Island were present, acknowledging the inspiration and friend this man had been to them. Laymen and women from area congregations — Lutheran and other — were there to manifest their love and respect for Clemonce and Glenice Sabourin. A string quartet played a Beethoven Sonata. A guest soloist sang arias from Handel's Messiah. The walls resounded as the congregation sang Martin Luther's "A Mighty Fortress is our God." The service was a mite long. No one minded.

And when it was over, people didn't want to leave. The mood was festive. There were affectionate hugs everywhere I'd look. And moist eyes. These people — members and guests alike — loved Glenice and Clemonce Sabourin. And three hours later a few of us were still sitting in the Sabourin living room while Clem and Glenice rehearsed for us some of the happenings during their years together.

And four and one half hours later the LHRAA member from Long Island (whose guest I'd been for this weekend) and I were still listening, long after everyone else had left. I was glad I had a traveling companion with me, because I needed shepherding to keep from getting lost in the big city. We got up to leave. Clem, near exhaustion after such an emotional day, rose from his chair, clipped back in place the clergy collar he had loosened and insisted on accompanying us to the train personally. He did not want us to be out in the night alone.

It was late. It was dark. The city's noise had subsided and it was almost eerily quiet. We saw a few night people. It seemed to us that they recognized and respected Clem. And he stayed with us till the noisy train shook and screamed to a stop, and we were safely boarded. There were so many of the day's happenings still to drink in, to absorb, to reflect on. We were quiet for a long while. We had been in the presence of a great man of God.

The Pastor from
New York
IV.
Never Quite Retired

some doors thought closed keep creeping open

The Sabourins moved to St. Petersburg in Virginia when Clem retired in 1977. We stayed in rather close touch with occasional letters and more frequent telephone calls. It was absurd to think even for one moment that Clem would disappear over the horizon like a setting sun.

Always a learner, Clem, with Glenice at his side, now had time to travel to distant places of the world. Back at his new Virginia home area he began attending church in a small community that once had been a stronghold of the world of segregation.

Patient with people, impatient with wrong, he became a light, leaven, and salt in that parish. The local pastor welcomed his collegiality and willingness to serve. So Clem would preach from time to time and he would participate in Bible discussion hours. And he would say what was on his heart and on his ready tongue — truths of Scripture and mooring posts of his faith, exposing the evils of segregation and the Godliness of genuine welcome to all of God's people at every level.

Clem was an engaging preacher, a persuasive teacher, a very genuine Christian and human being, with a twinkle in his eye, a smile on his lips and a resoluteness that would not accommodate any compromise of truth. And the people in that little congregation grew to love him and respect him.

When they would come to the altar and kneel there to receive the Lord's Supper and hear this African American minister say so very personally that the Lord Christ is *"for you,"* they were participating in a Holy Integration that many white Christians have never experienced.

Grateful for the Sabourins' ministry among them, this parish also wanted to celebrate the fiftieth anniversary of Clem's ordination.

For this occasion too, the good people of Hopewell invited me to be speaker. In the liturgy that followed my homily, Pastor Carr incorporated a bit of ritual with which I'd not been acquainted. It somewhat reenacted the traditional Lutheran Service of Ordination. Other ordained pastors, garbed in clergy robes, participate. Late in the service, the new ordinee makes public confession of faith. Then, before the altar, each minister places a hand on the head or shoulder of the candidate and speaks an appropriate word of Scripture. This then constitutes the ordination. After a prayer the one newly ordained turns and pronounces a blessing upon the gathered worshippers as a first official pastoral act.

Hopewell's Pastor Carr had invited neighboring pastors to attend this special service. All robed, they filled the two front rows of the little church. Following the sermon and subsequent hymn, Pastor Sabourin stepped forward to kneel at the altar as he had at his ordination, to publicly declare his faith, as he had then. All the ministers stepped forward to participate in "the laying on of hands" and each spoke an appropriate word of Scripture. Since my chair had been in the chancel, I was the last to step forward. As I rose I saw Harry Haysbert sitting directly behind those two vacated pews where the clergy had been sitting.

Harry Haysbert had attended Immanuel in Greensboro with Clem long ago. The bond of friendship between them was strong. Harry had been ordained a Lutheran pastor too, almost as many years ago. But when he became married, the all-white Lutheran Synodical Conference Mission Board determined that his salary should be lowered because his wife was employed, earning income — albeit small — as a teacher. The Haysberts were not able to survive on this arrangement, so he was obliged to withdraw from the ministry and seek some other employment.

Pastor Haysbert was a gifted man and many of his attributes and skills qualified him for working with the Boy Scouts of America. He became an executive in the organization's national offices in New York. However, he remained active in the church, and occasionally he would substitute in the pastoral role for nearby clergy who were ill, vacationing, or in other ways indisposed.

Through all these years Clem and Harry stayed in touch, encouraging and affirming each other in their vocational pursuits. Mrs. Haysbert had since died and Harry had moved to Princeton, New Jersey, in his retirement. There he helped the University Lutheran campus pastor in his ministry and also assisted as liturgist in Sunday services, especially in the observance of Holy Communion. More recently he had been the victim of a wretched automobile crash that left him severely impaired.

249

Pastor Haysbert was sitting out there in the congregation now. Instead of going directly to the altar, I stepped down into the center aisle, took him by the arm and steadied him as he limped his way to the altar. There he raised his hand to place it on his dear friend and to speak his word of blessing on this veteran servant of God.

Again, when the service ended, no one seemed to want to leave. There was food, and more joy and congeniality than one could have possibly expected. It was, in a phrase I invented because none other would be quite adequate, "A Sabourin Event."

One more Sabourin event —

Three days before his eighty-first birthday, Clemonce Sabourin died.

The little church was full again. And Harry Haysbert was there too.

And Dr. Richard Hinz, the regional president of the Lutheran Church was there. He spoke. They were good words. Clem's pastor spoke — and his were good words. And others spoke too. And theirs were good words.

But in the quietness that hung over us, as the strains of our farewell hymn trailed away, the word that Clem had had for us, and the word he was to us, were clear to us.

Glenice and I visit together often, mostly by phone — and from time to time Harry talks with us too. Mainly, we remember Clem and the things he was saying to us when he was here. And we remind each other that the words are still here for us to remember.

Good words.

Poet Indeed

simple, simply doors

The Springsteens met as students at Valparaiso University in Indiana. When Bob would be introduced he'd tell how he was from Harvard, and with a grin he'd add, "Harvard, Illinois." His dad was a railroad engineer.

Anne came from Baltimore. Her mother was a church organist and taught piano as well. Her father was an architect whose particular accomplishments included designing palatial motion picture theatres in large Eastern Seaboard cities. He also was conductor of his church's choir. It was a very musical family.

Bob was already a senior when Anne enrolled. Their widely divergent backgrounds provided no barrier to a reciprocal fondness that quickly developed once they met. Bob's talents in his field, business, enabled him to find a position with McGill Manufacturing in Valparaiso. They married before Anne completed her academic requirements while she also was editing the University's yearbook. World War II disrupted any immediate plans they'd had for homemaking, as Bob was whisked off for service to his country.

The military experience helped Bob cultivate his administrative skills and upon completion of his military stint, he accepted University President O. P. Kretzmann's invitation to become the school's business manager. I still marvel at the comprehension Bob had of the entire workings of Valparaiso University. I recall one time, in later years, when we were faced with an enrollment at a summer institute that far exceeded our earlier estimates. We, in semi-panic, approached him for help. Without looking to his desk or any files, he calmly assured us that the problems were solvable. Without notes, he recited to us statistics, telling us precisely how many beds and mattresses were available in specific storage areas he named, and explained what kind of adjustments in personnel assignments would make it possible to accommodate the increased numbers we were expecting.

Several years and four little Springsteens later, our family moved to Valparaiso. We were desperately looking for a replacement for the little prefabricated house into which we had crowded — with half our furniture still in storage. A vacant lot near the University became available and, together with a special loan program of the Ford Foundation, some smaller loans from relatives, and our own meager savings, we made the purchase and contracted for erection of a home of our own. We soon discovered that our immediate neighbors, whose front door was hardly a hundred steps from our garage door, were the Springsteens.

Their own house, of their own design, was, literally, their own house. And for years after we moved in, Bob would hurry home from the university and don work clothes to resume building activities. Patiently he would lay brick upon brick. He installed electrical fixtures himself. He'd be on top of the structure, carefully laying out the roof. He would always be busy, tending to the 1,001 tasks that constitute building of a house. In the most fiercely hot weather Bob would be outside on the job, perspiration pouring down his face like a stream.

Of course, Anne would pitch in wherever she might feel useful. But rearing four children is no small assignment. And she put her magnificent talent for writing to use. Pieces she would write were so well received that it took the people at the University only the shortest time to engage her services as associate editor of the University's magazine, *The Cresset*. She worked closely with Dr. John Strietelmeier, himself a skilled writer and the *Cresset's* editor. The University's administrators were so impressed with her work that they appointed her University Editor.

Especially in mid-mornings and mid-afternoons, when our four and their four would be in school, Anne would often be at our kitchen table sipping coffee with my wife, Esther. They'd frequently be talking about things she'd been reading. If I happened to be home, I'd want to sit in on their conversations too. And she would want us to share with her, too, what we were learning as we became more and more involved in racial confrontations that were intensifying day by day.

Meanwhile, more and more people were learning of her writing and editing skills. Concordia Publishing House in St. Louis appointed her to a special literature review committee and she was asked to contribute to a collection of pieces called the *Lutheran Book of Prayer.*

Deeply spiritual, Anne was somewhat — make that *very* — disenchanted with what we'd refer to as "the formal religious language" that marked so much Christian literature. She had the knack of choosing words and turning a phrase so that conversation with God sounded as if it were coming from very human beings. And she would do this without resorting to slang and without forfeiting an appropriate dignity that attends standing in the presence of God.

A short book she wrote, *It's Me, O Lord,* won an eager audience of people who readily identified with Anne as she shared on the printed page her own simple prayers. Like this *Thanksgiving* prayer:

> *Lord,*
> *keep my mouth shut awhile.*
> *All these blessings counted,*
> *praises sung,*
> *beat with too great a noise*
> *against my inner ear*
> *and make it hard to hear.*
>
> *Lord,*
> *shut my mouth awhile.*
> *Put tongues in my hands,*
> *voices in my feet.*

Or this evening prayer she entitled *This Quiet Night:*

> *Life has come to a close, Father.*
> *I will sleep and be as close to death*
> *As I will ever willingly come.*
> *This day of grace has ended,*
> *and I know only a very little*
> *about what it all may mean*
> *for tomorrow or next year.*
>
> *But You have been with me in everything.*
> *Now I put this day aside,*

254

with everything that happened
wrapped in Your forgiveness.

Whatever this day will become
for me and others
I put in your hands.

We in the Lutheran Human Relations Association could hardly overlook such a gifted, bright, and generous friend, living so close to us — and, besides, her husband Bob was our treasurer. So we would ask her for "small" favors from time to time, like editing the printed proceedings of our annual Human Relations Institutes, and the addresses delivered there.

In 1968, when we were overwhelmed with work and underwhelmed with limited financial resources, we brazenly asked Anne to serve as unsalaried editor of our bimonthly periodical, the *Vanguard.* She loved editing, welcomed our promise to give her a free hand, and she was totally committed intellectually and spiritually to the ministry of LHRAA.

One morning she walked into my office and said, simply, "I would like to work here — whatever the pay, whatever the job." I probably looked as surprised as I actually was. I'd never even expected any turn of events like this. She went on to explain that she was seeking new ways of giving expression to the life she was eager to live for her Lord. She proved a wonderfully helpful colleague, filling the role of administrative assistant. Quietly, in a style quite her own, Anne, in soft gentle humor brought with her fresh perspectives and a spirit that inspired and enriched all of us in our ministry together.

More than carrying a crowded agenda for the Association, Anne carried heavy personal burdens. She and Bob had opened their hearts and home to Anne's mother in her final months and days, and later, to Bob's mother who carried the weight of ill health and deep unhappiness. In those days also, for one full year, they welcomed into their family circle Debby Armstrong, lovely young African American from Chicago. Sharing quarters with the two Springsteen daughters, Janet and Margaret, Debbie was able to attend Valparaiso High School, enrolled as its only non-white student.

Then in the closing days of 1974 came the devastating news of Margaret's death.

Margaret, second oldest of the children, had been high school co-valedictorian with our son Steve. She had graduated with highest honors from American College in Washington, D.C. and was now in her early days of graduate study in law at the University of Minnesota.

So bright, so unselfish, so warmly caring about the needy and victims of injustice, so considerate and thoughtful!

So suddenly.

Never could the bond of love in that family have been more evident than in that final service when we gathered to celebrate in stunned sorrow the death of Margaret. To the strains of the recessional chorale, "Jesus, Still Lead On, Till Our Rest Be Won," the worshippers rose as the family slowly made its way towards the narthex. Janet, Rob, and John appeared emotionally fatigued, their hearts torn by separation from that sweet sister. Tears streamed from Bob's eyes. And Anne — pale and exhausted, stubbornly refusing to display her heart's anguish, appeared almost expressionless.

We were to discover later that the enormity of her grief, at this moment, had been too great even for her to comprehend, let alone, interpret to others.

It was only a few weeks later that Bob's mother died too. Enough of death and funerals, Anne and Bob traveled into the far southwest to be alone, to gain new perspective in desert lands of quiet.

Some time later, when returned to their home, this loving pair could once again pick up the loosened strands of their years together. Anne invited a group of her close friends and neighbors to a room she'd had set aside at the University. Some twenty of us were there, not quite sure of what we might expect.

Anne explained briefly that in the "after Margaret" days she had, in her contemplation, taken pen in hand to write reflections on what had happened and what was going on in her mind and heart.

256

She had gathered them into a booklet, which she named *Handful of Thorns*.

In low, calm voice, Anne began to read aloud the feelings of her soul. No tears, no choking up — she read slowly, clearly, completely in control.

The rest of us, her listeners? We sat in quietness and soberness. And an occasional clearing of throats or quiet weeping. This was heavy listening. There was no quick and easy calling on the old familiar comfort passages of Scripture. No circumventing the reality of her bruised and shaken heart. No holding back her disappointment, no concealing of her anger at the God she could not help but feel had drawn away his hand of love. She wanted to assure us she had not been a brave survivor, silently bearing her cross. She spoke of going off to a lonely place and wailing there in grief. She insisted that God had left her with a handful of thorns, and journeying through grief's desert, one ultimately must realize the aloneness of that journey.

And yet in all her plaintive lines she still discerns the thread of God's constancy, concluding with the words:

> *God sits deep*
> *Deep in the marrow of my bone,*
> *A stubborn infection in my blood*
> *That I cannot shake off.*
>
> *God sits deep in my bone,*
> *Saying nothing;*
>
> *In and out of my desert*
> *We go in silence,*
> *Remembering each other . . .*
>
> *The memory of God is wide*
> *And very long*
> *For names and faces,*
> *For thorns and desert places.*

We left in quietness. How generously she had welcomed us into her most intimate privacy — as she never had, or possibly could have — in simple conversations.

Poet indeed. And teacher. Two of the maxims I learned from her:

> *Each person's death is new, different; none has ever been just like this one.*

> *People who are younger than you aren't supposed to die.*

When she was still very, very young, Anne Springsteen was distressed by a malady the doctors diagnosed as Hodgkin's Disease. She responded favorably to treatments and the condition passed into remission to free her for long years of home-making, mothering, word sculpturing, and being a wonderful neighbor and friend.

In 1985 the Hodgkin's assault returned. It was November — the Thanksgiving season, which Anne knew how to observe so well. I came to pray with her again. She had just breathed her last breath and she lay there in her pale beauty, her frail, weary frame stilled, leaving me with far more thoughts than in my prayer I might ever have brought to her.

Returning home I chose to read again a poem from her book she'd called *It's Me, O Lord!* — one which she titled "This Night":

> *I'm tired, Lord.*
> *I want to sit still and not move.*
>
> *No more meetings or questions or decisions.*
> *No more children watching me and learning.*
> *No more poor, hungry, desperate people*
> *   standing in front of me.*
> *No more friends expecting me to be and do.*

A little while ago it was different, Lord.
It was easier.
We had a comfortable, nodding acquaintance,
     You and I.
I was happy and peaceful.

But you have changed that now —
You and Your judgment,
     You and Your mercy,
     You and Your incredible love,
     You and Your tireless walking
          around the world.

I tire quickly, and I must sleep a little.

```
┌─────────────────────────────┐
│                             │
│      The Church Leader      │
│             I.              │
│    Facing a Different World │
│                             │
│                             │
└─────────────────────────────┘
```

reluctant doors

One never got the impression that becoming President of the Lutheran Church — Missouri Synod was for Oliver Harms a mark of high achievement in his career. On the contrary, he seemed to regard his election as a bestowal of a sacred trust.

I never really got to know him in any kind of social context. The occasions for our being together were either in prearranged appointments or in churchly meetings where we both happened to be in attendance.

He was a humble man, really. And very human. And exceedingly pastoral. One never sensed he was any moment not a pastor.

When I would be scheduled to meet with him, he would know well that I was going to be bringing to his attention the reluctance of the church to give full and genuine welcome to people who were non-white. In a sense then, he knew that the visit would be uncomfortable in what would likely be a confrontation.

In working with the Lutheran Human Relations Association of America, I had on several occasions met with Dr. Harms' predecessor to discuss these same issues. In those meetings the president usually had two or three others with him in the office, in a sort of defensive stance. And those meetings were usually strained, polite, and brief — and not particularly satisfying to any of the participants.

Not so with Dr. Harms. He asked if he might call me by my first name and invited me to call him "Ollie." I could never quite bring myself to do that — I couldn't quite explain it, but I felt a great reverence for the man and the way he conducted himself in his high office. When his secretary would show me in, he would rise from his chair, walk around his large desk to shake my hand. After closing the door, when we were quite alone, he would stay with me on my side of the desk, draw up a chair to give me his complete attention. With pen and pad in hand, he would ask me to share with him things he said he needed to know.

Dr. Harms' life experiences had primarily been developed in his years as a Texan. He enjoyed being teased about that. But that also implied a deep immersion in the segregating ways of the South in days when racial discrimination was not only allowed, but legally enforced.

He was not blind to the developments of the day. The Supreme Court's 1954 school desegregation decision had been a wake-up

262

call to all America that "Times, they are achangin'!" But this man's pastoral heart reached out with compassion for the people caught in the old system's web, for whom the superiority of whites had always been accepted as absolute truth. But, though he'd not had frequent concourse with non-whites, he realized more and more that those attitudes and practices could no longer be tolerated.

However, he was the head of this large church body — whose membership was predominantly white, and he felt that the church's unity must not be threatened or jeopardized by changes too swift or abrupt. This was truly a struggle for the man. Yet he never discouraged me in my ministry, and, in fact, encouraged me to help and be supportive of his ministry.

Our organization pursued every avenue possible to alert the church to its responsibilities — and its opportunities — for sharing God's grace, God's penchant for justice, God's commitment to reconciliation and peace.

Each time that church body would meet in national convention, LHRAA would present proposals for resolutions regarding the church's role in human relations. And the conventions invariably would make these formal resolutions the official position of the church.

I remember receiving a letter from Dr. Harms on one occasion, commending me for my spirit, but indicating that the general membership was not ready for drastic change. He was pleading with me, "Don't rock the boat, Karl!"

We kept on having our meetings. I remember urging him to form a special Advisory Committee to make recommendations to him in dealing with human relations issues. He appointed members of the church, representing different parts of the country, and brought them to St. Louis for a first meeting.

The members of the committee could not help but recognize and respect this man for his honesty and genuineness. Together we reviewed current human relations issues and how these in turn impinged upon the agenda of God's people. As the day wore on, the conversation drifted into discussion of practices of the national offices of the Missouri Synod. The committee learned that the Missouri Athletic Club had awarded Dr. Harms a free membership, entitling him to all its privileges. These included the right to use the Club's meeting rooms and dining services, and to lodge special overnight guests. Its facilities were quite elegant and, in addition, the Club was only a few steps away from Synod headquarters.

One of the group interjected, "Doesn't the Missouri Athletic Club have a policy of including only whites in their constituency?"

The President answered that that was indeed their practice, but most of the people with whom he met were white, so that had not been a consideration. And he did not even realize that in saying this he was acknowledging patterns of exclusiveness that had marked — make that *marred* — the practices of the Synod through the years.

Someone in our group tried to clarify the issue and remarked that this meant that *this committee* would not be invited to meet there because not all on our committee were white. Does that not imply that this group — or at least its non-white members — were not quite at the level of acceptability that "all white" committees of the church enjoyed?

That surely was not President Harms' feeling, he protested. He pressed on, observing that the people at the Club really were being very generous to him and he would not want to rebuff their kindness and the convenience they offered. He acknowledged that he would not want to convey an image of himself favoring racial exclusiveness. In fact, he indicated that by his retaining his membership, he might eventually persuade the administrators of the Athletic Club to develop a "more open policy."

He just didn't get it.

The meeting adjourned on a sadly disappointing note. And, one by one, the members submitted letters of resignation from the committee. The group disbanded.

This was tremendously disappointing to the President. It was almost as if I had given him bad advice. Yet he always had an open door, and he'd still come around to the front of his desk with pad and pen when I'd return. He desperately wanted to be an honest listener, a faithful leader.

So I made another suggestion. After all, Missouri Synod Lutherans had a far more impressive record than either of the two other major Lutheran church bodies of the time in reaching out to include African Americans into membership. Why not, I proposed, call a meeting of all pastors who served congregations with African Americans on their membership rosters? In sort of a forum they could contribute their experiences and their ideas to produce a pool of recommendations for the church's leadership in the matter of racial concerns.

Once more he agreed.

There must have been 75 or more people in attendance at this Chicago meeting. Some of these men had never before had opportunities for such a direct hearing. They were made to feel free to speak out their concerns in this forum setting.

Some of their stories revealed pain and hurt and disappointment at the behavior of certain all-white congregations and their members. Others told of obstacles that hampered their ministries, because the Church had failed them. The meeting went on for hours.

The President and his Vice President took turns chairing the sessions. They tried desperately to respond to the complaints and criticisms raised. In doing so they became defensive as they tried to explain away tensions, excusing misbehaviors and justifying inaction. In effect they unintentionally had come to take on the identity as the very culprit this group of churchworkers was criticizing.

It was a horribly demoralizing and emotionally draining experience for those leaders. So much disunity had surfaced in this confrontation — the last thing this president wanted.

When it was over, Dr. Harms said, "Karl, I'm very disappointed in you. You didn't even defend me."

I thought I had in sincerity and honesty acknowledged strong leadership in his assembling grass roots people so that they might have a hearing. But I could hardly counter the truths these people were reciting as they spoke their hearts.

I liked Dr. Harms. I was deeply disheartened that I so often found myself in what appeared to be an adversarial position.

I remember his inviting me on another occasion to "come back again." He asked me what would be the best thing he could do to give leadership to the church, without endangering its unity.

I then asked him — not in a challenging way, but intending to seek his personal reflection and assessment, "What do you see as the essential responsibilities of a church body president?"

He thought for only a short moment, and then said, "That's easy. I have to try to keep the congregations, the clergy, and the laity faithful to the Scriptures. And my second responsibility is to strengthen the unity of the organization by carrying out the by-laws and resolutions of Synod. My task is to find the most effective ways of doing all that."

His answer prompted me to propose that he authorize a printing of all the resolutions of Synod's past conventions, intended to give guidance to the churches in racial concerns. He agreed to finance the printing (as a legitimate expense of his office). Lutheran Human Relations would do the editing and actual publishing of the pamphlet, and the Synod offices would be responsible for its distribution to the leaders of all congregations.

A neat, concise, green-covered booklet came off the press shortly thereafter. It included eleven specific resolutions of the Synod. The earliest among these came from the 1956 convention; the most recent, also known as *The Mission Affirmations,* had been passed in 1965. *Lutheran Hour* Speaker Dr. Oswald C. J. Hoffmann had this to say about the production:

> *Here is the expression of the church itself, based upon the clear insight of Holy Scripture regarding one of the deeply troubling problems of this age — thrusting people apart and feeding the flames of disunity which sinister forces throughout the world are striving to keep alive.*
>
> *This brochure is published to help put into practice what we preach....*

Dr. Harms may have received a small flutter of criticism from some quarters. If he did, he never told me. He felt good about what we had done together. And I felt good.

The Church Leader
II.
Human But Full of Grace

being a doorman isn't easy

Some congregations in the South found the very idea of deseg-regation distasteful. A regional head of one of those judicatories also feared that in some instances the pressure for change was too severe, too insistent. This churchman found the activities of Pastor Joseph Ellwanger particularly troublesome. He felt that this young activist was obstructing his administrative work and compromis-ing his leadership.

This judicatory head appealed to President Harms for help. Recognizing the seriousness of the matter, yet wishing to be to-tally fair, Dr. Harms arranged for a special meeting in Birming-ham. This plaintiff, the Southern regional leader, and Pastor Ellwanger would receive a public hearing. Presidents of the two larger seminaries, editor of the Church's official paper, and other synodical leaders were to be present. Both participants in the face-off were invited to bring with them advocates who might supportively complement their presentations. Joe asked me to at-tend as his ally.

Pastor Ellwanger, who served St. Paul Lutheran Congregation in Birmingham's African American community, had been outspo-ken in his support of desegregation efforts in his city and his state. He was an officer of the Lutheran Human Relations Association of America. He had participated in demonstrations and personally helped lead a small procession of fellow whites, native to Alabama, to the Courthouse in Selma, seeking compliance with federal laws banning segregation.

His critics did more than complain about his concern for de-segregation. They attempted, in this arena of ecclesiastical leaders, to discredit his ministry. Of course he hadn't apprised his regional head of all his activities. And, as if to mount their clinching point of discreditation, they accused him of "unionism," pointing to his participating with clergyfolk of other denominations in protesting racially discriminating practices. His accusers even charged him with worshipping and praying with other-than-Lutheran people — even with Jews — in the devotional portions of civil rights gatherings.

I was really "in-raged" — I coin my own word to connote "keeping my *out*rage within." Then, in all the calmness I could muster, I requested permission to respond. I asked the audience to indulge me in a thought that had just struck me in these moments. I did not intend to be irreverent, and if what I was about to say would prove to be invalid — or in poor taste — I promised, I would never use the illustration again. This would be a first — and possibly last — time trial:

> A man was traveling from Jerusalem to Jericho, and while he was on the road some brutes attacked him and left him weak, wounded, penniless.
>
> A short while later another traveler, en route to his church's convention, spied the abandoned man lying there. Possibly recognizing the dangers of the road he stepped to the farther side of the road and hurried on.
>
> A second man, hurrying to conduct a worship service in Jericho, paused briefly and saw the hopeless figure lying there in his discomfort. He realized that to get involved might entail more than mere giving first aid. Rather than risk being late on his mission, he turned quickly, resuming his travels, determined to pray for the poor fellow in the service he'd be leading.
>
> Still a third man came along. He too saw the man lying there in his distress. Without regard for his own safety and not even considering the inconvenience, he reached into his large pouch and retrieved a small bottle of brandy and some handkerchiefs. He gently applied the liquor and washed the blood from the man's wounds, covering them with the white cloths he had now folded into bandages. With soft voice he assured the distressed man that he would not leave his side.
>
> Meanwhile, he wondered to himself, I am so short and I barely weigh 150 pounds. This poor stranger must easily push the scales to 250! I cannot hope to move him. Just then he looked up and saw another man walking toward them on the road.

As the stranger drew nearer, the man who was now holding his injured friend's head in his lap called out, "Come over here, please!"

He judged the newcomer to be about his own size and said, "Sir, this man has been badly injured, but I'm sure, with your help, we can get him atop my donkey so I can take him on to a wayside inn a little ways ahead.

Each grasped the injured man at his armpits and behind his knees. They began to lift their heavy burden. Breathing heavily, they grunted their words as they strained. The newer man asked, "This is nice of you to have stopped to help. Tell me, to what church do you belong?"

"I don't belong to any church, and I'm a card carrying communist."

Hearing that, the questioner gasped and let the wounded man slip through his hands to the ground. The other man tried as gently as possible to ease his own portion of the burden to the grass. And he commented to the other, "You know — I rather think you must be a Missouri Synod Lutheran!"

Wiping his fingers on the grass the other man replied, "Well, yes, how did you know?"

"Well, I've often heard it said that Lutherans take the Scripture verse, 'and do not be unequally yoked together with unbelievers,' with such devotion that they often ignore God's command to love the neighbor. I'm sorry if I offended you by asking your help. Go along now. I'll have to wait for someone else to come this way who will help me do something good for my neighbor, something too big for me to do alone."

No one made any comment whatever, as I recall.

Dr. Harms arose and quietly announced adjournment of the sessions until the morning.

As the session closed I hurried to Dr. Harms' side, before others could crowd him with other agendas. I asked him if he would possibly give me some time so I might introduce him to a very dear friend of mine who was eager to meet him. Always gracious, he agreed at once. After attending to a few necessary details, he gave his briefcase to a friend to take to his hotel and he came with me to meet a little blue Volkswagen Beetle that had pulled up at the curbing.

I introduced him to the driver, my friend Chris McNair, who offered to show him a little bit of Birmingham. I folded myself into the back seat and Dr. Harms tucked himself into the front seat. We didn't talk about the meeting. Instead Chris began pointing out different landmarks of the city and he offered to take us out to his house for a cup of coffee. Dr. Harms said he'd welcome that. I concurred. We were continuing on our travelogue when Chris abruptly slowed down and said, "I want to show you this, Doctor Harms." I saw the sign identifying Sixteenth Street and at once knew what Chris had in mind.

"This is the Sixteenth Street Baptist Church that was bombed. This is where my daughter Denise and her three little friends were killed." It was dark but amid headlight glare I could see Dr. Harms' face as he looked at Chris in a distressed silence. It was a long quiet. I knew he had to be recalling the night I had telephoned him and told him that one of our Lutheran members in Birmingham had experienced that ultimate in racial hatred, and how I'd supplied him with the McNairs' address so that he might express his feelings to them directly. It was all coming back now, the pieces fitting together. Finally, Oliver Harms could clear his throat and speak.

"That must have been a horrible experience for you!"

Then Chris told about his childhood days in Arkansas, how on Sundays that little brown radio in their home got all the family's

271

attention as his dad would tune in *The Lutheran Hour.* There were no Lutheran churches near where he lived, but Chris was determined that someday, wherever he might be living, if there were a Lutheran church there, he'd join it.

Oliver Harms chuckled, "And we're glad you did!"

Chris continued. "There are several churches in Birmingham but St. Paul is closest to our home and that's where I belong. There's an awful lot of segregation in Birmingham. So it was gratifying for us, on the day Pastor Ellwanger was installed as our pastor, that white Lutherans from other congregations were on hand to celebrate with us the welcoming of our new pastor. By the way, he has been a great pastor, and we are grateful to have him as our minister.

"Well, you probably heard how, on the Sunday after the bombing, Pastor Ellwanger had asked the pastors of all the Lutheran churches in the city to speak a prayer for comfort for the bereaved on the following Sunday. The proposed prayer, however, was also to include a petition of penitence, asking for forgiveness for the way we've all tolerated and condoned racial divisions that could result in something so horrible. These pastors responded as he asked. Yet, as you probably know, as a result of his leading such a prayer in his church, one of those pastors was asked to leave his church — he was put out."

Recalling this ugly confrontation, Dr. Harms shook his head in regret, agreeing with the enormity of that shame.

"Well," Chris continued, "eventually, that church seemed to have regrouped. For many of us a lot of healing had taken place, we were eager to get on with life — to have a life together in a community where decency and common sense could again have a chance.

"When I heard that that congregation was getting a new pastor, I thought to myself, why shouldn't I take the first step in showing I have no anger, no malice towards those people? I want to rejoice with them as they begin a new chapter of their lives.

"So that Sunday afternoon I got into my little bug and drove toward their church. As I came close I saw a sign outside that identified it as *The Church of the Lutheran Hour.* That already made me feel good. I found a little space where my car would fit in near the

272

front of the church. Before I could even climb out of my seat, two men who'd been standing in front dashed over to the car and said, 'What are you doing here? You're going to spoil everything!'

"Now *that* really hurt deeply, Doctor Harms!"

By this time we had turned into the drive at the McNairs'. Everything about the house seemed very new. Our host invited us into the living room. He disappeared for a moment and then returned to tell us that his wife had not been feeling well and had therefore already retired. He would prepare some coffee.

He turned the lights up and stepped into the kitchen. Dr. Harms and I started looking at all the walls, pictures of Denise of course, along with a message of condolence from the President of the United States. There were framed communications from other notables and among them, a letter from the Lutheran Church — Missouri Synod, signed by Oliver Harms. He was obviously grateful to see it displayed so prominently.

Then Chris called me to come into the kitchen. He asked me if I would hold his tiny daughter, who had awakened, while he finished preparing the coffee. I took the sweet infant and rejoined Dr. Harms and handed him the child, explaining that this was the gift that God had given the McNairs to help them in their sorrow. Would he mind holding her a bit while I would help Chris? And I left the two alone. Of course Chris didn't need me. And after a bit the child started to murmur and Chris took the little one back to lie aside her mother.

And we drank coffee. There wasn't much more to say.

Next morning the sessions resumed. I cannot really recall with any precision just how the meeting ended. But it seemed clear to me that there was a new sense of urgency and clarity of purpose reflected in the way Dr. Harms conducted and concluded the meeting. He did not once mention the night before. I believe for him it had been a deeply personal, a holy moment.

———————

It had been the custom in the Lutheran Church — Missouri Synod for convention assemblies to re-elect, term after term, its president, until either death or the impairments of aging required replacement.

Until the time of Oliver Harms.

Dr. Harms presided during a time of great change. He endeavored to guard that church against interior crumbling. But he was equally committed to prevent its failure to meet the challenges that a changing world imposed. This called for alterations and adaptations, changes in program, structure, and also in relationship with other Christian ministries.

Some disgruntled clergy found allies in a few influential laypersons and they organized a campaign to discredit the President and his staff. In a kind of shrewd manipulation, not previously observed in the Synod's history, delegates were found who could be — and *were* — instructed how to vote.

Quite unprepared — and unwilling — to resort to political machinations in order to counter this movement, President Harms chose to address the issue in his regular column in his church body's periodical, *Lutheran Witness*. He wrote in his customary gentle style his word of response.

In the article he lamented that people were hearing — and believing — rumors that Oliver Harms had changed.

He pleaded with readers to realize that he was the same Oliver Harms who had been baptized and confirmed as a child, the same excited boy who began his studies for the ministry, the same young man who had been Pastor of Trinity Lutheran Church in Houston, Texas. He explained that he was still trying to be faithful to the Lord to whose service he had committed himself. He still was devoted — and to no lesser degree — to serving that Lord. And he gave an account of his unchanged faith. He insisted that He had not *changed*.

But, he noted, he had been *growing*; and he had not yet stopped growing; and he hoped people would know that none of us are ever to stop growing, in learning, understanding, and in our capacity to serve God more and more faithfully in God's changing world.

Not many months later, in a convention in Denver, an instructed majority of delegates cast their votes early in the sessions to unseat Oliver Harms. He was deeply hurt. But he was not vindictive. He was very gracious. So much so that some of the delegates who now were able to hear and watch this kindly gentleman as he chaired the meeting, wondered aloud why ever they had been persuaded to vote him out. If given opportunity, now that they had observed his wise and evenhanded presiding, they would surely have voted for his re-election.

I've not found an overabundance of people who are truly humble and yet stand exceedingly tall. Oliver Harms was one.

The Large Tall Man
I.
Opening of Eyes

---

replacing frosted door windows

When Andrew, my mentor and colleague, returned from his trip to northern Minnesota, he was bursting with excitement. He had accepted an invitation to a meeting of clergy and other church workers who were serving residents on Indian reservations. He pointed to the tall hurdles these workers faced as they were dealing with a people whose history for decades had been marked by poverty and oppression.

He lamented the low priority the church community assigned to the issues involved, and how frustrating — though enlightening — this exposure had been for him. It was clear that the stories he heard from Indians varied little in essence from the kind we'd been hearing from African American voices during all our years of ministry.

Then he added, "Karl, since I'm going to be spending much time on writing in the months ahead, and since these people could very well benefit from learning of our experiences and procedures, I'm asking you to take the responsibility of offering our services to them."

At the time I was enrolling, organizing, and coordinating the work of 42 LHRAA chapters across the country, developing and teaching new courses at the University, and trying to support individuals in racial confrontations, especially in the South. However, an overloaded schedule had never deterred Andrew from taking on new challenges as they arose, so I agreed to do my best — as he surely would have.

At my first meeting with the group I was at once impressed with the commitment and dedication of these people, but a bit troubled that the discussion focused on attending to the symptoms of disarray in the lives of Native Americans, rather than root causes and problems. One such item prompted an expanded discussion of working through ways in which a family might deal with a father's drinking problem.

In a subsequent meeting we moved into the more basic theological problem of exploring possibilities for grounding this ministry. We focused on the Scriptural mandate calling for the whole Christian community to exercise a vital, loving concern for *all* the people of God's world.

Some voices proposed that we organize into a chapter of the Lutheran Human Relations Association of America, since that organization was already in full operation, helping Christians as they encounter discriminatory exclusiveness. Furthermore, LHRAA, like our group, was "pan-Lutheran" and free of some of the official institutional limitations that often encumbered other ministries.

Of course, decided advantages would accrue from such a merger. I was obliged to tell them, however, that the impending racial turmoil surfacing in so many places in the country might pre-empt so much of LHRAA's agenda, that its offices might not be able to devote the kind of energy and rigorous attention that current Native American issues deserve. The increased occurrence of protests and demonstrations and other interracial confrontations would be absorbing so much of LHRAA's focus in the immediate months ahead that the concerns of the American Indian community might easily become marginalized and shaded from view because of the front-page prominence black/white issues would have generated.

I was eager that they realized that the matter of Indian concerns needed to be brought directly to the attention of the church, its leaders, and its members. If we did not have a voice of our own, raised with clarity and persistence, our message might surely be smothered or ignored.

Most of the early meetings were with church workers who may well have had the prayers of the church — but not the ears. Also there'd be a mere handful of Lutheran Indians present for our meetings. For the most part, these people were appreciative of their Lutheran Church, but — probably for a lot of reasons — were somewhat passive in their participation in our discussions. I remember one of these meetings when only one Indian was present. More and more, we came to realize that, as usual, a few clergy were doing most of the talking. That might have been expected — most who were there were ministers. There was no intent to stifle or to usurp the Native American voice, yet we simply weren't tuned in to hearing any.

We resolved to remedy that situation and make it possible for such voices to be heard. We organized. As if to ensure that our role in this arrangement would be that of listener and learner, we named our organization, *Lutheran Church and Indian People,* (LuChIP) consciously and intentionally anticipating that some of the Indian voices that deserved hearing, necessarily, might not be Lutheran.

By this time stirrings on the black/white scene in the country were spilling into the church. In LHRAA we were busy addressing the Lutheran Church — Missouri Synod in its national convention, proposing resolutions that identified practices and policies which ran counter to the Gospel and recommending remedial actions. We LHRAA staffers were off addressing regional conventions of the Lutheran church bodies. We were meeting highest officers of the church bodies. We were running to different cities to support courageous people who were harassed and threatened because of their stands on justice and concern for all God's people.

Besides all this, my Valparaiso University President was asking me to devise an exchange program with Miles College, (a member of the American Negro Colleges) and Dr. Lucius Pitts, President of Miles, to arrange for my teaching there on a part time basis, taking northern students to Birmingham for a week. In return, I was to bring Miles students to our Chicago area for lectures and a week's study of conditions in the North.

Those responsibilities really were enough to warrant my full time attention and to justify my backing off from LuChIP, which was increasingly asking for a greater slice of my schedule and energies.

However, the more I became involved with Indian concerns, the more convinced I became of their neglect and their urgency. I found myself intrigued and excited about possibilities, so when asked whether I'd chair LuChIP, I quickly agreed.

Only a short time later a Minnesotan in our LuChIP circle, Ms. Twila Osborn, brought to a meeting in Sioux Falls, South Dakota, two non-Lutheran Indians. They were to serve as resource persons for a planning session. The two, Al Wensman of the Twin Cities and Charlie Deegan from Chicago, proved particularly helpful in our task. Pastor Walter Weber of Sioux Falls, (probably the most knowledgeable and best-informed Lutheran churchman in the matter of Indian concerns relative to the churches at the time) joined us in a committee of five to draw up a slate of possible invitees to a larger meeting. Purpose of the planned event: to make possible a conversation between church leaders and people in the Indian world.

With so many tribal backgrounds from which to choose, and such a wide variety of perspectives, we necessarily leaned heavily on committeemen Wensman and Deegan to nominate Native American invitees. Once that roster was completed we would have to contact church leaders who would agree to attend, leaders whose organizational resources might be tapped to underwrite the expenses of Indians invited to participate. We could hardly expect these representatives of the Native American world to pay their own way to perform a service *we* were requesting.

The plans materialized in an assembly held at Augustana College in Sioux Falls in 1969. I was to serve as chairperson, supported by a hard working LuChIP Board that had helped make most of the arrangements for the event.

We were elated. Church leaders had taken us seriously and agreed to underwrite the costs. Executive officers from all major Lutheran church bodies were on hand and lay organizations were represented by their leaders too.

The meeting room was a large one. It was almost filled. There must have been almost fifty Indians present. Among these were a sizable representation from the American Indian Movement (AIM), a group just coming into its own with chapters in different parts of the country. Most were probably in their twenties and thirties, articulate and outspoken, and beginning to be known more and more for their disruptive, confrontational style.

Though some of the Indians who came were Lutheran, other denominations were represented as well. Some who came belonged to no church at all — some sought to find a faith in the spiritual traditions of their forebears.

This was not the type of meeting any in the room — white Lutherans or Native Americans — had ever experienced before. The atmosphere was one of almost nervous expectancy. What now would be happening? What would be said?

The Large Tall Man
II.
Confrontation

directing doorway traffic

Everyone in the room had a printed copy of the agenda the committee had prepared.

My opening words referred them to the agenda, slowly — intentionally so. I'm not sure people realized I was stalling, hoping to set the stage for what happened next. Finally, key leaders in AIM, Dennis Banks and his partner, Clyde Belcourt, came to stand between me and the microphone (I'd witnessed such "takeovers" in other protests and more than half way was expecting something like this — I thought at first they'd never come!) In angered tones they said that this was as it always is. "When whites meet with Indians they always bring their own agenda. Well," they said, adding a few colorful words of their own, "we're supposed to be here as your guests. This time we're going to decide for ourselves what we're going to say to you. So now we are going to have a caucus just for ourselves. When we're ready, we'll come back and talk to you."

En masse, all the Indians in the room exercised solidarity and rose to follow to the caucus. The whites were aghast — and not a little offended — at such conduct, and were quite at a loss as they emptied the room and we were left behind.

Almost a straggler, as the last to leave, a very tall gentleman turned toward us who were still sitting there. He had a parting word for us. A man up in years, he was himself a Lutheran, as I recall. He stopped, turned slowly toward us and began speaking. He told how in his early years he had been a truck driver. Then he said, "I noticed that, as our young friends spoke, some of you seemed shocked at their language and some of the words they used. I wasn't shocked. I've known words like that for a long time, but I don't choose to use them. Some people use them when they're at a loss for words to say what's heavy on their hearts."

He concluded, adding, "By the way — I know several Indian languages and there is no Indian equivalent for some of the words they used. We simply don't have those words — so, you see, they must have learned them from white people." And quietly he left.

There was edginess and lots of fidgeting among the abandoned white Lutherans. I tried to answer their disturbed questions (with dubious profundity):

"Where are they going?"

"I don't know — somewhere off to themselves."

"When are they coming back?"

"I don't know — likely when they've decided how and what they wish to tell us."

"Well, what are we supposed to do now?"

"We can have our own caucus and decide what kind of questions we'd like answered. Or we can go out for a walk. Or go to our rooms and read. Or we can just visit with each other."

"Well then, what time should we back here again?"

"There's no way of knowing; but we should be here and ready whenever they do come back."

As hours passed some of the church leaders were clearly miffed. Some called the experience rude and demeaning; others, a horrible waste of time they could be putting to far better use if they hadn't come. Yet everyone there was intrigued by it all and curious about how the situation would be resolved.

A particularly moving moment occurred that evening when we finally reassembled. Eddie Benton arose somewhat hesitantly, and unsure, made his way to the front. He appeared to be speaking with great difficulty. There, at the microphone, he began speaking slowly and very softly. We strained to hear him, and I remember whispering to him, "Eddie, are you okay?" He nodded, cleared his throat and continued his eloquently simple account of his own personal experiences from childhood through the present.

Lights had been dimmed in the room and the audience was totally absorbed in the moment, no whispering or coughing or shuffling of chairs. He himself was so absorbed in the telling of his story that he would pause occasionally, as if he'd not be able to continue. He was almost overwhelmed in his recall of incidents that, already in his childhood, had crushed his spirit, that saw his parents shamed by the crude behavior of arrogant whites, and impoverished by a systematized degradation devised, implemented, and enforced by a government that hailed itself the land of the free, with justice for all. He wept as he told of friends of his younger days who, with high ideals, had enlisted in the military, only to experience insult and abuse and, in some cases, battlefield injuries and even death in loyalty to their country.

He told of the disillusionment of some of those young friends who had lost all sense of self worth and slipped into the grip of alcoholism. And his voice, almost empty now, lamented the doubtful future of little Indian children.

When he returned to his seat, the room was heavy with sober quietness and we all slipped out to our rooms. No more needed saying.

In the next day's session — which of course began when the Indian contingent decided to arrive — Indians asked official church leaders to report and give an account of what their respective church bodies were currently doing to address the needs of America's Indian community.

This in itself was a strange request. Church officials would readily acknowledge their accountability to the government and to the church bodies and contributing members — but to people who would be beneficiaries of their services?

Arnold Tiemeyer of the Lutheran Church in America spoke first and acknowledged how painful it was for him to admit that compared to the enormous needs, his church, to its shame, had done virtually nothing.

The Indians who had raised the challenge felt his comments vindicated their claim that the church had failed them.

Jim Cross spoke for the Missouri Synod, pointing out that his church's efforts had been so pitifully few that they didn't deserve mention in the face of needs not yet attended and tasks not even begun. The challengers welcomed that admission too.

Then Russell Helgesen rose. He was the American Lutheran Church's staff person assigned to monitor and coordinate his church body's activities in ministering among Native Americans. He had carefully done his homework. Anticipating the opportunity of reporting to this assembly on the ALC's involvement in these ministries, he had assembled a full and detailed account of his church's expenditures in the area of Indian concerns. The report shamed the poor performance described by the two previous speakers. Literally, the ALC had spent thousands of dollars, much of it — probably most of it — designated to support pastors and workers serving Indian congregations.

That was all that the militant ones present needed in order to launch a tirade against white people and their penchant for writing the agenda for Indian people. Almost relentlessly, one voice after another spoke out, charging that whites and white dominated institutions — churches too — always have had to exercise control. Without consulting the Indian community, whites through the years have unabashedly decided what Native Americans' needs were and with shameless arrogance have ranked priorities among these needs as *they* determined how any kind of funding be distributed or spent on behalf of Indians. And, they insisted, this style has prevailed, because — of course — whites felt sure they were better able to make such decisions.

Poor Russell! The Church with the least bad record became the target for a devastating verbal clobbering. There really wasn't much dialog. The mode was pretty much one of "We talk; you listen!"

Before the conference adjourned, the Indians emerged from their caucus with a list of challenges to the Lutheran Church bodies. The Church officials who had come responded somewhat positively, but somewhat warily. After all they were hardly in a position to make commitments for their churches. They were not vested with such authority. They begged for more time, since many of the issues raised would call for decisions by boards and different offices and would also involve the meeting of different church heads with each other.

In the view of many present (white Lutherans too), however, their response was lame and evasive.

In effect, the Indians said, "We'll give you one year."

———————

The second convening, in 1970 — again at Augustana College in Sioux Falls — significantly outdrew the previous summer's event. Registrations exceeded the 300 mark, and more than 200 of the conferees represented dozens of tribes and Indian organizations from as distant places as California, Florida, New Mexico and Alaska.

Stories about the previous year's gathering had made the rounds in the Indian world and piqued the interest of people eager to learn more about what had been such a momentous experience.

Prime concern of this second meeting: what had the churches done to respond to the *Challenges* submitted last summer? These had called for the following items to be placed on the Lutheran agenda:

> Establish a "national board of Indian concern" for the church, three fourths of its members as well as its chairperson to be Indian;
>
> Pledge commitment (by that board and the Lutheran Churches) to support Indians in determining their own needs, priorities, and appropriate programs and actions;
>
> Designate a contribution of 7.5 million dollars by Lutheran Churches over a ten year span, supporting programs and projects designated by Indian Americans; and
>
> Lend church support to legislation beneficial to Indian Americans.

LuChIP's new president, Larry Martin, a Chippewa from Minnesota, chaired the session and invited the conferees to respond, to speak their hearts. For the most part their remarks reflected bitter dissatisfaction and disappointment. Women and men alike rose to tell of anger growing among their people and among tribal communities they were representing here. They cited instances of abuses and injustice, broken promises, procrastination by government and other institutions. And they were offended by the ignorance, paternalism, apathy, and duplicity that have characterized the churches' relationships with Indian Americans.

There were voices that threatened to disengage from the entire conversation because church people had not taken them seriously during the year that had elapsed since the previous summer's meeting.

More measured voices conceded that, indeed, far less had been accomplished than hoped. Yet, they reasoned that the amount of time, energy, and self already invested in our effort to achieve meaningful conversation deserved more than walking away from its possibilities at this time.

The assembled participants themselves voted into being a "National Indian Conference." The structure provided for a total roster of 24 members. Six were to be selected by reservation representatives. Six were to be chosen by urban Indians. Six more were to be selected by Indian youth — three of these to be from urban communities, three from reservations. The final six were to be persons elected by Lutheran conferees (two of the six elected for this category were themselves Indian Lutherans).

The organizing of this structure proved a useful, constructive development. The success of the process itself hinted at the inherent potential in this action. Clearly what had happened held promise for future collaboration.

It was then that the conferees addressed the touchy subject of financial contributions by the churches. Setting aside the "ten year proposal," the conference pressed for immediate commitment, for this calendar year, to allocation of $750,000 from the three major church bodies, asking that a show of good faith be given within 90 days.

The idea of confronting a church body or its leaders with an ultimatum was, to say the least, novel. No great imagination would be required to anticipate the resentment and resistance this kind of presentation would generate.

Those among the Lutherans present, who knew even the slightest about finance proceedings in the church bodies, could quickly grasp what an audacious move this was, and how great the unlikeliness of its implementation. Nonetheless, the church executives that were with us promised they would present the challenges as effectively as possible to the appropriate respective church leaders. Hearing those pledges of commitment, the conferees chose to adjourn.

Well, most did.

Forty-two, who were more militant, were skeptical. They wanted no part in waiting till next year, only to hear then that the churches wouldn't have quite found themselves ready to respond as had been hoped.

So, while other conferees were carrying their suitcases to their cars, these forty-two gathered themselves in Augustana's Bergsaker Hall. They locked the doors with chains, declaring their intent to remain there, day and night. They vowed not to leave until they could be assured that their newly elected Board would immediately receive official recognition by the churches, and, in turn, be entrusted with the responsibility for administering the $750,000 to be allocated for the concerns of Indian people.

Obviously, the churches were not used to this kind of procedure, and, amid pouting and injured feelings, leaders were faced with an altogether new problem in the matter of church administration. And many insisted, "We simply cannot do this."

Close colleague of mine in all this, Pastor Walt Weber, then LuChIP's Executive Secretary, offered this perspective:

> *"This 'lock-in' ought be seen as the willingness on the part of these people — after all of their bitter experiences with white people, government, and other institutions — still to take the church seriously, to give it a chance to show the genuineness of its preachments."*

The Large Tall Man
III.
Churchly Response

---

squeezing a church through a door

To the credit of the Lutheran Churches, in earlier days its leaders had ingeniously established a new structure designed to explore and employ ways of collaborating to meet opportunities for service. Not only did this new Lutheran Council — USA help to eliminate duplication of expenditures and efforts, it also prevented neglect of needs that might have resulted, should one of those churches have presumed erroneously that either one or both of the other churches already might be attending to that particular issue.

Even in all the efforts that preceded the Augustana College meetings, LCUSA staff persons were already providing much help in convening, structuring, and helping to cover the costs of these conferences. And how fortunate that LCUSA stood ready to help in this instance!

President Balcer and his Augustana College had been gracious hosts to us on many occasions, and certainly in these two major gatherings. However, he was faced with the beginning of another academic year. He needed every bit of time available in the next few days to prepare for the arrival of students. The buildings needed readying — the usual cleaning and painting attention. With the takeover of a residence hall, he was hardly experiencing any gratitude in return for the hospitality Ausgustana had provided.

LCUSA immediately dispatched staffer Osgood Magnuson to South Dakota. He, with LuChIP's Walt Weber, coordinated the sequence of steps required to resolve the deadlock. LCUSA convened the church body presidents, presumably by conference calls. These leaders could readily empathize with President Balcer's predicament and set themselves to some constructive planning. The recognition of the new national Indian board was a troublesome hurdle logistically, but not insurmountable.

LCUSA agreed to create a staff position, to be called an "Indian Desk."

Probably most fortuitous of all was the suggestion of Dr. Martin Poch who headed the LCMS office of World Relief. He reported that an extraordinarily generous response by Missouri Synod Lutherans to an Alaska disaster had resulted in a surplus amount that presently lay unused. I do not remember the exact figure but it was significantly high enough to almost guarantee LCMS's contribution to the $750,000 figure. Presidents Robert Marshall (LCA) and David Preus (ALC) were encouraged by this development and indicated their intent to seek similar support.

It remained only therefore to report that kind of news to those who had been holding the dormitory hostage. When they heard the news, they felt great gratification, unlocked the doors, returned Bergsaker Hall to Dr. Balcer, and left for their homes.

By now it had become increasingly difficult to coordinate, manage, and control all the activities that our meetings and actions had generated over an almost nine year span. The accomplishments had been significant, but had resulted almost entirely from the devoted efforts of volunteers. We could no longer rely solely on volunteers to build on and to sustain the momentum achieved thus far.

What had finally been born on Augustana's campus was now going to need full time attention. The person charged with this assignment would have to interpret Indian needs, feelings, and experiences to a church community that was woefully uninformed. The task called for helping people in pulpit and in pew to see ways of exercising the concept of Christian family as it pertains to their Native American brothers and sisters. It would be necessary to try to make Lutherans worthy of Indians' trust in church people, trust that repeatedly had been shaken or shattered through the years. And there'd have to be meetings with Lutherans of different groupings that had often shown distrust for one another.

The conferences had made it strikingly clear that any one who would be assigned to the "Indian Desk" should indeed be a Native American. And this person would have to be someone Indians themselves would deem trustworthy.

To find such a person would indeed be a large, tall order.

However, those who had met at Augustana could recall one person, a rather large, tall man, who, though he didn't speak often, spoke with considered thoughtfulness and logic. His words manifested sensitivity to others. His comments were marked by wisdom and warm humor. He was fiftyish, a member of the Sisseton Sioux Tribe, and he was the Director of the Omaha Indian Center in Nebraska.

Eugene Crawford was the son of an ordained Presbyterian minister. His wife Evelyn, an elementary school principal in Omaha, was of northern European heritage. Her family had deep roots in the Danish Lutheran tradition.

Gene was LCUSA's choice. Of course, LCUSA told the 24 member Indian Board that the ultimate selection would be theirs. Some in the group took exception to rubber stamping a white institution's decisions, or, in this case, appointment. When other names were proposed for the post however, one suggestion after the other prompted responses that took exception to these nominations. In each instance voices would cite these nominees' inadequacies, lack of experience or credentials, or tainted political connections. At length, the group agreed that no other person nominated quite measured up to Gene Crawford and his qualifications.

I was one of the four on the National Board whom Gene with good humor referred to as "our blue eyes members." I thought I had been well informed on Indian issues, and probably I did understand things more clearly than many other folk in our churches did. However, my very earliest conversations with Gene Crawford revealed how close I was to kindergarten level in comprehending the full range and complexities of Native American concerns.

I remember that at almost all the gatherings I'd attended through the years I would feel a bit uncomfortable as I sensed that people who hadn't known me regarded me with uncertainty and suspicion, wondering whether I could be trusted. I never felt that way in Gene's presence. His stance always seemed to say, "I really don't know much, if anything, about you. But there's a lot to do. Let's see if we can find ways to get at what's before us and do it together — as soon as possible."

Gene was clearly a "take charge" sort of person, but while he'd be offering clear assessment of situations and suggesting practical

294

strategies for response, people working with him neither felt trampled nor undervalued for their input.

Already at the first organizational meeting we discussed choice of a name for our board. Almost everyone agreed that since we were functioning collaboratively with the Lutheran Churches, the name Lutheran should be included. On the other hand because most board members were not Lutherans we should not be called a Lutheran Indian board, we'd be more accurate in naming ourselves the National Indian Lutheran Board.

There was something a bit heady about realizing that we 24 were to be entrusted with the responsibility of distributing a very large sum of money. An unusual perspective surfaced already in our preliminary deliberations. There was a clear awareness about our accountability in this role of awarding funds. Uniquely, we were less concerned with a need to answer to the churches for how we would distribute "*their* money" than feeling conscience bound to be accountable to the Indian world, to divide what had been entrusted to us for addressing the needs of all Native Americans.

Most of us who were Lutherans on the Board took on the role of listener and learner, as the lively discussion by our colleagues tried to develop guidelines for the award granting process to ensure fairness and prevent abuse. Rules we imposed on ourselves originally included these provisions:

- Proposals will be considered only if submitted by organizations with a Native American executive officer and whose board membership has a Native American majority.
- No grants shall exceed $4,000.
- Progress reports on expenditures and project development are to be made quarterly.
- No second grant will be awarded till first grant is used.
- Other stipulations were no less rigid. The group was determined to see to it that these funds would be managed to achieve maximum and optimum results for Indian people.

So conscientiously did the Board pursue this concern that, with Gene's guidance, they would actually seek out smaller groups with particularly burdensome needs. We would help them plan an appropriate project and help them prepare a proposal to insure its implementation.

The Indian Desk was to get the word out so that eligible applicants might submit their proposals before the Board's next meeting.

When NILB members next assembled, Gene Crawford entered the room with his very capable assistant, Shirley Canchola. She held in her hand a carefully organized stack of several dozen proposals. Gene commented that some of them had been submitted by organizations to which our Board members belong. He noted too that there was nothing wrong with that, because all the projects listed for support seem both valid and appropriate, and the rules established for submitting proposals had been followed.

Some Board members expressed their personal discomfort in the possibility of criticism of NILB as giving preferential treatment to its own members. A further uneasiness surfaced as, after two hours of deliberating, we'd not yet dealt with two thirds of the proposals, and the rest of our agenda hadn't yet been even touched.

The Board accepted a suggestion by Gene that the Board delegate the task of awarding grants to a committee of four, composed of one reservation person, another from the urban category, a third from the Youth group, and one of the Lutherans would be the fourth. Each of the groupings selected its own representative.

We on the new committee worked late into the night on our assignment and were able to report before the next day's adjournment so that the entire Board might review our work. They were obviously pleased and voted unanimously to affirm and ratify our decisions, parceling out thousands of dollars to tribes and organizations that had submitted requests to support their programs.

More and more we discovered qualities in Gene that equipped him so well for his role.

Whether in formal meeting (and he had the good grace of bringing an informality to these) or in personal conversation he'd always be bringing information to us about happenings (he would often say, "in Indian Country"). He must have maintained a thousand or more contacts who kept him updated. He would have true-life stories that kept us from forgetting troubled lives and he would provide insight into the emotional struggles of people.

One sensed also that there were people with especially fine minds, experienced, skilled, and wise with whom he would consult and on whom he would draw. He pursued a continued self-assessment so that his performance would always be the best. And yet, he would appear disarmingly casual and relaxed, so people could feel comfortable, as he'd begin his conversations with them.

And what a complex audience was his. There were church body and regional area leaders. There were country parsons and pastors of big suburban parishes and college and seminary professors. There were people immersed in Native American history and others who'd never before spoken to an Indian.

And there were people from reservations and some who lived in cities and some who maintained their tribal ties and others who left all that behind. There were militants and conservatives, people who returned to Native Religion and others who stoutly rejected such practice.

When Gene was engaged for his task, probably no one articulated for him the range of people to be influenced by his work.

A self-effacing person, Gene would chuckle, "Some people they call doctor, some president, some executive director. Me? Me they call 'Desk!' I'm the Indian Desk!"

Gene knew full well the vital role he was filling. He would begin what might appear to be a light, casual conversation over coffee and the head of a church body would unknowingly become a student. And Gene would walk away with a promise of program funds, or an invitation to address a national convention, or at the very least, a word of affirmation, encouragement, and assurance of support.

Gene would be a bit apprehensive when meeting with church leaders because almost always they would be interested in learning whether there were any results of improved relations between church and Native Americans — and specifically, were any joining the Lutheran churches.

Gene would have a simple but graphic way of responding. He repeatedly said that his concern was to help church people know and understand Native Americans, and to make possible communication between the two groups. He then explained, "Your concern is more with altar, candlesticks, and hymnbooks. That's not my area of proficiency; that's for the church to attend to."

————————

Gene spent a lot of time on the road. And on the phone. And on the job. One could never get the idea that his intense concern for people and particularly Native American matters was ever pushed to some distant corner of his mind. And few people in the Lutheran Churches ever came to realize how his ministry had helped thousands of Indian people to recognize Lutherans as friends.

I would love hearing his voice when I'd answer my phone. Invariably he would want to enlist me for some task or other. I never dreaded that. It was an honor to work with him. And gratifying. When I'd leave, I always felt something significant had been accomplished.

In the late hours that would follow those first meetings, most of them in Minneapolis, when all the others had finally disbanded, Gene and I would often resort to the Coffee Shop. Gene was always willing to have us stay at the former Curtis Hotel, because he knew I liked strawberries and the Curtis Coffee Shop served fresh strawberries all year round.

Some of the conversation would deal with facets of his work that didn't get into the formal reports. On one occasion he told how funds we had awarded a tribal group in Nebraska had gone to purchase from the U. S. Army a recreation center being dismantled at a nearby camp. The recipients had only to lay a foundation for installing the facility; the Corps of Engineers would transport the building to the site and place it on the footing.

While in transit, the engineers encountered a blizzard that prevented them from advancing any farther on their mission. So they left the building there on wheels, at the side of the road, until the rigors of winter would subside. Weeks passed and the snow and cold persisted with severity.

The reservation people who lived nearby found their own fuel supply low, and some entered the abandoned building and removed a few boards for firewood. Some other neighbors did the same, taking out just a little, piece by piece.

When the snow finally melted and the engineers could resume their project, they attached their tractor to ease their trailer from the road's shoulder. The frame started creaking and groaning and suddenly the walls, roof and all collapsed, because all supporting timbers had been removed.

Gene said, "You know, it's really a pathetic story and sort of funny too; but I can't tell people that that's how some of the money the churches gave was wasted."

I reminded him that it's okay to concede our humanness and our capacity to make mistakes. But I also suggested that maybe more good came from the warming of little children in their homes than might have been derived from a recreation center.

He would want to hear about my ministry, and together we'd plan how we might collaborate with and support each other. I'd do writing and other chores for him — he'd come and speak to my classes and to assemblies at the University.

———————

More and more in Indian Country the name Lutheran was being spoken with respect, as a community of church folk who wanted to prove themselves genuinely involved in exploring answers to the question raised in the Scriptures, "Who is my neighbor?"

Some of that was lost when the Lutheran Church — Missouri Synod chose to sponsor its own ministry with Native Americans withdrawing from LCUSA and brought the Council and NILB to an end.

So many leaders, like Sol Bird Mockicin, Sid Beane, Ramona Rank, Paul Schultz, Vine Deloria, Floyd (Red Crow) Westerman, Rose Robinson, Joan Bordman, Larry Martin, Marilyn Sorenson-Bush, LaDonna Harris, Marlene Whiterabbit Helgemo, Cecil Corbett, and literally dozens more gave so much of their time, their expertise, their wisdom, and their very selves to the formation of

NILB and its ministry. Though many of these themselves were not Lutheran, they helped give the Lutheran community a reputation as a credible ally to Native Americans. To permit NILB to disappear from the scene so cavalierly has surely tarnished that image, and detracted from the rich contribution Gene Crawford made — and was — to us. When Missouri made its decisions to disassociate with NILB, probably little thought — if, indeed, any at all — was given to the possibility that people of the Indian community might regard the step as a rude discourtesy and an utter lack of gratitude for these people's contributions and services.

Many Lutherans never did become aware of this bright moment in Lutheran history that came with Eugene Crawford. He stood large and tall.

It was a good while before his death in 1986 that Gene called to tell me that he was so impressed with what the Lutherans had done with Indian Concerns since his arrival on the scene in 1971. He wanted to be a part of that church and he had become a Lutheran now himself.

Long before, I had learned that this mentor and friend was a brother of mine in faith. I keep remembering him with gratitude and with a warm joy.

The Young Bishop

so many doors

In the early 1980s, Valparaiso University's president, Dr. Robert Schnabel, added to my teaching responsibilities the appointment to the position of Director for Church Relations. In the administrative structure the position was fit into the Division of Public and Alumni Affairs. A particularly advantageous aspect of that arrangement called for my attendance at the meetings of the Alumni Board of Directors.

At one of these meetings the chairman, as was customary, asked for nomination of candidates to be honored by the University for special citation. Year after year we would recognize former students whose record reflected favorably on the University. Awardees of past years had included people of a wide variety of careers. I could not recall, however, that the citation had ever been awarded a member of the clergy.

When, therefore, the name before us for consideration was the Right Reverend Craig Barry Anderson, the group's response revealed an arched eyebrow sort of puzzlement. Valparaiso University has often been referred to as the "Lutheran University" — not that all who attended or taught there were necessarily Lutheran. And besides, Valparaiso was not a seminary. Its founders had intended this school to prepare young men and women for roles of service in their respective careers and communities as responsible Christian citizens.

So each question raised received due attention. Yes, he was a member of the clergy of the Episcopal Church. Yes, he had attended Valparaiso University, class of '63. Yes, he had indeed been recognized in his field — and had been appointed Bishop of his Church's South Dakota Diocese, currently youngest of all its bishops. Duly impressed in their learning about Bishop Anderson, as more of his virtues and achievements were rehearsed, the Board unanimously and enthusiastically chose him to receive its citation of honor.

The Board also felt that in presenting the award to the young bishop in South Dakota, we would be letting people of his area know about Valparaiso University and the respect this young man's peers and this school had for him.

302

Admittedly, staff members regarded travelling to other parts of the country as offering more excitement than Sioux Falls, South Dakota. My colleagues happily were altogether agreeable to my offer to represent the University and its Alumni Board in making the award presentation. After all, I had been one of Craig Anderson's teachers and I welcomed the opportunity to be meeting with him again after all these years.

It was a wonderful meeting, that Saturday evening I arrived. The Andersons warmly welcomed me. We dined. We talked. Barry was eager to be brought up to date on happenings at his alma mater. He especially wanted to hear about two of his favorite Valpo profs — Dean Tuttle and Willis Boyd. And I had question after question for him, asking what had been happening with him in the days since he'd left Valparaiso.

He recounted events of his life-after-Valpo, about his studying for the ministry in Tennessee, about his serving as a campus pastor, and how in his more recent years he had come to South Dakota as Bishop.

He surprised me with statistics that pointed to the high number of Episcopal Congregations in South Dakota located on Indian Reservations. This also accounted for the large number of Native Americans in the state who were Episcopalian.

The young bishop himself had been studying the Lakota language. This made it possible for him to engage in communication with the Native American community — especially its older citizenry. It demonstrated how genuinely serious he was about giving expression to the unity that must surely be pursued by any Christian community that seeks to be faithful to its purpose and calling.

Next morning I sat with the Bishop's gracious wife and their young daughter in a pew near the front. The processional was in every way appropriate, marked by dignity, and the mood was festive. Together with acolytes and other assistants the Bishop, carrying the Shepherd's Crook of his office, made his way to the altar, accompanied by a small retinue of others whom the Bishop this day would be inducting into diaconal ministry.

After the reading of the Gospel, the Bishop stepped forward to the pulpit and began his sermon.

I could hardly conceal the gratification that was mine as he started speaking.

He told of the awkwardness he was feeling as he would be endeavoring to bring the message of the day's Gospel while a man who had been his teacher in the Gospel readings was sitting before him in this audience of worshippers. And then he told how important his days at Valparaiso University had been for him. What he had learned there, he said, had been important in establishing the moorings for his faith and ministry.

His presentation had all the qualities of a really fine sermon, lucid and earnest. I could sense the appreciative response of the congregation and the strong rapport he had with his people.

We had agreed earlier that I would make my presentation after the ritual of induction, and at that moment he invited me to step forward, and accorded me a more formal introduction.

I told the worshippers it was not my intention to submit them to still another sermon. I did, I explained, want to tell them about the school that was honoring their Pastor and Bishop this day.

I told them that the University was not founded to be either a seminary or a school of pre-ministerial study. It was rather intended to fill a role not unlike that of the Gospel Reading of the day. It was the message of Jesus in which he portrayed himself as a mother hen. She ruffles her feathers to welcome into safety and warm shelter her young chirping chicks who have just encountered their first frightening experience with drops of rain and flashing lightning and pounding thunder. The University, I explained, seeks to prepare young men and women to survive all the unexpected challenges they face as they launch into a world they'd not before experienced.

I told of the gratification we who teach there have when we see our alumni move into their new settings and perform faithfully, with a high sense of responsibility to God and to neighbor.

It is a special bonus, I explained, when occasionally someone who passes through our halls pursues the call to pastoral ministry. While among us such students have found the strength and support in early life to commit themselves to bring Christ's reliable and sustaining presence to others as new challenges in faith and life confront them.

This is why Valparaiso University chose to honor Bishop Anderson in this way. And, I added, it was my special privilege this day to observe this highly regarded alumnus in his role of equipping his parishioners to be both faithful and conscientious in their role of caringly "clucking" among the tired, confused, and troubled people they encounter.

At that moment I held high for all to see the handsome bronze plaque which I first read aloud and then presented to the Bishop.

I had always been of the impression that Episcopalians were somewhat — if not very — reserved. So I admit to having been a bit startled when the congregation rose and enthusiastically applauded. I turned to give the Bishop a congratulatory embrace. Whispering slightly, yet loud enough so I could hear him above the outburst, he asked me to remain with him there in the chancel. When the congregation had once again settled into the pews and a semblance of order restored, he had a word for the congregation.

It was clear that he was deeply moved, and he chose to say a bit more about what Valparaiso meant to him. However, he also told them about me and my ministry with the Lutheran Human Relations Association of America. He noted how, though that work had initially focused on the difficulties of African Americans in our country, I had, in recent years, been very much concerned with issues facing Native Americans.

He observed that possibly none of the people present were aware of my activities with the National Indian Lutheran Board that had involved me directly with Native American issues in South Dakota.

"So you see," he said, "he's already been a partner with us in ministry here." With that he reached forward and attached to my lapel on oval pin that bore both the Bishop's name and the name of the diocese, as he declared me an honorary Episcopalian and member of his diocese. Once again the congregation rose to its feet and applauded loudly.

Once the plaudits had subsided he reached into a shelf in the lectern and drew out a green book, explaining, "Every real Episcopalian is a hymnal toting Episcopalian." I was so pleased — and doubly pleased when I opened its pages and found the hymns to be printed in the language of the Dakota Tribes.

The celebration of the Eucharist followed, and I remembered the counsel of St. Paul to the congregation in Rome, "Welcome one another, as Christ has welcomed you." I had been welcomed.

Early, on this visit, Craig showed me about — and I remember a brief conversation we had had when we visited the diocesan school. He had not been in office long before he visited the various classrooms when school was in session. He had noticed only a very few Native Americans among the students.

He made it very clear to those administering the school that this was indeed intended to be a diocesan school. However, since such a large number of South Dakota Episcopalians are Native Americans and are not proportionately represented among its students, the school might well be making a statement that we are favoring non-Indian children and that would be counter to the Gospel.

The Bishop said that, were the situation not remedied by the beginning of the next term, he would close the school.

I questioned whether such an ultimatum may not jeopardize his future effectiveness, coming so early in his tenure here, while he was yet so new in office. He explained simply that a principle of his church is "Once a bishop, always a bishop." Then he said, "They cannot strip me of my office for doing what is right."

I was driving through South Dakota and had been unable to reach Craig in advance, but late at night I tried to phone him once more. He had just returned from overseas, and that accounted for the unanswered calls. I told him we were leaving early in the morning and so it seemed unlikely that we could get together. I'd be getting into Sioux Falls at seven and would have to continue to

306

keep an appointment that evening. And I knew he'd be tired from all his travels and I didn't want to prevent his "sleeping in" the first morning he was back.

He wouldn't have it otherwise. He didn't want to make me late for my meeting, but he didn't want to miss the opportunity for visiting, so I was at a breakfast table with him next morning at 6:15.

It was stimulating to be with him — it always has been. But on this morning, after all the initial "catching up," he told me how he'd been supportive of efforts to help Indians reclaim lands due them by treaties, and in the midst of all this he had received threats of a bombing. He was unwavering, while yet caring about the safety and well being of his family. This wasn't just a display of bravado seeking recognition or approval. He was manifesting his own experience of walking through dark valleys, but wanting to be assured of the guidance of his Shepherd and companionship of others who care.

———————

Our friendship has continued — a visit to our campus, a stay in our home, a stay in his home in New Hampshire where he serves now.

———————

Experiencing the confidence and the respect of leaders in other Christian communions as well, Bishop Anderson has also been serving difficult terms as President of the National Council of Churches in an endeavor to help church leaders persist in efforts to respond with resourcefulness and faithfulness to the prayer Christ prayed shortly before his crucifixion,

Father, I pray not only for these [disciples] but also for those who will believe in me ... that they be one ... that the world might know that you sent me....

307

Through the years churches have spent little effort on seeing that prayer implemented. Far more energy and time have been spent highlighting the differences among Christians and nurturing those divisions.

In his life and ministry — even now as he directs a school for some of God's young ones — Craig Barry Anderson has been for me a symbol of great and devoted faithfulness, open to new ways of enriching his life, serving his Lord, and caring for others.

Norman and Helen

God's kind of doorman

We wanted to be at Midway Airport in Chicago by noon, so we decided to slip into St. John Church in Gary for worship on the way into Chicago. Helen and Norman were already there in a pew to the right, up front, near the lectern.

Eightyish now, thin, frail, he sat there in his black suit, dignified, ready for the service to begin. Helen leaned over to whisper to him and found the appropriate page in the hymnal and held it up to share it with him. As the singing began, it was clear that he had little need of the book. He sang along without looking down at the page. He knew all the stanzas of the hymn.

It was a familiar hymn, so I didn't have much need of the hymnal either and found myself watching Helen and Norman as I sang along.

And a wave of memories washed across my mind.

I'd first met Norm when I began my seminary years in St. Louis. He was well liked and much respected and had been elected student body president. Unassuming, modest, warm — a gentle man — Norman Brandt would surely be a fine pastor some day.

It was almost eighteen years later when I had moved to Indiana. I was immersed in preparing myself for the double assignment I had accepted. Beyond my teaching tasks at the University, I also had to learn the diverse facets of administering a national voluntary human relations ministry. When members from this same St. John Lutheran Church asked me to assist them by conducting Sunday services until they would be getting a replacement for their pastor who had accepted a call to serve a parish in Illinois, I could hardly refuse them. Their hopes for finding a new minister did not quickly materialize, and I became more and more involved with the congregation's leaders in their plannings.

Gary, once a virtual United Nations of many ethnic groupings, with the expansion of the steel industries, had been attracting more and more African Americans into its borders. Whites who had also benefited from employment opportunities and had the financial resources to move elsewhere did just that. The fever of inhospitality and racial tension increased as surely as it did in neighboring Chicago and so many other major northern industrial centers.

310

Unsurprisingly, this oldest of Gary's Lutheran churches had not found ways (nor apparently even looked for ways) of welcoming their new neighbors into its community or its congregational life.

I suggested that minimally members of the congregation might make door to door visits to these new residents' homes, assuring them of friendship and inviting them to make use of the services of the church. We set a gathering time for volunteers willing to make such calls. Only nine of us showed up (five of these, well beyond their seventies, still are faithful in their membership at St. John).

The little sortie into the blocks immediately near the church proved rewarding. We were warmly welcomed and the congregation began laying plans for a midsummer Vacation Bible School.

A few in the congregation were excited, a few encouraged, a few reluctant, a few aloof, and not a few resistant.

It was clear — no whites were moving into the area, more and more of the original St. John members had died or moved to warmer climes, and some others had already moved to all-white suburban communities. If St. John were to flourish — or even survive — its program necessarily would have to be intentionally inclusive to all in all its ministerings.

But without a full-time pastor? I had told them about this young pastor in Milwaukee who had been active in youth programs of our church body, had served as a pastor of a church in Detroit's inner city, and also had been involved with university students as campus minister in Lawrence, Kansas — and now in Wisconsin.

St. John issued the call. Norman Brandt came.

And, on this Sunday morning, almost forty years later, here we found him, sitting in the midst of his flock of loyal, faithful members who love him and respect him so dearly. Most of them are African American, and a handful are some of the original members of St. John whom Norman had inspired.

There aren't many such congregations around, churches that stayed in the midst of change and tension to be a resource in their community to meet needs, and to be a symbol of integrity and genuineness, a reliable friend to the people there.

Don't discount the strong-spirited devotion and faithful, visionary commitment of these members who constitute St. John of today. *They* certainly do not discount the role Norman Brandt and his wife Helen have played in the life of this great church — and in their own lives.

It is clear that Norman is tired. Sweet Helen gently leads and supports him as he shuffles slowly towards the altar to receive the Holy Supper. As he turns to find his way back to their seat he shows weariness in his thinned and tightly drawn face. And there are stories, more than I can ever know behind that tired countenance.

But I know a few.

Norman would often call me, expecting me to give him another perspective — or affirmation — with regard to what he was planning or doing at the moment.

Helen had been a student aiming at a career in nursing when she first met this handsome young pastor. Several years his junior, she was drawn to his unpretentious, genuine care for people in their struggles with the problems they encounter. And Norman was wise enough to ask her to be his life partner. Obviously she agreed.

Three children later (Monica, Christopher, and Maria), the young couple felt deeply moved and restive upon hearing a TV special.

The program vividly depicted, as a critical problem of the day, an overabundance of tiny black children needing a home. There was little question that the Brandts would accept the challenge and in their open-heartedness, they submitted their offer to adopt such a child.

Rebecca was a beautiful child and they were so eager to bring her to our home for a visit that we might get to know her too. However, when they arrived, Helen was in near tears, and Norman was obviously hanging somewhere between the feeling of "new-father pride" and a heavy, troubled heart.

They began to unfold the series of happenings that had thrown such a cloud over their new joy. Neighbors who were upset at such

312

transracial intermingling launched an assault of harassment that reeked of hateful vengeance. Shovels-full of gravel and dirt thrown on their porch, Helen's clothesline cut down, abusive and threatening phone calls — all these were upsetting enough. Even far more painful to them were expressions of resentment by members of their own church.

Helen and Norman had earlier addressed a letter to the congregation, announcing the impending adoption.

In presenting their rationale for their decision, the parents acknowledged the profound responsibility they were assuming in taking this precious child into their home and into their lives. They stated their need for the help of their Lord in this undertaking, and pleaded with the congregation to support them with their help and their prayers. They particularly expressed their hopes that the members would be on hand to participate in the Baptism of Rebecca.

Almost as "boycott," several families refused to be present at the worship service when the Baptism was celebrated. One formal protest came in a letter, in which the writer explained that if someone chose to make a decision like this, one might understand; however, that a pastor, who *should* be a shepherd and example to the congregation, would do such a thing would be unthinkable and reprehensible.

People were running roughshod over the sweet, beautiful innocence of this loving couple. They were shattered, and Helen sobbed as Norman placed his hand on her shoulder as she held the little child.

It was very quiet. If there were words, they were few, soft, and awkward.

Our front door was open and we heard a child singing. Of course it was Beth. She was the Loomans' daughter. But she really was the daughter of everyone in the neighborhood. She was everyone's Beth — even the kids in the neighborhood would take her by the hand and return her to home when she'd wander off to look for a flower or to visit a neighbor. And when she would be making her walk through the place where they'd be playing ball, they'd stop the game till Beth had made her way across the field. She had Downs

313

Syndrome, and she brought with her a contagious love, a sweet innocence, and laughter that everyone welcomed.

Beth came up our steps and pushed the doorbell and came right in. She walked directly to Helen's chair, leaned closer and said softly, "Pretty baby!" and gently kissed the infant's forehead. It was as if she came into the moment of turmoil and said "Peace!"

And with little more on her agenda, Beth left and skipped down the drive to her home — of course, singing.

Later, the Brandts opened their home to another young stranger — this time a young Sioux, one who was older and who entered his adolescent years with great difficulties in working through the issues of his personal identity. With boundless patience — and much personal sacrifice and pain — they worked with young Tim in his personal identity struggles. Even now, as Tim has grown and himself is a father, he has had to face the severe problems that so many American Indians experience. Through the years Norman and Helen have maintained close contact with Tim, visiting him and his family in their South Dakota Reservation home.

All this I remember as I sit in church and watch the back of Norman's slightly balding head.

And I remember the late Saturday night phone call to which I chidingly responded, "Norman, what are you still doing up? You should be home to get some sleep and be ready for tomorrow's sermon!" I knew however that this had to be serious. He would never have called me at such a late hour if it weren't.

He told me then he didn't quite know how to explain to Helen why he still had not come home from his office at church. And then he told what had occurred.

He had heard a crash at the intersection in front of the church and rushed out to see what had happened. He saw a car fleeing the scene and in the other car a young man — possibly seventeen years old behind the wheel. He appeared somewhat dazed. Norman offered to help.

The driver slowly climbed from his car. Norman reached out, offering a hand. Then suddenly, altogether unexpectedly, the fellow struck Norman, knocking him down to the pavement.

The police were arriving by now, and after Norman had picked himself up and identified himself to the officers as pastor of St. John, the officer asked him to press charges against his assailant.

Norman simply said, "No," explaining that the young man had obviously been over-excited and, in anger, had just lashed out — simply because Norman was white. "Well," said the policeman, "then *we* will charge him with assault," and, putting him in handcuffs, drove him off to jail.

This was Norm at his pastoral best — eager to help, quick to understand, never vengeful, not wanting Helen to be worrying about him.

To no one's surprise (except possibly some Gary policemen) Norman was down at the jail the next morning to visit the prisoner. But he was turned away. As I remember, the mother of the young man did manage to visit with Norman, expressing her appreciation for the way he'd treated her son.

Word got around — this man Brandt and his family are decent people, they are friends, they take their Christian faith seriously, and they live it.

Norm was not always placid and unruffled. I had seen Norm angry. I saw him bristle when people would badmouth Gary. I saw him initiate a program and secure grant money to help revive a neighborhood commercial community that deserved attention and support. I saw him become actively and publicly involved in programs seeking to make adequate housing available for needy families and pressing for the curtailing and eliminating of racial segregation in residential development.

In the life of St. John's Church itself Norman had been involved in other memorable and dramatic moments. Not the least of these was to be seen in Norm's determination that this great old building on the corner of Tenth and Taft Streets not become decrepit and shabby. Before he would retire, the structure, the stained glass windows, the roof, and all the interior would be in vintage condition. He wanted the church edifice to be an architectural statement — that in the midst of chaos and change, St. John intends to be here for people, a place where human life is valued, where hope, encouragement, and the love and care of Christ can be found and shared.

Maria Brandt, my goddaughter, honored me by asking me to share in the performance of her marriage some years ago. I was to speak the homily and Norman was to perform the ceremony. At the appropriate moment, when the music indicated such a move, I stepped from the vestry into the chancel. Norman followed me and together we stood at its gateway, looking down the aisle awaiting the procession.

Norman was elated — and excited. There had been no nuptial rehearsal, so I whispered, "Norm, are you giving away the bride?" In semi-shock his jaw fell open and his eyes opened twice-normal and he said, "Oh, my! Hold this!" and, handing me his service book, he slid back into the vestry. Moments later he appeared in the rear of the church to carry Maria's arm in his down the aisle, before resuming his place next to me.

But Norman also had a capacity for staying calm.

I wasn't in on this episode, but Helen reported it to us shortly after it happened.

It had been a mid-week evening and fifteen or so members — mainly women — had come to the church for a Worship Service. Because of the lighting — and the heat distribution in the large church, they all sat together in the very last two pews. Norman himself stood between the pews, two rows ahead, leading the informal worship.

They'd sung a hymn and had just begun the hour, when the door in the rear of the church opened. The group at first did not turn around because it does happen upon occasion that one or more will arrive a bit late for church. However, this man was clearly no regular worshipper. He wore a ski cap over his face and was holding a gun. He shouted, "Everyone get on the floor and pass down your wallets and your purses!"

Norman made it clear to the people that this man was probably not kidding, and so he told them to do as the man said. Then while the intruder was gathering his loot, Norman led the people in prayer, asking God to have mercy on this man, to help him become penitent, and to help the victims to be loving and forgiving.

Upstairs, Helen who had accompanied the singing of the hymn, had heard what was going on and was hiding behind the organ, much frightened. And then she heard Norman close his prayer with an Amen, and add, "Sir, are you still here or are you gone?" When there was no answer, he peeked out and made sure the culprit's exit had been effected and told the people they could once more get off the floor. It was his intention to resume their worship. But the women would have none of it. One protested, "He's got the keys to the car; my husband's going to be angry!" Norman thought better about his earlier decision and dismissed them all.

I don't remember that they ever found the burglar or that he has yet paid for that particular sin.

Norman Brandt —
What a man. What a ministry. What a pastor. No wonder, long after his active years, his very presence in the congregation that Sunday morning was a powerful message about faithfulness, innocence, courage, steadfastness, commitment, and hope — for his people — for me.

Since I wrote these pages, Norman has died. I do not begrudge his leaving. Heart difficulties, failing memory, and a physical tiredness had begun to diminish his life significantly. He had used his talents faithfully and spent his life well.

The day before his funeral service, his family, members of St. John, neighbors, and countless others gathered at the church to bespeak their profound respect and admiration for this saintly pastor.

As we were about to leave and I pushed open the front door of the church, we were a bit startled to see a huge fire truck, engine running, double-parked at the front steps. These uniformed men quickly mounted the stairs, politely brushed past us and soberly made their way to the casket near the altar to express their good-byes to this man everybody obviously loved and respected.

Next day at the service worshippers crowded the church. Among them were officers of his church body, city officials and civic leaders, other Lutheran pastors as well as ministers of other denominations. And Pastors Frey and Halvorson, seminary classmates of Norman, both in their eighties, came from Cleveland to be there.

Several people rose to speak their final tribute to Pastor Brandt. One young high school lad walked to the front. The presiding pastor held the microphone to him and the young man started to speak, but could not make a sound. Choked up, with the supporting arm of the pastor on his shoulder, he finally gained his composure (and we all breathed a sigh of relief!). He told us his story of his once having missed a session in his confirmation instruction. As "penalty" his pastor gave him the assignment to gather all the debris near the church and its parking area. It seems that, after only a minute or two, Pastor Brandt joined him in the task and, when they had completed it, he invited the boy to go with him. They crossed the street and together they cleaned up paper and bottles and cans from a vacant lot there. It was obvious to every one of us in that congregation — this boy really loved his pastor.

Helen and her children were sitting in the front rows. When the little children came to sing the song they had prepared for the service, the song they knew their pastor loved, Helen and her children were singing along with them.

"Blessed are the dead who die in the Lord. They rest from their labors — and their works follow them."

EPILOGUE

I confess that I find it necessary to stifle an impish urge that teases my piety each time I am at table and someone suggests, "Shall we say grace?"

This immediately suggests the wild possibility that a lengthy and heated debate might ensue, with rationales presented for either side of the confrontation, to pray or not to pray — when that is not even the question!

To succumb to my alternative urge would be even less responsible, by answering the host's invitational greeting by simply saying aloud, *"Grace!"*

I suppose what prompts such thoughts is a bit of my impatience with our use of the word *grace* without giving the concept any second thought.

Eager to find a summation appropriate for what I've written, I tripped across a phrase that opens a portion of Saint John's writings, *"Count it all JOY. . . ."* It comes close. But maybe the earlier question *is* in order: "Shall we say GRACE?"

So in reflecting on these pages I say with excitement, "Count it all Grace!"

Grace connotes "gift." These people and my experiences with them have been gifts. And the very word "gift" presupposes and infers a "Giver."

I cannot thank God enough — with excitement, "Count it all Grace!"